BEING CHURCH

NML NEW MONASTIC LIBRARY
Resources for Radical Discipleship

For over a millennium, if Christians wanted to read theology, practice Christian spirituality, or study the Bible, they went to the monastery to do so. There, people who inhabited the tradition and prayed the prayers of the church also copied manuscripts and offered fresh reflections about living the gospel in a new era. Two thousand years after the birth of the church, a new monastic movement is stirring in North America. In keeping with ancient tradition, new monastics study the classics of Christian reflection and are beginning to offer some reflections for a new era. The New Monastic Library includes reflections from new monastics as well as classic monastic resources unavailable elsewhere.

Being
CHURCH

Reflections on
How to Live as the
People of God

JOHN ALEXANDER

Edited by
JONATHAN WILSON-HARTGROVE

CASCADE *Books* · Eugene, Oregon

BEING CHURCH
Reflections on How to Live as the People of God

New Monastic Library

Cascade Books
An Imprint of Wipf and Stock Publishers
199 W. 8th Ave., Suite 3
Eugene, OR 97401

www.wipfandstock.com

ISBN 13: 978-1-60899-869-2

Cataloging-in-Publication data:

Alexander, John.

Being church : reflections on how to live as the people of God / John Alexander.

viii + 258 p. ; 25.4 cm. —Includes bibliographical references."

New Monastic Library

ISBN 13: 978-1-60899-869-2

1. Church. 2. Christian life. 3. Church renewal. I. Title.

BV 600.2 A30 2012

CONTENTS

Contents

The book you're holding is a book that was written before its time.

But I'm glad you're holding it, because this is a book whose time has come. From conversations about "emergent Christianity" to the proliferation of house churches to the "new monasticism" movement, Christians are experimenting with new ways of doing church in America. However they say it, a new generation is dissatisfied with modern church forms and the fruit they produce. So much of what gets proclaimed as good news in America's churches seems hollow and irrelevant. But what is the alternative? What would it look like to live as the people of God in America today?

Being Church . . . is a manifesto of hope about how to move beyond criticism and become the church we long to see. It is, in many ways, a fitting conclusion to the life and work of John Alexander, who first became dissatisfied with the church tradition he had inherited when evangelical Christians lined up on the wrong side of the civil rights movement in the early 60s. Together with his father, Fred Alexander, John started *The Other Side* magazine and was for years a leader among progressive evangelicals.

But in the mid-eighties John reassessed his life and ministry. As he said it, "I eventually found progressive Christians' rights orientation (by then, *my* rights orientation) to lack depth. Their litany of who was violating their rights and the rights of others grew boring and had a stunningly different tenor from Jesus' teaching. Besides, they were no better than schismatic fundamentalists at getting along with folks, and often their sexual stance was roughly as destructive as nuclear war." John began to suspect that both the right and the left in American Christianity were missing something.

Then, at the Church of the Sojourners in San Francisco, he found a group of people experimenting with a new way of being church. He and his family relocated. John left *The Other Side*, left the Christian speaking circuit, and took up residence in a 24-7 live-in church.

John's story reminds me of Henri Nouwen, the well-known academic and spiritual writer who left his teaching post at an Ivy League divinity school to join a community of people with mental disabilities who were living together with others who not only wanted to care for them, but also to learn from them. By every account (including his own), Nouwen struggled with the transition. But it opened his eyes to the truth of the gospel. However hard it was for him to live this new truth, he wrote beautifully about it.

In the fall of 2006, I visited the Church of the Sojourners and talked to folks there about John Alexander. After ten years with them as member, mentor, and pastor, John had died very quickly from cancer in 2001. Within a very short window of time, the community lost another important elder. They had wondered if it would be possible for them to go on. But, somehow, grace sustained them. They kept going.

Having worked through their grief and found a way forward, the folks at Church of the Sojourners said two things about John. First, he understood what they were doing and articulated it in a way that captivated all of them. They loved him for that. But they also noted that, like Nouwen, he struggled to live this vision. To the very end, he was trying to learn to love the people God had given him.

Because John trusted the vision that had captivated him, he stuck with it until the end. He wrote and re-wrote his best expressions of it, trying to say exactly what it was that had claimed his life. This book is a carefully distilled manifesto of someone who spent his whole life thinking about how to become the church. And it is, as such, a great gift.

But this book is also the vision of a man who was being transformed by love. It's the confession of someone who had a lot of good ideas, but still struggled to live them well. John worked on this book until his death, leaving it almost finished. But one of the things he wasn't sure of was what to call it. He'd liked the title *Stop Going to Church and Be the Church* . . . It summed up nicely his radical idea. But the more he tried to live it, the more he thought he should probably just call it *The Love Book*.

"Love in action," Dostoyevsky said, "is a harsh and dreadful thing compared to love in dreams." But that's exactly what the church is called to be—exactly what we've all been invited to become. This is an idea whose time has come. I pray we'll find the grace to live it.

Jonathan Wilson-Hartgrove
Lent 2012

PART ONE

The Nature and Purpose of Churches (What's the Problem Here?)

ONE

Growing into the Stature of Christ
(Whatever Happened to the Kingdom of God?)

Paul says that Christians will grow into "the full stature of Christ" (Eph 4:13).[1] He doesn't seem to mean sometime in the distant future or way off in heaven. He seems to mean here and now. Which is an astonishing thought. It seems almost heretical, but the text says exactly that. It teaches that Christians will normally become saints.

In the New Testament, "Christian" wasn't yet a common word. So do you remember how the New Testament writers most often refer to Christians? As saints. For example, "Paul and Timothy, servants of Christ Jesus, to all the saints in Christ Jesus who are in Philippi . . ." (Phil 1:1). Fifty-nine times the New Testament calls us saints. Fifty-nine times. The word isn't just for Mother Theresa or St. Francis. It's for all of us. And it means "people who are holy."

Of course, it could just be a change in how we use words. Once the people of God were called "saints," but it was a proper name whose meaning was largely forgotten, as is the meaning of most proper names. (Take Smith for example.) But now we use "saint" literally so it refers only to extraordinarily virtuous people. But I doubt that that's what's happening. No, the New Testament is full of extravagant promises and extraordinary expectations. It really does promise that we will become holy. It expects it. It expects ordinary Christians to ordinarily become saints.

That's the normal Christian life.

For example, the night Jesus was betrayed, he prayed to his Father that those who believed in him "may be one, as we are one, I in them and you in me, that they may become completely one" (John 17:22–23). That is, Jesus prayed that we would be as united as the Trinity—united with him and therefore with each other. Once again, his words don't seem to refer only to a distant future off in heaven. He seems to include the here and now.

As I said before, this is so astonishing it's almost heretical. And it's similar to Paul's talk of growing into the stature of Christ. If we're in unity with each other and God, then haven't we in fact matured in holiness to something like the stature of Christ?

---

1. Unless otherwise noted, all biblical quotations are from the New Revised Standard Version.

Or try this statement of Paul's: "I have been crucified with Christ; and it is no longer I who live, but it is Christ who lives in me" (Gal 2:19b–20a). Here Paul isn't praying that something will happen or promising that it might in some future conditional subjunctive. He is asserting that it is in fact true of himself at that moment. He says flat that he has been killed and Christ is living his life. So since Christ is living in him, he has presumably grown into something like the stature of Christ.

Then there's, "You are the light of the world" (Matt 5:14a).[2] Which wouldn't be a surprising thing to say about Jesus, since it's referring back to the suffering servant (Isa 49:6). But this is Jesus talking to his followers:[3] we are the light of the world. Paul and Barnabas make the point even more clearly by saying, "For so the Lord has commanded us, saying, 'I have set you to be a light for the Gentiles, so that you may bring salvation to the ends of the earth'" (Acts 13:47). Apparently the people of God as a whole are to be transformed into light to bring salvation to the world. We are somehow a stand-in for Jesus, the suffering servant. Or to be more precise, we *are* his body in some sense that's not merely metaphorical. As such, we grow into his stature.

Then in Ephesians, Paul says not that we are the light of the world but that "by the church" even "the rulers and authorities in the heavenly places" will come to know God's "mystery hidden for ages" (3:10, 9). Clearly, the New Testament expects the people of God to be extravagantly transformed—or at least to have some power we don't think of ourselves as having.

The Sermon on the Mount also points toward our becoming saints. What it's full of isn't extravagant promises but extravagant commands: commands we can't possibly do. It tells us to turn the other cheek, not to look on a woman to lust after her, not to worry about where you're going to get your next meal (this to a crowd that included poor people who genuinely didn't know how they would feed themselves tomorrow), and on and on. The extravagance of the commands is so extreme that books have been written on why Jesus would give such commands when we can't possibly live up to them. Some people think their purpose is to drive us to despair so that we will throw ourselves on God, and others think they exist as ideals to point us in the right direction even if we never get anywhere near the destination.

But as worthwhile as those perspectives may be, it's hard to find them within the Sermon on the Mount itself. That is, it's hard to believe that Jesus or Matthew primarily meant us to read the Sermon on the Mount either of those ways. After all, the Sermon on the Mount ends with a warning to those who don't pursue its commands: "And everyone who hears these words of mine and does not act on them will be like a foolish man who built his house on sand. The rain fell, and the floods came, and the winds

2. Compare this to the similar, even more poetic statement: "But thanks be to God, who in Christ always leads us in triumphal procession, and through us spreads in every place the fragrance that comes from knowing him. For we are the aroma of Christ to God among those who are being saved and among those who are perishing" (2 Cor 2:14–15).

3. Actually, his listeners aren't even all disciples. They're the collection of people listening to the Sermon on the Mount, a pretty motley crew. I suspect he's telling them that they are the people of God (they're probably almost all Jews) and are therefore the light of the world.

blew and beat against that house, and it fell—and great was its fall!" (Matt 7:26–27). Matthew, not to mention Jesus, seems to think that these commands are for us, that we can make a meaningful effort to obey them, and that we darn well better.

And to get the larger perspective, don't forget that Jesus came announcing the kingdom of God. It was at hand, he said. And the writers of the New Testament clearly thought that the kingdom had come substantially with the crucifixion and resurrection of Jesus. At that point, God gave his people new hearts with his law written on them. That fulfilled the promise of a new covenant in which God assures us, "I will be their God, and they shall be my people" (Jer 31:33).[4]

According to Jesus, according to Paul, according to John, according to Matthew, according to the whole New Testament, the normal Christian life is for us to become saints.

Ordinary Christians ordinarily grow into something like the stature of Christ.

So what's going on here?

Unfortunately, it's not at all clear that the New Testament is right. It's not at all clear that most of us are saints or even that we're on the way. In fact, it's pretty clear that we're not. People like Mother Theresa are pretty rare, and I'm not referring to the power of her personality. I'm referring to her holiness. The fact is that few of us even approach holiness. And our churches are often about as unified as the Democratic Party right after losing an election. Which is a long way from growing into the stature of Christ.

The New Testament promises so much. What can it be up to? What can Jesus and Matthew and John and Paul have meant? How can their teaching be so disconnected from our reality? Is the gap between their promise and our reality an unbridgeable chasm?

Don't misunderstand me. I'm not so much disturbed by the poor performance of us Christians as about whether we know what we're up to. Fans of the Chicago Cubs don't seem to mind too much that their team plays badly and drops the ball from time to time. But what if in the middle of a close game, the Cubs sat down in the infield and started playing tiddlywinks? Or eating lunch?

No doubt, the illustration will prompt all kinds of supposedly entertaining remarks about the Cubs, but when the people of God forget what they're about, it's not entertaining. Dropping the ball is one thing. We all do that. I certainly do. And the most casual reading of 1 Corinthians or of Revelation 2–3 prepares us for churches that drop the ball. Often and badly, even. But I'm not sure it prepares us for churches playing the wrong game. Playing the wrong game is very odd and very troubling.

In fact, it's the most troubling thing I know—this gap between today's churches and the New Testament. But what's troubling isn't that churches fail. That's very New Testament. The kingdom is not yet here in its fullness. So I don't expect Christians to

---

4. This passage is quoted in Hebrew 8:10 and 10:16, and the idea is referred to as fulfilled in places like Romans 7:22, 8:5–8, and 2 Corinthians 3:3.

leap tall buildings at a single bound. Or to catch every fly ball. Or to die rather than let Jews be taken to concentration camps. That sort of thing is great when it happens, but the New Testament gives us little reason to expect heroics of ourselves or of other Christians. Peter seems to have failed with some regularity. Besides, I'm a pastor myself and have learned not to be too stunned by the sin and failure of the folks I pastor. After all, my own record isn't that great. It's God's grace that is great.

So, for example, I don't expect us to live up to the Sermon on the Mount. But I do expect us to fail in such a way that people watching us will know what we're reaching for, what we're failing at. By now I don't expect us to be as united with each other as Jesus is with the Father, but I do expect us to live in such a way that outsiders will be able to tell that being united with each other is what we intend to be about.

I may be undercutting my own argument, but my problem isn't that we fail. Nor that we do church badly. It's that we're doing something else. We seem to be playing the wrong game against the wrong team at the wrong time. Not always, but pretty often. Maybe especially on Sunday mornings.

Depravity

The Bible is full of extravagant promises and extraordinary expectations, but it's also full of accounts of extraordinary human sin and extravagant failure. The Bible is as aware of the chasm between promise and practice as I am, as is the most critical among us. Both the Old and New Testaments are unwaveringly honest about the disturbing state of humanity, including the people of God.

So how do you pull together the Bible's abundant promises with its unflinching report of sin and misery? It would be impossible to take the Bible seriously if it were full of promises but had no sense of the holocausts that humanity seems to choose. At least we can be thankful that, unlike some people today, the Bible isn't naive.

Some years ago, I noticed something I thought odd: the parts of the Bible that make the wild promises are fully in touch with the width and depth of sin. It's not that the promises are in one part of the Bible and the misery in another. For example, the Psalms are full of glowing promises about green pastures and the Lord being our shepherd, our rock, our refuge, our shield, our salvation, and on and on. Then the very next Psalm and sometimes the same one will say, in effect, "God, if you're so great, where are you? Why do I feel so alone while my enemies overrun me?"

Take Psalm 79 (chosen almost at random):

> O God, the nations [the heathen, not the chosen people] have come into your inheritance; they have defiled your holy temple; they have laid Jerusalem in ruins. They have given the bodies of your servants to the birds of the air for food, the flesh of your faithful to the wild animals of the earth. . . . How long, O LORD? Will you be angry forever? . . . Let the groans of the prisoners come before you; according to your great power preserve those doomed to die. (Ps 79:1–2, 5a, 11)

Here the Psalmist believes in God's great power. The power of the heathen is just an expression of God's power. But God isn't acting yet; so he wants to know how long he has to put up with the mess.

The same sort of thing is true of Paul and John. Both have a dual sense: God's promise and humanity's sin.

Perhaps there's a clue here in the way biblical writers hold the agony and the ecstasy together. For example, the Bible practically starts with Adam and Eve's rebellion. But, even before that, the Bible offers great promise: God creates a wonderful universe, declares it good, then declares it very good, blesses it, and, finally places Adam and Eve in the best part of it, the Garden of Eden. This framework of promise is the frame for the whole rest of the biblical story; everything else that happens in human history happens within the context of the universe being God's good creation, blessed by him.

Now of course, as I've already said, almost immediately Adam and Eve choose to rebel (Gen 3), and the promise is thrashed. In their willfulness, they're driven from the Garden, losing much of their intimacy with God and, from then on, having to do long hours of hard labor just to survive. Their idyllic existence is over.

Or is it?

Well, maybe the idyll is over, but the Bible then proceeds with a mix of great promise and of our choosing sin and misery. I suggest that it's somewhere in this mix that much of the power of the Bible lies. That's the clue. If the promise were all, the Bible would be romantic idealism, toothless pietism, a Hollywood romantic comedy. Movies like *An Affair to Remember* or *Pretty Woman* are great fun, especially for those of us tired of hearing how depraved and miserable we all are, but you better not try to live your life by such amiable unreality. If the Bible were such a book, it would not have survived Israel being conquered, even the first time. Instead, it's still with us thousands of years later.

By the same token, if sin and misery were all that the Bible recorded, it could inspire only sodden hopelessness. And in fact, it couldn't even do that, because few would bother to read it. *Cinema noir*, the French version of unblinking depravity, never runs at United Artists Cineplex 20. It's always at an art cinema that seats thirty-five and then only for two nights. Then the theater goes on to some depressing Ingmar Bergman flick. (My wife is not alone in being tired of accompanying me to his marvelously miserable black and whites.)

Besides, anyone can catalog the mess that is humanity. That takes little imagination. Much of the secret of the Bible is that it holds on to extravagant hope while cataloging the reality of sin.

And the Bible doesn't seem to find that self-contradictory. The wonderful promises are available, but we human beings keep choosing evil instead. It's up to us. It's a matter of freedom, of choice. We can live the wonderful lives God promises, or we're free to be a mess. Don't ask about the Holocaust, "Where was God?" Ask, "Where were we?" It was people who murdered Jews, Poles, Gypsies, gays, and the disabled, and it was other people who let them be murdered.

God's Word holds onto the promise of victory in the midst of defeat by telling us that the choice is ours. Free choice is what allows tragedy and ecstasy, is what makes the Bible the Word of God and not the scratchings of some scribe. There are no guarantees of holiness because we're always free to make bad choices. But ordinary people can become holy. We just have to choose it.

The Bible's stance is, "Ordinary people can ordinarily become saints. It's up to you. Any person can choose to become Mother Theresa." How that happens we'll have to struggle with for the rest of this book, but the Bible's answer is unequivocal. Holiness is within our grasp. We truly can choose holiness (wonder and beauty), but we're also free to choose sin, misery, and ruin. Which human beings generally do. That, however, doesn't make the promises empty. It just makes their fulfillment up to us. It's all about the freedom God gave us.

Eden or Auschwitz? Our choice.

Mind you, I know that's not fully satisfactory intellectually. Philosophers have been struggling with this issue (which they call the problem of evil) for over two thousand years. And none of them has an answer for it, whether they're Christians, atheists, or Zoroastrians. Scripture can help us think about the problem of evil, but the burden of this book isn't to solve an apparently unsolvable theoretical problem. It's to point toward ways we can do better at becoming holy.

I also know that this answer isn't fully satisfactory emotionally either (especially as you walk through the gates of Auschwitz). No wonder romantic comedy is so popular. The ruination that historians and the Bible record makes some of us not so sure we want to be in this story. We'd prefer the victories guaranteed from the beginning of each Harry Potter book. Harry Potter may not be great drama, but altogether too many great dramas are tragedies. What if I don't want to live out my tragedy, even if it is a great one?[5]

But what are the alternatives? Increasingly our culture sees the alternatives as the pretense of romantic comedy or the depression of *cinema noir*. Did you ever wonder why we have so few good movies? Hollywood has all the money imaginable and can buy almost any talent they want, and yet they have a hard time making a movie worth sitting through. Why? It's partly that there's a mystery to art that interferes with its being created for money, but it's mostly that sin dumbs us down and blinds us. (See Romans 1 and John 15.) Our culture is losing the idea that free choice holds together the promise and the tragedy; so our movies and literature get less and less satisfactory.

Conclusion

Now I realize that few people understand these problems just the way I do, and even fewer experience them with the intensity that I do. Nonetheless, I think my experience is indicative of where many Christians find themselves. We have a sense that there

5. Editor's Note: This book was written before the final Harry Potter books were released. Had John lived to read the final book, perhaps he wouldn't have used it as his example here.

must be something more than we're experiencing and more than we're seeing around us. We may remember a time when we were part of a small church or some other Christian group (perhaps in college), but it ended or got bigger or went bad, and we've never been able to find anything like the original. Or perhaps we tried spiritual disciplines once upon a time but have since quit because life got too busy or God seemed pretty distant.

I talk to people all the time who are discouraged with their spiritual life and no longer know whether it's worth the effort. Down deep they hope it is, but they've pulled back for the moment. They've lost their enthusiasm. Many of them failed badly and others just didn't experience the kind of growth they expected. Whatever the reason, many of us have pulled back.

This book is for such people. It points toward hope and gives concrete ways that we can begin again to seek God and in fact become holy in the way the Bible promises. And it does it in such a way that even failure will draw us closer to God rather than pushing us farther away.

The New Testament promises so much. What can it be up to? What can Jesus and John and Paul have meant? It would be nice to imagine that the New Testament is a wonderful book to be read for inspiration and fine poetry, that we can grow as we absorb its moral insights and lofty vision. But the New Testament makes many factual claims that are either true or false. Just think about the examples we began with:

1. We Christians can grow into the full stature of Christ.
2. We can be as unified with each other as Jesus is with the Father.
3. We can die to ourselves and let Christ live our lives.
4. We are the light of the world, from whom even principalities learn.
5. The kingdom has substantially arrived.

Either these claims/promises are true or they aren't. Either they're an accurate description of the normal Christian life or they aren't. And if they aren't, then those who made them are not wonderful moral teachers; they're dangerous people who are deceiving themselves and misleading their followers. As someone said as early as the second century, "If the world has not changed, the Messiah has not come."[6] If that's the case, then honest people need the courage to say that Jesus made a huge mistake: he honestly thought the kingdom was just around the corner, but in fact it never came. This is far better than the sentimentalism and foggy-mindedness of those who claim to revere Jesus while living lives of spiritual mediocrity that deny the power of the gospel.

---

6. Lohfink, *Jesus*, 175.

TWO

The Secret of the Christian Life
(Whatever Happened to the Church?)

My father used to say that the secret of the Christian life is that there is no secret. We just have to keep putting one foot in front of the other trying to be faithful to God. There are no magic bullets. No quick solutions. No easy answers. It's a matter of slogging out our discipleship day after day, year after year, decade after decade.

When we've given up supposing that our problems can be solved by having a mystical experience, finding the right spouse, speaking in tongues, or finding a ministry that uses our gifts, then we can get on with the gradual process of growing into the stature of Christ. Which is the only secret there is. A long obedience in the same direction.[1]

My college pastor used to say that the secret of the Christian life is an alarm clock. That annoyed me to no end because I was in a romantic phase and valued spontaneity, but I think he meant what Dad did. There are no quick fixes, only getting up every day and seeking God's Word for us and then doing our best to live it. Day after day after year after decade. That's how we grow into the fullness of Christ. Like training to run a marathon or to play Major League ball. You don't master a sport overnight—or ever for that matter. Why should we think we can grow into the fullness of Christ without practice and discipline and hard work?

Holiness is possible, but it requires a long obedience in the same direction. That's why Luke's Jesus talked about taking up the cross daily (not once and for all, and not yearly). And that's why Paul talks about dying every day.[2] Maybe that's what we're missing. Part of it anyway. The modern desire for spiritual mastery in thirty days and five easy lessons closes the Word of God to us, and guarantees that we will be spiritual midgets.

---

1. This is the title of an excellent book by Eugene Peterson, *A Long Obedience in the Same Direction: Spirituality in an Instant Society,* Downers Grove, IL: InterVarsity Press, 1980.

2. Luke 9:23 and 1 Cor 15:31.

The cost of discipleship

Which is another way of saying that the whole New Testament is clear about the cost of the Christian life. Each of the Gospels contains some form of the saying, "If any want to become my followers, let them deny themselves and take up their cross and follow me." (Matt 8:34; compare to Matt 16:24, Luke 9:23.) Even John, which gives many fewer requirements than the other Gospels, gives a form of this one (John 12:24). That this saying is in all four Gospels suggests its centrality.

The context in each of the first three Gospels makes its centrality even clearer. Peter has just identified Jesus as the Messiah. This is the first time the disciples have used that word for Jesus. It's often preached as a moment of victory and insight, but instead of celebrating with his disciples, Jesus seems to think they still don't understand. They apparently think the Messiah will be a military king who will drive out the Romans and establish again an earthly, independent kingdom of Israel. So Jesus warns them that instead the Messiah will suffer terribly. Then in Matthew and Mark, Peter rebukes (!) Jesus for this, and Jesus calls him Satan. Apparently to deny that the Messiah will suffer is to deny the faith. Jesus then goes ahead and says that not only will he suffer but that he's to be their model. They will suffer too, as will anyone who wants to follow him. His disciples must choose the cross as he is about to do. That is at the core of their faith.

Jesus is asking the disciples to reimage what it means to be the Messiah and therefore what it means to follow the Messiah. Following him isn't going to be like being Caesar's right-hand man. It's going to be like being a suffering servant. Lest we miss the point, Matthew and Luke repeat the saying in another context (Matt 10:38; Luke 14:27).

This is so hard for the disciples to accept that each of the Gospels repeats the point again and again, as do most of the other books of the New Testament. Apparently, it wasn't just the disciples who couldn't accept this; it was also the people Paul was writing to originally, and those John and Peter and James were writing to.

Not to mention us. We may think it strange how hard it was for the disciples to understand this, but my impression is that most of us still don't understand. We don't have much of a clue that following Jesus is costly business. At least, I'm doing well if I understand it half the time. (Not that cost is the only thing to talk about; joy and freedom are there, too. But I will get to that in a moment.)

So the New Testament devotes itself to trying to explain the costliness of discipleship. Documenting this could be a book in itself,[3] but I can only illustrate it here. The Sermon on the Mount and the Sermon on the Plain are devoted to some of the details of how life with Christ will be costly (Matt 5–7 and Luke 6). Both of them end with the story of the man who built his house on the rock and the man who built his house on

---

3. In fact, that is the main point of my book, *Your Money or Your Life*. It's not his only point, but it's well summarized in Richard Hays' *The Moral Vision of the New Testament*. His biblical arguments are frequently better than mine.

sand. The point of this story is that those who don't live out the incredibly high standards of the sermon just preached will have their house come crashing down around their heads. "And great [will be] its fall" (Matt 7:27).

I learned that much from my fundamentalist father when I was in junior high. He preached a series of sermons back then growing out of the Great Commission: "Go therefore and make disciples of all the nations, . . . teaching them to observe all things that I have commanded you" (Matt 28:19a, 20a). His point (and now mine) was that Jesus never commissioned us to make converts. He commissioned us to make disciples who would follow all the incredible things that he taught. More importantly, his point was that we Christians usually just don't take Jesus' commands as things we can or should do. As a result we're spiritual midgets.

Lest we imagine that this is just for special disciples or special times, the New Testament picks up these themes almost everywhere. Romans 12 picks up most of the themes of the Sermon on the Mount. 1 Thessalonians, 1 and 2 Corinthians, Hebrews, 1 Peter, Revelation—they all emphasize how much suffering Christian living includes, how much it has the shape of the cross. In fact, the whole New Testament emphasizes this point.

For years I argued, along with my father, that this teaching is what is missing from our Christian lives. I argued that our failure to try to live lives of costly discipleship is the secret we're missing. Day by day, step by step, we need to be aiming ourselves in that direction, and too often we aren't. There's no shortage of proof-texts for my point and no shortage of sophisticated arguments from the structure of the New Testament. I wasn't wrong.

But by my mid-forties, that answer began to seem inadequate. I didn't reach that conclusion by the study of Scripture, I'm sorry to say. I was driven to it by my own continuing spiritual failure and by what seemed to me to be the parallel failure of those (like my father) who believed the same thing. Something was still missing. This book is the record of what I believe that is.

THE EXTRAVAGANCE OF THE CHURCH

What I believe is missing I found mostly in Ephesians. Not that it's only there, but that's where I first found it. In Ephesians I found two things that I had understood only peripherally before. I found a teaching on the nature of the church and an assumption of extravagance. I started with the teaching on the church and was gradually lured by Ephesians into the assumption of extravagance.

I suspect that this teaching on the church is the best-kept secret in the New Testament. As a matter of fact, the best-kept secret in the history of the world. More secret than the oracles of Delphi. Only the church isn't meant to be secret; it's meant to be a light set on a hill. Not that the New Testament is obscure the way the oracles of Delphi were. It's perfectly clear about the church. Well, maybe that's not quite true. The New Testament is rarely perfectly clear. Especially Ephesians, and Ephesians is the book with the most specific emphasis on the nature of the church. The author of Ephesians gets so excited about the church (and about Jesus and about most other things) that he sometimes loses control of his sentences. (The authorship of Ephesians is disputed, but I'm going to say Paul wrote it.)

Ephesians has the two longest sentences in the whole Bible. Many years ago, I was editor of *The Other Side* magazine. If Paul had sent me the manuscript of Ephesians, I would have sent it back to him. I'd have told him he had some great ideas, but he needed to find someone to write them up. You see, modern editors like short sentences (and low expectations). Which are not things that ever occurred to Paul. Or if they did, he forgot them when he was excited. Which, judging from his writing, was often.

So Ephesians has monster sentences while modern editors have something called the fog index. You calculate the fog index partly by the number of words per sentence, and the number you arrive at tells you the number of years of education required to read the passage with ease. Hemingway, *Reader's Digest*, and *Time* have low fog indexes. If you want modern people to read your work, your fog index better not be any higher than eight.

Well, Paul's fog index often runs around thirty. (As do Karl Barth's and Immanuel Kant's.) So you can read Paul with comfort if you have a mere eighteen years of education beyond high school.

In a way that's too bad. But in another way it shows the grandeur of Paul's thought. Hemingway could have a low fog index partly because he had such small ideas.[4] (I won't comment on *Reader's Digest* and *Time*.) But Paul, he had ideas of such enormity that you can build a life around them. In fact, the very kingdom of God is reflected in them.

I suspect that that's the heart of what's missing in our lives and in the walk of the people of God: the grandeur of Paul's vision, made concrete in the church.

THE EXTRAVAGANCE OF EPHESIANS

But before talking about the church, let me talk about the structure of Paul's thought in Ephesians. After greeting the Ephesians, Paul starts his letter to them with a twelve-verse, 206-word sentence.[5] He then proceeds with a three-chapter prayer as full of praise as the Psalms and as full of theology as Calvin's *Institutes*. And he concludes his letter with three concrete chapters on the daily life of the church he was writing to.

Here's the start of the prayer: "Blessed be the God and Father of our Lord Jesus Christ, who has blessed us in Christ with every spiritual blessing in the heavenly places" (Eph 1:3). Right away we're in a foreign land. (Or is it home, and we're in exile in a

---

4. On the other hand, Shakespeare's fog index is low, too. Part of the reason Hemingway and Shakespeare have low fog indexes is that they have a lot of dialogue, and in realistic dialogue, sentences are short.

5. 1:3–14. Of course, Greek doesn't have periods, so the notion of sentences isn't as obvious as in English. Still, all twelve verses have only one independent clause. The rest is a series of dependent clauses.

foreign land?) Note the cathedral Paul assumes: we have every spiritual blessing. Is this a slip of the pen, or does Paul mean it? (Maybe the reason we can't imagine growing into the full stature of Christ is that we don't believe we have every spiritual blessing.) And what does he mean by "in Christ" and by "in the heavenly places"? This guy is up to something quite foreign to common sense.

Paul tells us God chose us "to be holy and blameless" (v. 4). He doesn't say God chose us to be mediocre; he doesn't say God chose us to be not too bad. He assumes something extravagant. Next he says, "In the richness of his grace, God has lavished on us all wisdom and insight" (v. 7b–8 REB). Now a modern editor would have to cut this down. Forget "richness" (it just adds to the fog index), and "lavished" seems a little flowery and extreme, while the hyperbole "all" will confuse modern readers. Besides, the talk of wisdom seems excessive. Let's reduce it to something like, "In his grace, God has given us some insight."

What do you think? Is something missing in the edited version? Whatever happened to hope and joy and excitement? Is that part of what's missing from our lives? Paul assumes an extravagant, wondrous cathedral here and now, but we reduce it to a hovel.

Later (vv. 18b–19a), Paul talks about "the riches of his glorious inheritance" (not just the riches of his inheritance, but of his *glorious* inheritance) and "the immeasurable greatness of his power" (not the adequacy of his power). Then Paul ends the chapter by talking about the church "which is his body, the fullness of him who fills all in all" (v. 23). I won't even start to unpack that, but I promise you that, whatever it means, it's extravagant.

Part of the very structure of Paul's thought is that God always gives extravagantly to his people. I'm building up to Paul's teaching on the church, but we won't be able to understand what he's saying about the church (or about the cost of discipleship) unless we grasp God's extravagance to us. I could keep illustrating this by quoting almost the whole of Ephesians, not to mention much of the rest of Paul's writing, most of John's writing, much of the Old Testament, and most of Jesus' teaching. Instead I will just say that extravagance and abundance are part of the very structure of Paul's thought because they are part of the very structure of Judeo-Christian thought. No, it's deeper than that: extravagance and abundance are part of Yahweh's character and therefore part of Yahweh's creation. Our God has always given his people a land flowing with milk and honey, and he always will. That's just who he is. He knows no scantiness, no scarcity, no pinchedness.

Neither do we—if our eyes and heart are open to the gospel. Jesus doesn't say, "Those who lose their lives for my sake, do so for a good cause." When he teaches about taking up the cross, he never stops there. He goes on to say, "Those who lose their life for my sake will find it" (Matt 10:39). "And everyone who has left houses or brothers or sisters or father or mother or children or fields, for my name's sake, will receive a hundredfold, and will inherit eternal life" (Matt 19:29).

Unfortunately, this theology of abundance is often picked up as some sort of manipulative, prosperity gospel: if you pray and tithe regularly, God will give you a Mercedes. But this leaves out (amongst other things) the foundational nature of the cross in our lives. Not as a way to manipulate God into giving us what we want, but as a recognition that godliness and joy are the sort of self-surrender that Jesus showed us on the cross. Then on the other side of that, we experience a new sort of prosperity. It's like laughter. When we laugh, we surrender control of ourselves, and yet when we stop laughing there is more of us than before. And it's like love. The more we give away, the more we have.

Paul was not a wealthy man. He gave up all for Jesus. Yet judging from Philippians, by the time he was executed, he was a man filled with joy. (And I'll wager that that's more than you could say for Nero, despite his vast holdings in gold.)

Besides, God's prosperity is more than emotional. By the time of his death, Paul was welcomed and loved in many of the cities of the Roman Empire. There he had hundreds of houses and brothers and sisters and fathers and mothers and children and fields. God gave him great abundance as he followed the costly way of the cross.[6] Here and now he gave him a land flowing with milk and honey.

EXTRAVAGANCE WITH THE CHURCH

And I suggest that God gives to us extravagantly, especially in and through the church. Let me give two illustrations from Ephesians, all getting closer to the core of the nature and purpose of the church.

First, in chapter 2 Paul tells us that through the cross God has broken down the wall between Jews and Gentiles and made us into one new person (2:14–18). Don't you suppose this is the unity of God's people Jesus prayed for in John 17? Don't you suppose it includes blacks and whites, men and women, rich and poor? I suspect that today's secular ideas on equality and cultural diversity are impractical precisely because they lack the cross of Christ.

That is, on an important level, our world longs for unity. It reaches for it by things as varied as racial integration and cultural diversity, the United Nations and the rights of women and of people with disabilities. But Paul is ahead of the world and teaches that such unity comes only to the people of God and only through the cross.

What a vision! What extravagance God gives the church. The unity that the whole world longs for is available to God's people as we choose to be the church.

Second (or is it still the same point?), in chapter 3, Paul tells us that God gives us this unity in a diverse church that "the wisdom of God in its rich variety might now be made known to the rulers and authorities in the heavenly places" (v. 10). Now think of our world, torn by racial and gender conflicts, by power struggles among different

6. I owe parts of this section to Ludwig Weimer and Arnold Stoetzel. They pointed out to me that this is said eloquently by Joseph Cardinal Ratzinger (now Pope Benedict XVI), *Introduction to Christianity*. See esp. 282ff.

interest groups, by war between Catholics, Protestants, Orthodox, and Muslims, Hutus and Tutsis, Israelis and Palestinians. Then remember sincere people debating racial integration, the free enterprise system, the welfare state, and military interventions by the United Nations. Finally, imagine a church set on a hill where the champions of liberalism and conservatism, of black power and white power, of Tutsis and Hutus finally see their dreams being lived out. And note that according to Paul it is from this united church that the spirits of the age, the principalities and powers, finally learn God's secret. (Are these just words, or is it a promise we can claim for ourselves?)

Then Paul ends chapter 3 with his typical extravagance. He prays that you will "know the love of Christ that surpasses knowledge" (I love oxymorons) "so that you may be filled with all the fullness of God" (3:19). Hello, what does that mean? "Filled with all the fullness of God"? That certainly surpasses my knowledge. Paul then prays for the power of God at work within us "to accomplish abundantly far more than all we can ask or imagine" (3:20).

THE SECRET MADE CONCRETE

Paul seems to think that being filled with all the fullness of God is the normal Christian life. He seems to think that through his people God will accomplish far more than we can ask or imagine. Is he right? Is this normal Christian life, or is it as empty as it is extravagant?

On bad days, Ephesians 1–3 seems like airy-fairy nonsense to me. Or maybe it's not about actual Christian life, but about how God sees us for the purposes of the Final Judgment. That's what many have argued, and I don't blame them. Others say it's the "not yet" of living between the time of the resurrection and the second coming. No doubt that's partly true. But in chapter 4, Paul gets specific. There he spells out the secret of the Christian life in a way that makes dreams come true here and now, at least in part.

He does it in a single monster sentence, the second longest in the Bible. It runs from verse 11 through verse 16. Six verses, 124 words (in Greek). It's the sentence where Paul suggests the extraordinary notion that this book starts with: our growing into the full stature of Christ. And he gives concrete, practical directions on how to do it. Directions to which we Christians haven't paid enough attention. Directions on how to go about being the church.

The basic idea of this complex sentence is that Christ gave his people an abundance of gifts, and if we use these gifts for each other, we will *as a whole group* grow until we are of Jesus' stature. He is talking about us Christians becoming as radically dependent on Jesus and on each other as are the parts of a body on each other. We are to devote our whole lives to giving ourselves and our gifts to each other—just as the parts of a body do. As each of us does this properly, we grow into union with each other and with Christ. Then, not as individuals but as a whole, we attain the full stature of Christ. Not in our own strength, but as a united body whose head is Christ.

Through grace and love, dependence and unity, Christ transforms his people into his body. Which of course has his stature.

What's so preposterous about that? Put that way, it seems quite possible. Maybe the reason we're such spiritual midgets is that we don't even try to live as a body. It's as if we forgot to read the directions.[7]

At least it's odd how rarely we even try to live as a united body, with our dependence on Jesus and each other growing till together we reach his stature. That's the game we're to be playing. Living as the body of Christ in all its depth, unity, breadth, diversity, and abundance. Anything else, no matter how noble, attractive, or effective, is the wrong game.

Let's look at the passage in more detail. Through his death, resurrection, and ascension, Jesus gave gifts to his people, and, according to verse 11, "The gifts he gave were that some would be apostles, some prophets, some evangelists, some pastors and teachers." Wonderfully, in Ephesians the gifts Jesus gives are not abilities or abstract ideas, but *people*—people with ideas and abilities and feelings. (In 1 Corinthians 12 and Romans 12, Paul gives a wider range of gifts, from speaking in tongues to administration to giving money, and there the gifts aren't people but the abilities of people.)

These gifts aren't for the individuals to whom they're given (or rather, who they are). They're for the whole body, "to equip God's people for work in his service, for the building up of the body of Christ, until we all attain to the unity inherent in our faith and in our knowledge of the Son of God—to mature [adulthood], measured by nothing less than the full stature of Christ" (4:12–13 REB). Growing into the stature of Christ is the result of incredibly diverse people pouring themselves out for each other in all sorts of rewarding and costly ways; it's the result of our using Christ's gifts for and on each other.

Let me put it more simply (and this is the core of this book): the secret of Christian growth and Pauline extravagance is the people Jesus has given us becoming one body and pouring themselves out for one another—together. By that I'm saying at least three things about the secret of growth. First, at the heart of growth is the extravaganza of people Jesus has given us. Second, this is not an individualistic process but is about these people starting to function as one, as a body. Third, this happens when the people stop serving themselves and begin pouring themselves out for the others, for the church.

So if something is missing, if we aren't growing the way Paul said we would, might it be because we aren't giving godly people a sufficiently central place in our lives? Might it be because we aren't living as the Spirit-filled, unified, diversified body of Christ, but as a collection of independent individualists trying to use our gifts for personal fulfillment? And might it be that our relationships with other Christians are mostly with those much like ourselves? Or that in our relationships with other Christians we're often serving ourselves rather than laying down our lives for the others?

---

7. Maybe it's because men run the church; women, I'm told, are much more likely to read directions.

In verse 15, Paul clarifies how this sharing of gifts—this growth—happens: "speaking the truth in love, we will in all things grow up into him who is the Head, that is, Christ" (NIV). Notice Paul's expansiveness: he doesn't just repeat that we will grow up into Christ. This time he says we will grow into him in all things. In every single conceivable way.

Paul is serious about us together attaining the full stature of Christ.

And he gets concrete about methods: we do this by lovingly speaking truth to each other. Now, obviously this doesn't mean we grow by telling Jane Christian what we think of her hat. Rather, we grow as we tell each other what we think of Jesus—the way, the truth, and the life. In context, it probably means that growth especially happens when evangelists, prophets, and pastors speak to us about Jesus.

But it's not just the pastors and evangelists. It's every single one of us. Paul says, "as each part is working properly, the whole body promotes its growth by building itself up . . ." (4:16b, REB). *As each part is working properly!* That means that if I'm not using the gift that I am for the church, then the whole body won't grow the way it could. It means that every single one of us has gifts needed for the church to grow. It means that we grow up in Christ to the extent that churches are functioning the way they're supposed to.

Yes, churches. Spiritual growth happens as churches function properly. That's the secret. Not as individual Christians function properly off by themselves. In private. Nor as groups of Christians function together independently of the church. The key is that it's corporate and that it's the church of Jesus Christ. And here's a second summary: *extravagant growth happens as diverse individuals learn to function corporately as the body of Christ.* That's the secret of the Christian life.

Now, that means that if you aren't doing your part, if the pastor isn't pastoring, if some of the parts refuse even to be part of the church and others keep their best for themselves or for things other than the church, then the body won't be growing the way it could. Maybe it's pretty clear why we aren't growing at a rate that will bring us to the full stature of Christ. It takes all of us giving our all toward being melded into one.

Paul goes on to say something even more important: this growth doesn't come from our efforts (even our corporate efforts) but from our Head, from Jesus Christ. It is from him that "the whole body promotes its growth by building itself up" (4:16b, REB). Jesus uses particular people to produce this growth, but he is the one doing it. Not us. We aren't just living as a body: we're living as the body *of Christ*. Learning to live corporately (as a body, from Latin *corpus*) won't be much of a virtue if we're living as some body other than Christ's! IBM's, for example. Or the Communist party's. Or as some community's body.

Notice, too, that Paul focuses on the nature of spiritual growth: "The whole body promotes its growth by building itself up in love" (4:16, REB). Concretely, that means we will love each other more and more as each part of the church works properly. Paul's spirituality isn't some airy-fairy, vague notion. It is growth in love among a particular people. We are growing into the stature of Christ as we grow in love for each other. Not as we grow in tolerance or in apologetic ability or even in Bible-reading, but in love.

The Christian life, then, is about Jesus. Who is about love. And we get there by the people Jesus has given us. By dying to ourselves and using the gifts of the Spirit corporately. The whole thing is extravagant, including the results. According to this passage, that's the how-to of growing into the full stature of Christ.

That, I suggest, is what we all sense down deep that we're missing. That's what we're all longing for. It's the game we're meant to be playing and often aren't.

Not that we're playing it badly. That's inevitable. The problem is that often we aren't playing it at all. Often we aren't even trying to function as a whole. Maybe especially on Sunday morning.

Conclusion

I understand myself to have made three main points, each of which partly explains our lack of growth into the full stature of Christ, each of which partly explains our sense that something is missing. First, God's gifts to us are extravagant, and we can expect full and extravagant lives. It will be like living in a cathedral. But that can't happen if we fearfully move out of the cathedral we've been given in favor of a hovel. We will then have a sense that something is missing. Second, among God's primary gifts to us are brothers and sisters in Christ. They are our cathedral. Or rather, together we make up the cathedral with Christ as our head. To do this, we all need to begin living corporately as the body of Christ. Until that happens, we will have the sense that something important is missing. Third, there is real cost in this. To become the cathedral, to live as a body, we must first die to ourselves. Unity is impossible if every individual's will is demanding its own way. So we must choose the way of the cross. That is foundational.

The cost is, in a sense, terrible. But in another sense, it is only the cost of the man who has been searching for a lifetime for a treasure. When he finds it in a field, "then in his joy he goes and sells all that he has and buys that field" (Matt 13:44). Or to put it differently, "For my yoke is easy, and my burden is light" (Matt 11:30). Until we grasp the extravagance of God's gifts to us and sell all to get them, we will continue to be spiritual midgets.

My understanding now of our earlier emphasis on the cost of discipleship is that, by itself, it is deadly. By itself, emphasizing the cost of discipleship tends to turn the Christian life into a pursuit of the miserable. But combined with an appreciation of God's extravagant gifts to us, we can experience the cross as a pearl of great price. And combined with an understanding of the Christian life as the life of a body, as something the whole church does together, the cost of discipleship seems hardly costly at all.

Paul's revolutionary idea in Ephesians is the central idea not just of Ephesians but of the whole New Testament—in fact, of the whole of the Bible. The idea is that God is gathering together groups of people to love God, to love one another, to die to self, to become one. When you think about it, the Bible is about little more than God's gathering a loving, united people to himself.

Now for one more piece.

These groups don't exist for themselves, so they can feel warm and fuzzy. They have a purpose. And that purpose is to gather the whole world into groups that are in unity with God and therefore with one another. And these groups attract others largely by their unity with one another and their love for each other.

So the purpose of the church, the purpose of Christians, is to love one another across our diversity so the world can believe. Our primary method is loving one another. Not verbal witnessing to non-Christians or devising brilliant arguments for the deity of Christ or doing great social service for the poor or even loving those in the world. Those things all have their place in evangelism—they're important, in fact—but they aren't the core of God's method. They will come to nothing unless people see in us the love God has given us for each other, unless they see Jew and Gentile, black and white, husband and wife, academics and uneducated, living together in peace. That peace is the light set on the hill so the world can see.

That's the game we're to play, the only game we're to play: loving one another for the sake of the world. Not hiding it, but finding ways to let the world see it. Extravagantly and with cost.

To turn it into a slogan, *The mission of the church is to be the church for the world.* That is, the task of the church is loving one another—not for our own sakes but for the sake of the world.

Those are our directions. Let's start following them.

THREE

Something Is Missing (How Did Churches Get Where They Are Today?)

Our failure to follow the Bible's directions about church is frustrating, but it's not hard to understand. In today's churches, how could we follow the directions of Ephesians and all use our gifts for each other? Churches today are rarely structured to make that possible. As most people know, in the New Testament, churches didn't even have buildings. They were generally neighborhood gatherings in the home of a believer. So people's lives presumably tended to overlap, not just for a few hours on Sunday, but also at work, in the market, on the street. When Christians are together during their daily lives, it's clear how they can use their gifts for each other.

But in modern culture, people's daily lives don't overlap enough to use the range of gifts much on each other. And our churches are often designed as performances to be observed. The gifts that matter are those of the performers.

Now I don't mean that no gifts are used in today's churches, that no part is working properly. Even the worst churches have parts that work. The essence of most of them is preaching and teaching, and while those gifts were never meant to stand alone, Ephesians (and much of the rest of the Bible) makes it clear that they're central to the life of God's people. So when preaching and teaching are done properly, spiritual growth will happen.

Other churches use other gifts. Some, for example, serve the poor, and while that wasn't meant to stand alone either, when it happens, spiritual growth will too. Some churches focus on worship (charismatics and those with high-church liturgies), and as they worship God together, spiritual growth will happen. And so on.

But few churches have a way to use anything close to the full range of Christ's gifts for his people. Fortunately, God honors our partial efforts, so good things happen in most all churches. But generally speaking, the fewer gifts we use for each other, the less we grow, while the more gifts we use for each other, the more we grow.

And you aren't using many gifts when a few people do the performing, when the importance of "each part working properly" is forgotten or neglected. That is, you won't be using many gifts when for every person standing in front, ninety-nine commute to watch. Especially when many of the ninety-nine won't see each other again till the next performance.

INSTITUTIONAL INERTIA

In other words, over the centuries our churches have developed in ways that leave their form nearly unconnected to the New Testament, and most Christians could even tell you so if asked. But nonetheless, we settle for our culture's form for church.

Which is more than understandable. The New Testament isn't meant as a handbook on the details of church forms: so use whatever forms work. Especially since changing an accepted cultural form is pretty tough. Most of us couldn't do it if we tried. (Especially not by ourselves, but I'm ahead of myself.)

And it's made tougher by inertia. Especially institutional inertia. In ways we have all experienced, institutions take on a life of their own—quite "innocently." Any form we give the church (or anything else) becomes an institution within hours. That is, it develops a tendency to perpetuate itself. Creativity and imagination tend to be resisted, change is looked at askance, and security rules. Anything that rocks the boat, especially the economic boat, is rebuffed.

This tendency toward institutional self-preservation is especially natural given the success of the church. It has grown into a vast, worldwide network of incredibly successful institutions that includes roughly two billion people. Never has an institution been more successful. The church has outlasted the Roman empire (and every other empire). In numbers, it's bigger than China, and in money it's no slouch. Perhaps the kingdom has come, and I'm just too negative to recognize it.

Undoubtedly that's partly true. The world has never seen success greater than the church's. So if it ain't broke (and its success suggests that it's not), don't fix it. And, boy, do the forms of today's churches work.

Or do they? Many Christians I know have a sense that something is missing. Something important. Interestingly, I suspect this is especially true of pastors; the people at the heart of our churches are often uneasy with what they're doing. And given my interpretation of Ephesians, they should be.

We have found forms that work extraordinarily well at numerical and economic growth. Unfortunately, these forms don't do as much to help us grow into the full stature of Christ. Which happens to be a prime function of the church according to Ephesians (and in different words, according to Matthew and John and every other part of the Bible). What is success anyway? Isn't it growing up as a body into Jesus, into love, joy, peace, patience? Our forms are extraordinarily successful—but not at producing the fruit of the Spirit.

What our churches succeed at is perpetuating themselves. And how do you fight success like that? It's like trying to set up an alternative government. Our present government/churches aren't what their founders intended or what anyone much wants, but given their vast inertia, what's the point of a few of us trying to do better? We should just keep the system, crazy as it is, and try to keep it from getting worse. Or drop out. Especially since even most of those who suspect we're right won't join in; they concluded long ago (and with some reason) that change is a utopian notion. Things can't be fundamentally altered.

This is sensible. But then, so were the Israelites at Kadesh-Barnea when they decided not to enter Canaan. They thought the inhabitants were too strong for them (Num 13). Which was true—if you leave God out.

Besides, if we're "sensible," we'll have to content ourselves with being spiritual runts. And not just us but everyone else, too. Depressed expectations destroy.

If not us, who? If not now, when?[1]

Before Constantine

How did we get to where we are?

People like me talk as if the Fall occurred in the early fourth century when Constantine became the Roman emperor. Offhand that seems unlikely.

Something nervous-making happened when Constantine slaughtered his rivals in the name of the cross of Jesus, but for now I'm not mostly concerned about his violence. I'm concerned about how Constantine changed the form and thereby the function of churches: he changed them in such a way that passages like Ephesians 4 began to seem odd, if not completely meaningless.

Let me suggest more fully the context in which Ephesians 4 made sense. First, we need to understand the form that churches took in Paul's time. The idea of local churches seems to have grown substantially out of the synagogues scattered wherever Jews were dispersed. They weren't temples where priests performed sacred or magical rituals. Rather, they were centers for the Jewish community: part place of prayer, part school, part social-gathering point, part market, part place for community elders to judge and make decisions.

In short, they were the center of life for Jews living outside Jerusalem. They were started abroad by lonely Jews—aliens in a foreign land. The parallel for Americans abroad would be if the American embassy, American Express, and the only English-speaking church in town were all in the same building, with a coffee shop included—only synagogues tended to be smaller than that would be.

Then when Christian Jews got into too many conflicts in the local synagogue, they started meeting in the home of one of the wealthier Christians. This limited their size to no more than those who could fit into the largest room of a large house.[2] When they got too big (as they apparently did in Rome), they would divide and start meeting in different houses.

1. Hillel, *Pirkei Avot*, 1:14. This bit of Jewish wisdom was made famous by Ronald Reagan in his second inaugural address.

2. For a more detailed discussions of this topic, see Del Birkey, *The House Church*. Robert Banks also has an excellent scholarly discussion of the topic, *Paul's Idea of Community*.

Second, the cost was clear. Indications are that the message of Jesus was still being preached: give up all and take up your cross. They preached costly discipleship, not salvation through easy believism or baptism. Besides, the average Jew was not enthusiastic about this new sect and neither was the average Gentile. Persecution was likely, martyrdom possible. The cost was obvious.

With these two ingredients (the cost of discipleship plus a house church model growing out of the synagogue), Ephesians 4 makes sense. It sets up the conditions for joining a new extended family. In this new family, you could experience love and honesty and intimacy as you'd never experienced them before. With this small group, you could have a deep sense of community and interdependence—emotional, economic, social, and intellectual. So deep that you could get the wealth of growing as close together as the parts of a body. (Whether you would or not is another question.)

With these people, persecuted like you, you could find your identity so that it no longer much mattered whether previously your story had been primarily as a Roman or a male or a slave, American or black or gay. You tended to become a sojourner in all other societies. With any social group (principality?) other than the church, you always felt a little foreign. You could not be quite at home in any empire, whether of Rome or of Israel, of wealth or socialism, of profession or class. Your identity and security were in God your father and Jesus your brother—and in the other brothers and sisters (gifts) God had given you as your new family.

Your identity (unity) with this family didn't grow just out of meetings or watching others perform. It grew the same way a family's does—from life together. From meals together, from sacrificing for each other, from mourning together the deaths of those you love, from celebrating births and victories together, from work together, from transacting business together. This identity grew like the camaraderie of sorority members or of those who hang out at the same bar or coffeehouse. It also grew like the camaraderie of soldiers who face the enemy together and watch their comrades go home in body bags.

No doubt, this is an idealized picture, one that rarely came fully to life in the first century or any other era. So don't misunderstand me: I'm not suggesting a return to the golden era of the New Testament (when we were all persecuted!). Passages like 1 Corinthians 11, Revelation 2–3, Galatians 2 (and on and on) make it clear that no golden era ever existed. The New Testament doesn't offer perfect people or perfect forms to copy. Rather it gives us the goals, points toward ideals, and reflects on actual churches in all their successes and failures. In this way, the Bible can function as a norm even when no actual person or human institution can. So you can learn what churches are to be (normatively) from reading about an imperfect church, if the failures are pointed out. That method is probably even clearer than reading about a perfect church.

Even with that qualification, the form of early churches and their social situation was supportive of becoming an extended family in a way that most churches today aren't. After all, early churches were house churches reminiscent of extended families in size and structure. And the cost was clear. They were not the sort of extended family that you could be born into, nor would you join one for social advantage. You had to choose personally, and it was costly. You never knew where you would lay your head, your biological family would probably be distressed by your lack of loyalty to them, and the state might well try to kill you. These sorts of things made the very nature of the church different from what we have today.

CONSTANTINE AND ALL THAT

Then came Constantine.

Not that Constantine was especially bad as Roman emperors went. And not that it was all his fault. Most church leaders must have forgotten what church was about before Constantine came along, or he couldn't have taken over so easily. The division of clergy and laity was already under way, and the hatred and division revealed by the hideous church controversies of that century can't remotely be blamed on Constantine. (My reading of the fourth century is that he is more a sign of the problems than the cause.)

But suddenly it cost nothing to be a Christian. Mind you, I'm glad not to have to worry about lions. But as F. F. Bruce says, "Christianity thus became fashionable, which was not really a good thing. It meant a considerable ingress of Christianized pagans into the church."[3] Earlier there had been "not many wise, not many mighty, not many noble" (1 Cor 1:26). Now there were many wise, many mighty, and many noble. Being a Christian paid. And no need to sojourn anymore. You could be right at home in the Empire and also right at home in your church. Nor was there any need for God's extended family; you could keep the one you were born into. And you can bet that with all the rich and mighty people in churches, sermons on the rich young ruler became rare. So a fundamental theological shift came inevitably when Christianity was legalized: the cost of discipleship was largely lost.

Then before long everyone in the Empire was Christian. Born Christian, in fact, so no choice had to be made. It was mandatory.[4] Which made churches grow wonderfully, at least numerically. Which destroyed the relationships and the sense of family. If you met a fellow Christian in the street, you no longer had that sense of delight in meeting a good friend: now everyone you met was a fellow Christian—sort of.

And the momentum for transforming churches into buildings increased. Living rooms were no longer large enough for get-togethers. Besides, the empire encouraged building buildings—impressive buildings.[5] Church architecture changed. Meetings moved from smallish rooms shaped so all could participate to huge buildings where the front was emphasized more and more. These buildings held so many people you

3. Bruce, *The Spreading Flame*, 295.

4. Constantine decreed the toleration of Christianity in 313, but it wasn't till 380 that Theodosius made Christianity mandatory.

5. Micks, *The Future Present*, 101–02.

didn't know everyone, and perhaps more seriously, only a few professional performers could actually participate except by sitting and watching. And paying.

At their frequent worst, these churches focused their meetings on a magical ritual from an altar that laypeople weren't allowed to approach. In Europe sermons were in a language that many laborers outside Italy couldn't understand.[6] Conversions were at sword point, and dissenters were tortured to death. Even in the monastic movement, the call was not for all Christians to lay down their lives and live in new extended families but only for unmarried people to do so, and then only if they had a special calling. The New Testament picture of the normal Christian life had been abandoned. And the form for producing it (the house church) had been lost.

Jesus would have been turning over in his grave—if he'd still been there.

From that moment the chance to use the gifts of the Spirit for one's brothers and sisters was all but gone for the average Christian. From now on, using the gifts of the Spirit was reserved mostly for professional clergy and others who stand up front. It was almost gone because the relatively small groups of persecuted Christians had been replaced by the religion of the empire.

In that process, two things were lost. First, we lost the idea of the cost of discipleship, that we serve Jesus with our whole being or not at all. It was now normal to call yourself a Christian while mostly serving the emperor or money or self. Second, we lost the idea of churches as relatively small groups who become the body of Christ and serve as your new family. With the loss of those two elements, the interdependence of a body taught in Ephesians almost ceased to make sense.

And over the next millennium and a half, the church has rarely recovered it. Or so I will argue.

Reformers

I'll skip over the next thousand years including the split between Roman Catholics and Eastern Orthodox because in that time the situation remained essentially unchanged with respect to the things I'm talking about. Parts of that history are horrifying: bishops "baptizing" people by holding a sword at their throat and kings converting (along with their whole kingdom) out of political expediency.[7] Throughout that whole period for both Catholic and Orthodox, church included little notion of discipleship and little sense of new family. The situation was often challenged but never successfully. But by the 1500s, it was clear to many in the West that Catholicism was malformed. This led to the Reformation and Counter-Reformation. The Reformation transformed theology and led to Protestantism; the Counter-Reformation transformed moral practice and revived Roman Catholicism. But neither attempted to address the function or form of the church taught in Ephesians, and neither recovered the idea of the cost of disciple-

---

6. This was less of a problem in Asia.

7. Details of this can be found many places. One popular source, readily available at the moment is: James Reston Jr., *The Last Apocalypse: Europe at the Year 1000 A. D.*

ship so clearly taught in the New Testament. Eastern Orthodoxy, perhaps even more under the sway of Constantine than Roman Catholicism and the Reformation, didn't address these questions either. And they all persecuted anyone who tried to call for the sorts of things I'm saying.

That is, the Reformation, the Counter-Reformation, and Eastern Orthodoxy kept a system in which everyone born in a certain area belonged to the church chosen by the government. So in Zurich and Geneva, you were automatically Reformed; in Wittenberg and Scandinavia, you were Lutheran; in Italy and Spain, you were Catholic; in Russia and Greece, you were Orthodox. No personal choice was required, or even allowed; the only cost was for dissent. Dissenters tended to be exiled, if not tortured to death slowly. Practically, neither the Reformers, the Counter-Reformers, nor the Orthodox had much concept of a believers' church, of a new family, or of the cost of discipleship. The Reformers taught the priesthood of all believers, but they kept the old forms for the church. Which made it clear who the real priests were. So after all the upheaval of the Reformation, large buildings remained the center along with professional performers, and being a Christian cost less than not being a Christian.

Steps weren't taken to make the priesthood of all believers practical; few steps were taken to adjust the forms of church to make it natural for the "laity" to share the gifts of the Spirit with each other. To put it differently, the distinction between clergy and laity made as much sense after the Reformation as before. But that distinction is fatal for living as a body, at least if the body you're trying to be is Christ's.

John Calvin (one of the most important Reformers and my personal favorite) gives two criteria for deciding whether a church is faithful: right proclamation of the word and right administration of the sacraments.[8] These are good criteria, but what he omits is interesting. His criteria don't consider the level of fellowship and interdependence within the church, the depth of their love for each other, or whether the group functions as a family or body. Someone else said, "By this everyone will know that you are my disciples, if you have love for one another" (John 13:35).

The Reformation didn't go far enough. Neither did the Counter-Reformation. We need a new reformation to restore the church. We need a new reformation to break down the clergy-laity distinction and restore the cost of discipleship so that we can all experience the richness of the gifts the Spirit has given. Then together we can grow spiritually as well as numerically.

ANABAPTISTS AND FREE CHURCHES

During the Reformation, some people went further. Their enemies called them Anabaptists (rebaptizers) because they insisted that only adult baptism counted:

---

8. *Institutes of the Christian Religion*, IV, i, 8–14. Calvin's concern here was to avoid writing people out of the church for trivial reasons, and on that perhaps he was right. But I think my point still holds. Somewhere, somehow Calvin and the other Reformers needed to emphasize the centrality of actually living as one body. They didn't.

you became part of a church only by personal choice as an adult. Both Catholics and Protestants were about as impressed as Nero and Diocletian had been with Christians. The resulting persecution clarified the cost of discipleship and contributed to Anabaptists' sense of alienation from surrounding cultures. It also helped make them good sojourners and drove them closer to each other—toward being an extended family. At their frequent best, their identity was in Jesus and each other, not in their country, their profession, or their successful church structures. (Today we know these people mostly as Mennonites, Amish, and Church of the Brethren.)

Throughout church history, others have had parallel insights (Donatists, Waldensians, Quakers, some Puritans, Moravians, early Methodists, Plymouth Brethren, and many more). But they were always a small minority and had little impact on the forms of the Protestant, Catholic, and Orthodox churches that most of us come from. In fact, the impact was usually the other way around. Over the centuries, most of these groups acculturated to the point that their practices and forms aren't that different from those of standard churches. So today if you join urban Mennonites for a service, you often have a hard time telling their forms from the church down the street that grew out of the Reformation, nor can you count on their teaching on discipleship being clear. They've acculturated well to the empires that surround them.

This is partly because on one or two crucial points the Anabaptists won. They were early advocates of freedom of religion. (If you believe that people have to decide personally as adults whether to follow Jesus, you almost have to let them decide "no.") And by now almost all Christians agree with this central claim, at least in the West. The rise and success of Baptists and other free churches (that is, churches that aren't state churches) guaranteed this. In the United States it was written into the Bill of Rights, and today even countries with state churches tolerate dissenters.[9] (Today, even words like "dissenter" and "toleration" seem quaint in relation to religion.)

So it's no longer as true that the local prince decides your church for you. In countries with state churches, the churches are usually sick or dying while in countries with "free" churches, the churches are more likely to be booming. We have won the right to freedom of religion, and many recognize the need for believers' churches that people choose into as adults. Constantine is dead.

If I had any sense, I'd rejoice in this and see it as yet another sign that the kingdom is here. But never fear, I'm going to whine about this too. For Constantine is also alive and well.

RELIGION AS THE ORGANIZING PRINCIPLE OF LIFE

The trouble is that freedom of religion (like most good things) has its underside, especially when cut off from other truths. Without a clear understanding of the cost of discipleship, Christianity easily becomes a tool of the economy and nation. (The devil puts even the best things into his service.) To put it obnoxiously, the local prince may

9. This is less clear with the Eastern Church.

no longer choose your church, but he[10] still chooses what you serve. At least, he tries to—and with far more success than we realize. He, or the spirit of the age, determines whether we serve our job (capitalism), the state (socialism), our pleasure (hedonism), or whatever. Then when we're done with that (with our religious service to our true king), we're free to go to the church of our choice. We can go to any church we like, providing we don't fundamentally challenge the surrounding culture, providing church is something we do in our spare time, providing we're mostly good little socialists or good little Republicans or good little devotees of art.

Anabaptists fought for freedom of religion because religion was so important that it of all things had to be freely chosen. Modern people have "freedom of church" because the principalities figured out that our churches are so unimportant they aren't worth fighting over. If the church-growth people are right, most people decide whether to be Presbyterian or Baptist much as they decide whether to use Pepsodent or Colgate. It's not a matter of truth but of private preference.

But when Catholics and Reformers and Anabaptists disagreed on religion, they were disagreeing on the organizing principle of life, on whom they were going to serve. That would be worth killing for if anything were.[11] But today church isn't like a synagogue that serves as the organizing point of life.[12] Church is usually what you do with your spare time. So it's less important whether you prefer Mennonite church services or baseball games. Why should the principalities mind if you prefer "going to church" to going to sports events?

So when the founding fathers of the United States guaranteed freedom of church, they weren't guaranteeing the freedom to organize our lives as we see fit. They were tacitly assuming that we would organize our lives in terms of democratic capitalism,[13] and they were making it hard for us to disrupt democracy and capitalism by minor matters like our beliefs about going to church.

The point is that at a deep level Western people are democratic capitalists. (Whether we're conscious of it or not,[14] we organize our lives economically—that is, around work and consumption, especially consumption as entertainment. Have you gone to any entertaining church performances lately?) So church persecution ceased (the Anabaptists won) the moment the rulers noted that persecution wasn't economically productive.[15] (Who is it that won?) The important thing is to keep people happy

---

10. I'm leaving the masculine pronoun because I suspect that women have rarely been allowed to play a real role in shaping modern religions.

11. Mind you, I don't know enough to argue this, but I suspect that even then wars of "religion" were fought more over economics and "tribal" hatreds than over faith.

12. Perhaps Jews keeping the form of the synagogue is part of the reason for their persecution. Religion still matters, at least to Orthodox Jews.

13. Chapter 4, and much of the rest of Part II, is devoted to defending and explaining this claim.

14. The things we believe most deeply we're often unconscious of. They're too deep down for us to be conscious of them.

15. My argument here may sound paranoid, but it's not controversial to say some princes used the Reformation for economic gain. If a prince chose one church, his neighbor (with a different church) had

so they will be good workers. And Mennonites and Methodists are great workers. Why persecute them? Why not induce them to acculturate?

Until recently, communists were another matter. They were worth killing. (So what is our real religion, and just how much freedom of religion do we have?)

So perhaps in this culture, the task of reinventing the church is finding ways to make Jesus, instead of democratic capitalism, the organizing principle of our lives. (Which doesn't imply that democratic capitalism is wrong.) And for some, our organizing principle may be something other than the economy. It may be being gay or the love of art or opposition to democratic capitalism or whatever. Nevertheless, our task is the same: how do we move Jesus back to the center, not just of Sunday morning, but of our whole lives? In a society with minimal persecution like the West, how do we remember that the way of Christ is the way of the cross?

But whether my claim about the organizing principles of our lives is true or not, free churches have acculturated in another, clearer way: the shape of free churches, too, is basically the one bequeathed by Constantine. Free church congregations often number in the hundreds or thousands, and their buildings have rows of seats all pointed toward the front. How can such a church live as an extended family, not to mention as a body? Especially if it's based on entertaining performances? Inevitably the identity of free-church members tends to be in something other than Jesus and the church.

This is a tragic process, but it's almost inevitable. Every generation must appropriate the gospel for itself, even if they've inherited the best of traditions. That is, every generation must reinvent the church for itself.

ON NOT GOING TO CHURCH

And here is what we have to reinvent. We have to turn church into the crossroad of life (like the synagogue). We have to reinvent ways to connect with each other so that we give to each other the gifts that we are. Let me say it yet another way: we have to reinvent ways to be the church instead of sliding into the inevitable process of going to church. Church is the way of the cross; it's a full-time occupation. It's not having your sins forgiven and then attending one meeting each week—or even three.

Church isn't the sort of thing you can go to. You can be the church, you can become the church, you can even do church, but you can't go to church. (Nowhere does the New Testament mention going to church.) One way of saying it is that church is the sort of thing that you become part of at the cost of your life. You're the church whenever you're with other Christians in such a way that you depend on each other enough that to do it you have to die to yourself. In that situation and almost only in that

---

an excuse to try to seize the territory. Whatever reason the citizens had for fighting, as far as the princes were concerned these were usually wars of religion only in the sense that wealth and power are the true religion of most of us. To use a different illustration, Henry VIII was not sorry to confiscate the vast estates of the monasteries.

situation, can you love each other, serve each other, live in unity, and speak the truth to each other in love the way Ephesians 4 teaches.

This sort of life doesn't happen mostly in buildings with steeples but in the street, at home, at work, in the creation of art, on the telephone, while you baby-sit or change people's oil or eat together. So for example, church is rocking the screaming baby of a fellow Christian and then later trying together to find ways that the baby might cry less. Church is composing an oratorio that brings the experience of the glory of God to both church and world.

Our task is to find ways to become the church together. I suggest that becoming the church is rather like becoming a baseball team. Players have to practice together enough to learn each other's strengths and weaknesses. Then they can use each other's strengths and play around each other's weaknesses. They sort out who can pitch, who can field, who can bat, who can coach. In the process, they learn to rely on each other, and somewhere along the way, rather mysteriously, they cease being just a collection of individuals and have a group identity. They become a team. They become the Cubs.

That's our task in reinventing the church.

Let me torture the team metaphor by spelling it out. First, when Ryne Sandberg was a Cub, he didn't "go" to Cubs games; he played the games. Going to them was something he could only do after he retired. He couldn't "go" because he was a participant—even if he was sitting on the bench waiting till he was needed.

Church is participatory in much the same way. But people are so stuck on the standard model of the church that when you talk about church being participatory, the only thing they can think of is making services more participatory or adding on more lay committees. There is something to making services more participatory and church government more democratic, but that's not what I'm saying. That's not it at all. What I'm saying is that church isn't mostly services and committee meetings. Both are important, but church is mostly crying with your brother in Christ when he learns that his son is disabled. Or helping your sister make her house more beautiful while talking together about the way, the truth, and the life.

Second, both in churches and on teams, it's crucial to identify people's gifts and weaknesses. A team won't survive long as a team if they use Ferguson Jenkins as a catcher or put Randy Hundley in to pitch. Naturally, church roles aren't always as clear as in baseball, but you better not normally send guests to stay with a couple who is terrified of people, nor should an intimidating person be used to comfort those experiencing failure. Church doesn't go well unless each player has a position that he or she can play "properly."

Third, being a team isn't the sort of thing you can do alone. The best pitcher in the world can't be a baseball team by himself.[16] A catcher would be nice, not to mention a fielder or two.

---

16. This is an adaptation of an illustration I learned from Rich Read. His illustration is how odd it would be for a football quarterback to think he could play football by himself, which is a better illustration.

This is obviously true of becoming the church, but I mean more than that. I mean that being a Christian isn't the sort of thing it's meaningful to do by yourself. I don't mean that it's a sin for a Christian to be a loner. (A Christian in prison or in Mecca might have no choice.) But God intends us to be part of a team, part of a body. This is of the essence of being Christian. So trying to be a Christian alone would be like Ferguson Jenkins trying to play baseball by himself. That wouldn't be merely arrogant; it would be silly. It would suggest he didn't know what game he was playing.

This is why we Christians are so often of such short stature. And why we need to reinvent the church.

Fourth, in neither baseball nor church is the building crucial. The church is wherever its people are; it's not the building they meet in. Remember, you can play baseball in the middle of the street if you want to. And having a stadium won't make you a team. Stadiums are about revenue for the owners and performers, not about baseball.

This may seem too obvious to need saying, but in English (unlike Greek and German, for example) the most common word for "church" covers both the people and the building. This is a tragedy that makes it easier for us to talk about going to church. Be clear: nowhere in the New Testament is church used of a building. That's why reformers in the English-speaking world have so often refused to call their buildings churches. Quakers call them meetinghouses, Wesleyans call them preaching points (or they did when they were Wesleyan), and English Baptists and Plymouth Brethren call them chapels.

Fifth, in both baseball and the church, people have to abandon their private pursuit of glory for the sake of the team. Obviously, professional athletes may fail at this even more than Christians, but the point holds. Teams play better when egos don't rule, when the person with the ball doesn't hog it but passes it onto the one with the greatest gift in a given situation. This is at the heart of the Gospel.

I could go on with parallels between becoming the church and becoming a team. In both, it's more a process than an event. In both, it's a matter of spirit. In both, the way it happens is rather mysterious. In both, coaching and mentoring are crucial. In both, not recognizing your need for others is disastrous. In both, there's a place for observing, but it's mostly for people not on the team. And so on.

But my real point is that if we're to grow into the stature of Christ, we must stop going to church and reinvent forms that help us become the church whatever the cost.[17] If Ryne Sandberg or you are sitting in the stands watching, you both better stop going to the game and start playing. There are limits to how well you can learn to play by watching others and listening to lectures.

Now, it may seem that my claim turns on a couple of interesting linguistic differences between Greek and English—and not differences of great importance. Who cares if in Greek you don't say it the way you do in English? After all, you don't say

17. For an extended reflection on church form, see Part III, "Reflections on Doing Church in America." In many ways this book is about trying to find forms that will help us be the people of God in America today.

anything in English the way you do in Greek. What matters isn't that you say it right but that you do it right.

That's true, of course. However, language shapes and reflects how we experience reality. And some ways of speaking reflect terrible distortions. So it's important (to understate the matter considerably) not to call black men "boys" and not to call adult women "girls." Such language shapes (and reveals) how we see our world.

As does talking about going to church: it reveals and shapes a fundamental disorientation. It's the sort of mistake you'd be making if you said someone slept slowly or came home in a taxi and a flood of tears.[18] How can we reinvent the church if we understand it so badly that we normally speak of it as something it's not, as the sort of thing you could go to?

Changing our language will help us reinvent church.

Conclusion

So whatever happened to church? By now that should be clear. We lowered the cost so much we could meet in large buildings with hundreds of people watching others perform. It's as simple as that. So we lost the sense of family, the sense of identity, of natural ways to die to ourselves and give ourselves (the gifts of the Spirit) to each other. The organizing principle of our lives ceased to be Jesus and his people.

Now, of course, every period had important exceptions. The most notable was the monastic movement. From the time of Constantine on, the church has been called to faithfulness by millions of monks and nuns trying to live as the body of Christ.[19] And in all periods, people in small churches can get to know each other, and in village churches the lives of people overlap enough that they can live as a body if they choose to. And large, contemporary churches often have small groups to make up for the anonymity of services where you mostly see the backs of others' heads. And though parachurch organizations make it harder for local churches to be as central as they need to be, they often provide connections to smaller groups and outlets for ministry superior to those in traditional churches. Furthermore, in every age faithful people find ways to live better than the structures that surround them.

Still, for the average Christian these things have had little impact. For we have quit playing the game given us by Jesus. Is it any wonder that we find it odd even to talk of growing into the full stature of Christ? Is it any wonder that we have a sense that something is missing? Something important?

---

18. English teachers call these syntactical errors (the grammar is fine). And philosophers call them category mistakes. See Gilbert Ryle, *The Concept of Mind*, 14–23. Ryle suggests that these errors are as important as logical errors because they help us think wrongly. Therefore, detecting category mistakes can help us see the origin of our mistakes and the way toward correcting them.

19. It's no accident that the monastic movement, with its high requirements, took root around the time of Constantine, precisely as the church was lowering its requirements.

What's missing is the church . . . functioning as the body of the Crucified One, with all the cost and joy that implies.

PART TWO

Things that Make It Hard for Modern Christians to Do Church Well (Reflections on Getting Culturally Absorbed)

FOUR

On Taking Attendance at Church
(My Personal Relationship with Jesus)

What do you think would happen in your church if the elders proposed taking attendance? What if they said that a member who missed two meetings in a row would have an elder call on her? And if she missed very often after that without explanation, her name would be removed from the roll?

In any church I've ever been part of, such a proposal would cause turmoil. Unless it turned out to be an April Fool's prank.

But we don't object to taking attendance at work. In fact, employers not only check on whether you come, they check on whether you come *on time*. So in most jobs you have to punch a time clock. And no one bats an eye.

Which is interesting. Why are time clocks in church so much more troubling than at work? Of course, I'm not literally proposing time clocks in church buildings; it would engender legalism. But I doubt that we're mostly distressed about legalism. At least, we tolerate all sorts of other legalisms in church.

I suspect that our problem here isn't fear of legalism but fear of commitment and accountability. We don't want to be that committed or accountable in church, especially in a particular church.

So while I'm not proposing a time clock in church lobbies, I am proposing that kind of commitment to a particular church. But as soon as you get that concrete, people begin talking about fanaticism or cultishness or legalism. Why? Is it fanatical or cultish for employers to ask people to be at work regularly and on time?

I suggest that the issue here is a notion of individual freedom that runs deep in our culture. We feel that a church taking attendance would violate our freedom. We feel that way (whether we think that way or not) because individual freedom is so basic to Western people. In fact, it may be *the* basic value of both modern and postmodern Westerners. Which makes it hard for modern people to be the church well.

Most of us are willing to surrender that freedom for work. Why not for church? Is it because we think work is more important? Is it because work pays and church doesn't?

The same sort of problem arises with marriage and family, maybe especially for men. People want sex (and maybe even intimacy), but without commitment or accountability. This is most obvious with abortion and teenage sex, but I've had more than one adult male tell me he's left his wife for the sake of freedom. His own freedom, of course.

Maybe I have some of the details wrong, but if church is to become all it's meant to be, if we are together to grow into the full stature of Christ, we will need to start taking church as seriously as we take work. Without commitment, we'll also be without spiritual growth, deep love, and meaningful intimacy. Commitment is essential whether in sex, family, church, or small group.

MY PERSONAL RELATIONSHIP WITH JESUS

Theologically conservative Western Christians tend to be centrally concerned with their personal, individual relationship with Jesus. Which is certainly better than being mostly concerned about church institutions and buildings. Given our paradigms, it makes all kinds of sense. In fact, if you combine traditional Christian views with modern paradigms, you have little choice but to believe that the only important thing for each human being is to make a personal decision for Jesus. And in some sense, that's true of course.

But in another sense, it's a set up. It's a set up to minimize the corporate. So we think that a street person has been saved if we get him to say a prayer asking Jesus into his heart. We then feel little need to disciple him, help him get a job, take him home, or even take him to church. If you believe in personal salvation, then in the standard Western paradigm, an individual's one-time decision for Jesus is more important than food, shelter, or church. Private, personal transactions are what matter most.

Within this paradigm, it makes sense for evangelicals to have mass evangelistic rallies without planning how to disciple the people who choose Jesus. If a private, personal transaction is what matters, then training people to live as Christians is, as a matter of fact, less important than converting them. So it's not unusual after crusades for the names of converts to be sent to any church in the person's zip code. (You couldn't get churches to cooperate unless they had an equal chance at getting "referrals.")

But what if some of those churches aren't designed to train new Christians or don't know what discipleship might mean? Many evangelicals worry about that, but we go ahead with our mass rallies anyway. We do it because we believe that what really matters is getting the private decision. It would be good to train converts, but if you have to choose between mass evangelism and discipleship training, it's a no-brainer. If you combine evangelical theology with Western paradigms, you can hardly reach any other conclusion.

That also explains why church isn't central for modern and postmodern Christians. What matters is my personal relationship with Jesus—not my relationship or lack thereof with a church. So if my employer wants me to transfer to another city, I don't need to check out the churches in that city. Once again, it's a no-brainer because my personal relationship with Jesus isn't going to change just because I move, now is it? By the same token, I don't need to ask my church how my move will affect them because how can my move affect their personal relationships with Jesus? Whatever happened to the second commandment?

Emily Dickinson puts the modern belief wonderfully:

> Some keep the Sabbath going to Church—
> I keep it, staying at Home—
> With a Bobolink for a Chorister—
> And an Orchard for a Dome—
>
> Some keep the Sabbath in Surplice—
> I just wear my Wings—
> And instead of tolling the Bell for Church,
> Our little Sexton—sings.
>
> God preaches—a noted Clergyman—
> And the sermon is never long;
> So instead of getting to Heaven at last—
> I'm going, all along.[1]

Dickinson puts this with her usual winsomeness. How could anyone disagree? Modern and postmodern people hardly can.

So not surprisingly, 63 percent of Americans think church attendance is unimportant. Nonetheless, I was astonished that 47 percent of evangelicals agree. I shouldn't have been. We live in a culture that has lost the sense of the corporate, and so naturally we have lost the corporate element of our faith. This isn't entirely our fault. It points to a basic cultural malaise—the same one pointed to by our discomfort at the idea of time clocks in church buildings.

Isaiah's personal relationship with Yahweh

But don't get me wrong. Our individual relationship with God is important. The Bible is always telling stories of personal encounters with God. Eve, Noah, Abraham, Moses, Gideon, Solomon, Isaiah, Mary, Jesus, Paul. The Bible tells dozens of such stories, maybe hundreds, and not just from one period of time or in one part of the Bible. These stories are throughout the Bible and throughout the history of the people of God.

But that's not the only thing in the Bible. It's just the only thing visible through conservative glasses.

---

1. Dickinson, *The Complete Poems*, 153–54.

Lately I've been studying Isaiah, and I've been struck by how odd Isaiah is for contemporary people—or rather how odd he would seem if we understood him. Apparently, Isaiah can't decide if he's a conservative or a liberal, whether the individual or society is more important.

Isaiah 6 records one of the great personal encounters between God and an individual:

> In the year that King Uzziah died, I saw the Lord sitting on a throne, high and lofty; and the hem of his robe filled the temple. Seraphs were in attendance above him; each had six wings: with two they covered their faces, and with two they covered their feet, and with two they flew. And one called to another and said: "Holy, holy, holy is the LORD of hosts; the whole earth is full of his glory." The pivots on the thresholds shook at the voices of those who called, and the house filled with smoke. I said: "Woe is me! I am lost, for I am a man of unclean lips, and I live among a people of unclean lips; yet my eyes have seen the King, the LORD of hosts!" (Isa 6:1–5)

The first part of Isaiah's reaction is one conservatives are comfortable with: "Woe is me! I am lost, for I am a man of unclean lips." But notice what he says next: "And I live among a people of unclean lips." What does that have to do with anything? Is he a liberal or something? In conservative paradigms this makes little sense; it's too corporate. Yet Isaiah treats corporate uncleanness as of roughly the same importance as individual uncleanness.

So while Isaiah seems to assume that personal responsibility is as important as conservatives think, he also assumes that corporate sin is as devastating to individuals as liberals think. He holds those thoughts together. It matters how we behave as individuals, and it matters who we live among. They interact.

To put it differently, we moderns draw sharp lines between the corporate and the individual. Isaiah (and the rest of the Bible) blurs those lines.

THE ASSYRIANS

Maybe even odder to us than Isaiah's blurring of lines is his reaction to his encounter with Yahweh. If it had happened to me, I'd go around trying to get everyone to have the same experience. Isaiah doesn't. His rhetoric is devoid of anything comparable to "having a personal relationship with Yahweh" and of "inviting Yahweh into your heart." What's going on here?

What Isaiah does is less individualistic; he calls the people of God as a whole to repent and trust God for political and military salvation. Or in his much more moving language, "In returning and rest you shall be saved; in quietness and in trust shall be your strength" (Isa 30:15b). This sounds like a good, evangelical verse, very individualistic, but in historical context it's saying something corporate and most unevangelical.

The whole world known to Israel was being devastated by the Assyrians. The ten tribes had already been carried off, and not much land was left for the others except

Jerusalem. At the time Isaiah was calling Israel to return and rest, either Jerusalem itself was under attack or they knew they would be at any moment. What Isaiah was saying was that Jerusalem as a city could only be saved from Assyria by trusting God.

Assyria's invasion was a corporate problem for Israel. Not that individuals were irrelevant, but no individual could deal with the invasion. They had to decide as a nation what to do. They had to make military and political decisions. So when Isaiah says, "In returning and rest you shall be saved," he isn't talking about the salvation of the individual souls of Israelites. He's talking about the nation being saved corporately from the military might of Assyria. Not that they wouldn't also be saved individually, but insofar as Isaiah bothers with the corporate/individual distinction, his focus here is on the corporate.

Now it makes sense to tell people that their personal salvation is in returning to God and resting in God. It makes sense if people are messing up their lives by adultery or by working eighty hours a week. Then you repent and rest. But what does it mean if the Assyrians are running amok? If the Iraqis are threatening germ warfare? In that sort of case, I'd advise against rest. Then you need to get you some big guns. (While preaching personal salvation, of course, because a lot of people are going to die. They need to be prepared to meet their maker—personally.) And I sure wouldn't criticize the government for making a treaty with Egypt or any other available superpower. Some outsiders need to be called in to help defend tiny Jerusalem.

But oddly, Isaiah doesn't agree. His message is corporate. It's military and political. "In returning and in rest, you shall be saved" from the military might of Assyria. When the Israelites refuse his message, they do it by saying, "No! We will flee upon horses." And he says, "Therefore you shall flee!" (Isa 30:16a). Here, not being saved means fleeing the Assyrians.

If there's any doubt, a few verses later he adds, "Alas for those who go down to Egypt for help and who rely on horses, who trust in chariots because they are many and in horsemen because they are very strong, but do not look to the Holy One of Israel or consult the LORD!" (Isa 31:1). God or military might? That's Isaiah's question. But we have all but lost the corporate element of our faith.

Isaiah hadn't. He didn't focus on individual repentance but on the corporate repentance of Jerusalem and Judah.

READING THE BIBLE INDIVIDUALISTICALLY

The problem is that evangelicals bring individualistic glasses to the Bible. Since our paradigms don't leave much place for the corporate, we just don't see it in the Bible (or anywhere else). Since it makes no sense to us, it isn't there. So when we come across, "In returning and rest you shall be saved," we naturally read it as if it were talking about private, individual salvation. We conveniently omit the historical situation and the actual meaning.

This obscures much of the Bible. It would take the whole book to argue this well, but let me ask some questions in passing. How much difference would it make to our understanding of Jesus' teaching if we understood how much of it was directed to Israel corporately? If we understood that the authors of the Gospels were writing to particular churches so that they would understand how to treat their sisters and brothers in Christ?

What if the Sermon on the Mount is mostly on how the people of God are to treat one another and not on how each individual is to treat every other individual "in the world"? What would a church-based interpretation do to "Give to everyone who begs from you, and do not refuse anyone who wants to borrow from you" (Matt 5: 42)?

And what would a corporate interpretation do to our understanding of the parables? What if the prodigal son is the (mostly poor) Israelites who weren't keeping the law strictly but were flocking to Jesus? And what if the older brother is establishment Jews who were keeping the details of the law while rejecting Jesus? It would then be warning seasoned churches, satisfied that they're OK, that they need Jesus. It would be a warning that those truly embracing Jesus are mostly new groups who may be pretty messed up but who are excited about joining Jesus' family.

What would it do to our understanding of the epistles to read them corporately? With the exception of a few of the shorter letters, they all seem to be written to churches. To corporate bodies, not to private individuals. And three of the four letters written to individuals (1 and 2 Timothy, Titus) are written to the leaders of churches telling them how to shepherd the church corporate.

The other letter to an individual is Philemon, who had a runaway slave. The slave has become a Christian and is returning. Philemon is supposed to forgive him and treat him as a brother. So Paul isn't instructing even Philemon on his private relationship with God. He's instructing him on how to deal with a broken relationship within his church. This letter is dealing with an issue within the body, within the church corporate.

Aren't all the epistles like that? They're about how churches are to live their lives corporately, growing each other up in Christ, not about keeping the individual's purity, not about how to treat the world (except by being a light). Do you know that the singular "you" scarcely appears in the epistles to churches? So those letters are almost meaningless to people living their lives outside church; if they seem meaningful individually and privately, it's partly because they're being misread.

Ephesians says, "Putting away falsehood, let all of us speak the truth to our neighbors" (Eph 4:25). Naturally, we read that as a general command to tell the truth to our neighbors, heathen or Christian. So we miss the end of the verse, "for we are members of one another." I'm not suggesting Paul would approve of lying to non-Christians, but I am saying that in this particular passage (as in the Epistles generally), we are being instructed on how to live with those in our local church. We are being told how to grow each other up. (This verse is only a few verses after the instruction "to speak the truth in love.")

And on and on.

Once again, don't misunderstand me. I'm not suggesting that our personal relationship with Jesus is a minor thing. I'm suggesting rather that it's not the whole story and that the strength of my relationship with Jesus can best be measured by my relationships within my church. That's the central argument of 1 John: "Those who say, 'I love God,' and hate their brothers or sisters, are liars; for those who do not love a brother or sister whom they have seen, cannot love God whom they have not seen" (1 John 4:20). In other words, John is saying, "Don't tell me about your personal relationship with God unless you love your brothers and sisters in Christ; if you don't love them, you don't have any personal relationship with God at all."

Without the horizontal and corporate, there is no personal, vertical relationship with Jesus.

THE CULTURAL PARADIGMS OF THE WEST

Our confusions about such things grow out of deep, culture-wide distortions. So it's hard for modern people to be the church well. Given the commitments of our civilization, our confusions are almost inevitable and inescapable. (Which itself is an excellent example of the importance of the corporate.)

The point of Part II is that we're profoundly shaped by the cultures we're part of. In many ways this is natural and healthy. Unfortunately, in a fallen and rebellious world, cultures as well as individuals are fallen and rebellious. So inevitably we learn lies from our cultures (as well as good things and neutral things). We'll only begin to get disentangled from the lies as we become part of a new people creating a new culture. There we can together struggle to discern what are lies and what is truth. This isn't mostly the individual's task but the task of the whole body. That's much of why it's important for us to become the church instead of attending church. We must become so thoroughly the church that we together develop new values that begin to leave behind the values of the world.

I'm not suggesting rejecting all of our culture. That's meaningless, impossible, and would disable our evangelism. The task of church requires us to be continually discerning what in the surrounding culture is valuable and what is less than valuable. This process is crucial both in seeking spiritual growth for the body and in our attempt to reflect the Light to the world. The idea itself is clear to Christians. That's why conservative churches regularly denounce X-rated movies and liberal churches regularly denounce racism.[2]

However, in Part II I'm concerned about cultural issues that are less obvious than racism and sexual immorality. You see, many of the most basic aspects of a culture tend to be invisible to those who belong to it. That's the reason for the old saw that water is invisible to fish: often only an outsider can show us the world in which we live and

---

2. Not as obvious as you might hope though. Those who tend to be sensitive to the evils of sexual immorality are often less sensitive to racism, and vice versa.

move and have our being. One reason it's so valuable to live in a different culture for a time is that when you come home, you see your own culture for the first time.

Human beings assume that how we do things is natural and inevitable when in fact more things than we can imagine are shaped by whatever culture we live in. We assume that everyone thinks and does things the way we do, and if they don't, they're wrong and inferior.

The value of escaping this ethnocentrism is obvious in evangelizing a culture as diverse as ours, but its value for our own spiritual health is comparable. Cultures grow out of basic values, and if those values are sub-Christian or anti-Christian and churches adopt them as their own, those churches then have sub-Christian values. Which undermines the whole functioning of church. Such values can work like computer viruses: they're invisible, but they can corrupt everything.

Detecting these viruses, these hidden values, is easier in the postmodern age than it once was. Postmodern thought presents many challenges to Christians, but it also gives us handles on what's cultural. Further, we live in the midst of so much diversity that we can often experience a different culture just by getting to know the folks across the street. So today we may have a better chance of determining which of our basic values are the values of Jesus and which are viruses.

FIRE

In my book *The Secular Squeeze*, I argue that a deadly virus is at the core of Western culture: FIRE (an acronym for freedom, individualism, rights, and equality).[3] People often moan that Westerners no longer have agreed-on values, but that isn't the problem. We have a thoroughly developed and almost universally-accepted value system; the problem is that our values are extra-biblical and rotten. They are our culture's paradigm at such a deep level that imagining anything else is almost impossible. So anything we read in the Bible or experience as Christians we read and experience wearing the glasses of FIRE.

FIRE is an ethical paradigm that addresses almost any issue that can arise. As a culture we may be unclear on the acceptability of sex outside marriage, but we're clear that people must be *free* to decide for themselves. It's the choice of each *individual*. And any attempt to legislate the sexual morality of adults (and maybe young people) violates their *rights* and may be unconstitutional. If anyone tries to tell me how to behave sexually, I ask, "Who are you to tell me what to do? Don't you understand we're *equals*?"

FIRE comes astonishingly close to being universally accepted, not only in the West but throughout the world. Whether you're black or white, young or old, hippie or capitalist, Russian or Guatemalan, you believe in FIRE. China appears to be one holdout, but the people there seem pretty clear that they want more FIRE, and the

---

3. Alexander, *The Secular Squeeze*, 197–219.

government insists that the people have more FIRE than they think. These days you can hardly find even a dictator who doesn't pay lip-service to FIRE: he's going to allow an election soon.

The primary holdout is Muslim "fundamentalism." And isn't it interesting how horrified everyone else is? Those Muslims deny FIRE, and it disgusts us. It's even profoundly distressing to other Muslims and to many within their own populations. Let's go to war with them.[4]

Right and Left

Perhaps the most surprising thing is that FIRE is agreed on by both the right and the left. The differences between these groups seem immense, but in important respects their disputes are actually in-house disagreements on how to apply the culturally agreed-on values. On the right, Adam Smith, the founding theorist of capitalism, was one of the earliest and most articulate advocates of FIRE. (It's great for driving an economy; people have a right to choose freely anything they as individuals want . . . to buy. Hence giant supermarkets and miles and miles of malls.) And on the left, the ACLU is the most notorious promoter of FIRE. They'll defend any individual's right to anything.

So both the right and the left agree on the centrality of FIRE. All they disagree on is who has a claim to which rights. These are in-house disputes. Take sex education in public schools. The left promotes it so that the free choice of young people will be informed. The right opposes it because it violates the right of parents to teach sex education. That is, the argument is over how to apply FIRE. But neither side thinks public schools should teach students sexual abstinence before marriage. That would violate our basic values (our rights and freedoms).

Or take prayer in public schools. The left opposes it because it violates the freedom of children who aren't religious. The right supports it in order to protect the rights of children who want to pray. Similarly, according to the left, farm subsidies are needed to protect the right of family farmers to exist, and according to the right, they violate the rights of taxpayers whose money subsidizes them.

Agreeing on Enlightenment values

Meanwhile, liberal philosophers proudly proclaim that Western democracies are value-free and that people from diverse cultures are welcome no matter what their convictions.[5] At the same time, conservatives bemoan our loss as a nation of agreed-on values. I don't know what either group is talking about. Let me tell you, freedom,

---

4. Editor's Note: This was written before the events of September 11, 2001 and the global "war on terrorism" that has followed. The ensuing years have only served to confirm John's analysis of how the acceptance of FIRE marks people as civilized/human in the modern world.

5. Violent overthrow of society is an exception.

individualism, rights, and equality are agreed on. And they're values. They just aren't biblical values. We agree on these values as much as the Puritans ever agreed on their values, and we're just as fierce, intolerant, and judgmental as Puritans are thought to have been whenever anyone dares to question our values.

What has happened here is that since most all of us agree on FIRE to a large extent even cross-culturally, it has become invisible. Like water to a fish. Everyone agrees—except inferior people.

Note: we didn't learn these attitudes from the Word of God; we learned them from Renaissance and Enlightenment philosophers—pagans and deists. In my paranoid moments, I suspect that the Devil engineered these gentlemen into inventing these values in hopes that it would make the idea of church unintelligible. That at least has been the result. If you want to know why we don't take attendance in church but do stress our personal relationship with Jesus, just ask John Locke and Tom Jefferson.

Notice I'm not discussing whether FIRE is a good system of government. My personal opinion is that in a fallen world it's better than the alternatives, though it needs to increase its emphasis on the common good.[6] But that's not my concern in this book. My concern here is the church. FIRE may be the best government can do, but Christians can't let FIRE control the church.

Unfortunately, we do. And it's deadly. So whether the Devil planned it or not, he couldn't have done a better job undermining church than by making FIRE invisible and thereby getting Christians to accept it whole cloth. And he got us to accept it not just for government, but for all of our lives, including our churches. So we have a hard time understanding what it would mean to live as the people of God. And as for doing it . . .

In different cultures and in different times, I suspect that different parts of the gospel are hard to understand and live. So in any culture being a Christian well will require paradigm shifts of some sort. But the shifts will vary from culture to culture. And most of the paradigm shifts in our culture revolve around FIRE.

In other cultures the hard part may revolve around breaking with strong families in favor of the family of God. But for us I suspect it will revolve around choosing to join a strong church family in a culture that doesn't allow for strong biological families, let alone a strong family of God. Modern and postmodern people will understand this as cultish and as an abandonment of the freedom that our culture has fought so hard to win. (And, of course, historically that has been one of the great dangers of strong churches.)

6. In my view, modern social views need to be modified along the lines proposed by people like Amitai Etzioni in *The Spirit of Community*. He leaves FIRE nearly intact while softening its more egregious manifestations by, for example, emphasizing personal responsibility and the common good alongside individual freedom and rights.

Freedom

Consider the effect of this version of freedom (the F in FIRE) on the church. If freedom seems essential to a person, she'll insist on floating from church to church. As soon as she gets bored with the music in one church, she'll change to a church with a better choir, and as soon as a better job beckons, she'll move to another town. Typically, she'll have little concern about how good a church she'll find in the new town and less concern about the impact of her leaving on her current church.

"Am I not free to do what's best for me?" As a result, churches regularly lose elders and members, and Christians have so few roots that few people know others well enough to speak the truth to them, let alone in love. And if a church prepares to discipline someone, that person will just go to a different church—and probably be welcomed with open arms.

In a culture that understands freedom in this way, commitment becomes odd and unusual. So most churches don't even ask for it. It would violate people's freedom. As a result, churches (and soon thereafter marriages) become sick, and intimacy becomes something for weekend encounters, whether ecclesial or sexual. As if you can have intimacy apart from commitment! Before long men are abandoning not only their churches but also their wives and kids.

By the same token, making freedom basic renders the idea of submission to each other almost abhorrent. This is partly because our culture parodies submission by constant references to Hitler and abusive husbands, but by now even the better sense of submission (listening respectfully and cooperatively to the rest of the people of God) seems odd to most Christians. How can we listen to each other without losing our freedom, maybe even our self-respect, for heaven's sake?

Instead of churches transforming our culture, they're being absorbed by it.

Individualism

Put differently, our culture has taught us to be independent agents, individualists. (The I in FIRE.) Our culture has instilled in us the importance of being John Wayne—rugged frontiersmen whom no one dares mess with. Living on our own so that no one will interfere with what we feel like doing, we float from job to job and from town to town, always asserting that we are in control of our lives and don't need anyone. Getting help is embarrassing. Many men can't even ask for directions at a filling station.

This rugged individualism is a foundational myth of Western culture, perhaps even *the* foundational myth for males. Which makes it feel wrong to try to live as dependent parts of the body of Christ, serving one another and regarding others as better than ourselves (Phil 2:3). On average, Christians aren't even conscious of the myth or its collision with the gospel. (Part of the power of myth today is that contemporary people aren't aware of them except in primitive cultures; so we think of movies mostly as entertainment.) As a result, we become so thoroughly enculturated that we can't point to a new way of life in which people depend on God and each other. In fact, we usually embody the old way.

Of course, in our culture we are in some ways more dependent on each other than ever before. I can't eat my Total for breakfast without depending on farmers, cereal-factory workers, truck drivers, and grocery clerks. And none of those people can do their jobs without other people drilling for oil and operating nuclear power plants, not to mention politicians passing laws about what farmers can plant where and how much to tax imports. I wouldn't be surprised if ten thousand people are somehow involved in the little box of Total on my breakfast table. Our economic lives can scarcely be understood except as a body in which each part must work properly. Just think what happens clear down in California if the wrong electric transformer shorts out in Alberta.

But a culture that starts with a Declaration of Independence doesn't teach us to see those parts of reality. That's especially true when that interdependence is emotional. If human beings are to survive as reasonably functioning personalities, we need a web of people who love us and support us and give us grace. If you don't believe it, just study family systems. We need other human beings who love us and love us well. That is, we need each other functioning properly.

For any culture to survive it has to put energy into strengthening these webs of loyalty and friendship and love. But in a culture of rugged individualists, that isn't a priority. How then can we do church for more than a couple of hours on Sunday morning? How do we become a people who are profoundly inter-relational and loving? We don't have time.

At times I suspect that I caricature Western culture (and at other times I think that would be hard to do). But in any case, I don't mean to deny the many strengths of FIRE. It's no accident that the Western world probably has less poverty and a lower percentage of people oppressed by the wealthy than normal throughout history. Horrifying as the level of abuse is in our culture, it's probably lower than in most cultures. Furthermore, I understand the attraction of urban anonymity: I'm horrified when I visit small towns where everyone speaks to everyone. But I can't finesse all that in this chapter. My concern here (whatever the advantages of FIRE) is simply how hard FIRE makes it for us to be the church.

Rights

One of the functions of the language of rights (the R in FIRE) is to avoid discussion. (Rights language was more or less invented by Enlightenment philosophers. There's not even a word for rights in Hebrew, Greek, or Latin.) If you claim the right to free health care or to no tax on tea, you usually feel little need to argue your claim. All you need to say is, "We hold these truths to be self-evident."[7] Rights seem self-authenticating to those who claim them, if not to those from whom they're being claimed.

---

7. Thomas Jefferson, *The Declaration of Independence*.

Epistemologically, it's all very odd. Often, a claim to rights is a claim to something no one has ever claimed before, and yet those claiming it say it's self-evident.

Talk of self-evidence is generally a sign that you have no idea how to defend your notion but you aren't about to give it up. If someone denies that you have the right in question, discourse tends to be brief: you repeat your claim. And if the person still won't give you your rights, many feel justified in attacking their opponent or in rioting and looting all the stores in the neighborhood. This description of rights may seem inflammatory, but ever since the Revolutionary War, rights have often worked that way.

Further, what people take to be their rights keeps growing. As new groups come into consciousness, one of their first steps is to claim a full set of rights. Immediately, battle lines are drawn up around that group, and those who disagree with them are automatically and instantly bad guys—racists, Nazis, commies, chauvinists, straights. (The "Puritan" response.) The rhetoric escalates with speed and without boundaries, leaving deeper and deeper divisions between smaller and smaller self-interest groups in a continually splintering society.

Some years ago I was teaching junior high in a poor section of San Francisco. The discipline problems were acute, the learning minimal, cooperation nonexistent. It gradually dawned on me that this was a logical outcome of all the talk of individualism, freedom and rights that I had so long advocated. These kids believed that their problems were caused by people violating their rights. They thought that what they needed to do was insist on their freedom and make sure no one violated their individuality. As a result, it was almost impossible for them to cooperate with anyone. Instead of working hard on their studies, they worked hard to see to it that no one stepped on their toes.

This sort of thing has prompted Amitai Etzioni to suggest balancing the rights we've accepted with responsibilities we also accept. He makes his case in a book significantly entitled, *The Spirit of Community*. He claims that a rights-orientation destroys community. (He means secular community, but the same is true of Christian community.) Rights set up competition instead of cooperation; they build walls instead of breaking them down. They set up a cycle of confrontation and insult, if not of conflagration and violence.

Beyond Rights

In a way superficially similar to the modern vision, Paul tell us, "There is no longer Greek and Jew, circumcised and uncircumcised, barbarian, Scythian, slave and free; but Christ is all and in all!" (Col 3:11). But Paul isn't thinking we'll get there by each individual fighting for her rights, the way modern people have done it since Jefferson and the Declaration of Independence. Those methods are the opposite of the church's calling.

In the very next verse after talking about there being no longer Greek and Jew, Paul explains how to get there: "Clothe yourselves with compassion, kindness, humility, meekness, and patience" (12b). Hardly the advice of crusading political reformers whether from the right or the left.[8] "Bear with one another and, if anyone has a complaint against another, forgive each other; just as the Lord has forgiven you, so you also must forgive" (13).

That's how Paul tells us to deal with racism and sexism in the church; that's how we're supposed to deal with violations of our rights. To modern Western people, that seems horrendous. Maybe even sick. That's because the Word of God smashes squarely into FIRE (and vice versa). We cannot be the church, we cannot live in peace with one another, unless we see how FIRE makes much of the New Testament seem gross and bizarre. Within the church, we cannot practice the politics of the secular state.

To put it differently, we cannot do church unless we take the way of Christ. For that's what we're talking about here: the imitation of Christ—his life and his death. Jesus came to take on himself the pain and suffering of sin, not to fight oppressors. (Or rather, he came to fight oppression by taking on the pain and suffering it caused.) And we are called to do the same. Peter puts it in a way that's extraordinarily offensive to FIRE people:

> Slaves, accept the authority of [submit to] your masters with all deference, not only those who are kind and gentle but also those who are harsh. For it is a credit to you if, being aware of God, you endure pain while suffering unjustly. If you endure when you are beaten for doing wrong, what credit is that? But if you endure when you do right and suffer for it, you have God's approval. For to this you have been called, because Christ also suffered for you, leaving you an example, so that you should follow in his steps . . . . When he was abused, he did not return abuse; when he suffered, he did not threaten; but he entrusted himself to the one who judges justly. He himself bore our sins in his body on the cross, so that, free from sins, we might live for righteousness; by his wounds you have been healed. (1 Pet 2:18–21, 23–24)

Not that Jesus was unconcerned about how Jews and Gentiles oppressed each other in the church. Not that he was unconcerned about the unjust treatment of women by men among his people. No, he was showing us another way of working for justice. By our taking on the suffering of others' sin and violence. As "Christ also suffered for you, leaving you an example, so that you should follow in his steps."

Christ's redemptive suffering reflected in our redemptive suffering (in imitation of him) is the only way to achieve peace with each other. If this makes no sense to you, don't join a church; just go to church on Sunday mornings. Because anything short of the imitation of Jesus the Christ will lead to the internal conflagration of his people.

---

8. As I've said, both the right and the left agree on the centrality of FIRE. That is, both are essentially pagan. One way of understanding how they disagree is who they are willing to extend rights to. The left has historically been more willing to extend rights to new groups, thus contributing to societal disintegration. The right has been less willing, wanting to keep rights for themselves. Neither is a particularly worthwhile enterprise.

Who is going to be our paradigm—Jesus or Jefferson, Isaiah's servant or Malcolm X, the crucified Christ or Gloria Steinem?[9]

Paul teaches, "Above all, clothe yourselves with love, which binds everything together in perfect harmony. And let the peace of Christ rule in your hearts, to which indeed you were called in the one body. And be thankful" (Col 3:14–15). A more incisive summary of what I've been saying about how to do church, I cannot imagine. Nor more impossible commands for those committed to FIRE.

To put it differently, the opposite of rights is grace. So in rights-based discussions of racism or gender roles, Christians can only participate Christianly if they first reject rights language and the worldview it expresses. We're called to extend grace to oppressors, to see ourselves in the same boat as the oppressors. We oppress people too, and would oppress people more if we had the power. So we can forgive oppressors because God forgave us. Then without anger and rejection, we call oppressors to repent (as we ourselves are trying to do) and be forgiven.

EQUALITY

As for equality (the E in FIRE), it's clear that God loves us all equally and that I better realize I'm not superior to junkies or anyone else. In the Enlightenment equality mostly meant that kings and aristocrats should live under the same laws as ordinary people, and it's clear that that is right.

However, equality doesn't mean that we all have the same gifts anymore than it means we're all of equal height. Some people are taller than others, some are smarter, some wiser, and some have better singing voices. While people can usually understand that only a few of us have voices good enough to sing in the Met, the parallel is somehow less clear when it comes to things like wisdom. "I'm as good as you are: why should I listen to you?" At which point church is dead, and all that's left is my personal relationship with Jesus. (And he better be careful what he tells me to do.)

This results in a peculiar sameness in egalitarian societies. The rhetoric of FIRE is supposed to encourage cultural diversity, but my experience is that once you get beyond skin color and how many rings people have in their ears, we are eerily similar. We all want personal fulfillment and to fight for our rights. And maybe to go to the mall.

---

9. I suppose that putting Jefferson and Malcolm X in the same league will offend some white people, but I suggest that Malcolm X merely applied Jefferson's talk of rights to the black-white conflict. Jefferson applied the notion of rights to the colonies and used that to justify violence against the British, and Malcolm X applied the notion of rights to black people and used that to justify violence against white people. However, toward the end of his brief life, Malcolm recanted much of this, which is more than you can say for Jefferson in his much longer life.

Others may be offended by my putting Gloria Steinem in the league of either of them, but I suggest that her role was similar: she applied Jefferson's notion of the rights of propertied white males to all women, and in that she had the same spirit as Jefferson and Malcolm, with the huge difference that she didn't advocate violence.

You see, equality is never enough. What we really want is to be better than others. We want to be God. And if we can't get that, then we want no one to be better than us. So one of the few things you can count on in this culture is that when you make a mistake driving your car, someone will blow their car horn. Or as the bumper sticker puts it, "Horn broken; watch for finger." Perhaps the middle finger is the symbol of the stance individuals take toward each other in our culture. And embroidered on our flag is, "Don't tread on me."

That's the way of a society contemplating self-immolation. The church must break with it, for it is not the way of Christ. We must live differently, turning the other cheek and taking on the suffering of others' sin so that the world may glimpse the Light that came into it two thousand years ago.

COMPOUND WORDS BEGINNING WITH SELF

We have looked at the four values of FIRE. I'm going to add a fifth. It's described by a whole series of compound words starting with self (FIRES!): self-fulfillment, self-expression, self-esteem, self-realization, self-actualization, self-improvement, self-pity. We may disagree with each other on abortion, but at least we all agree on the importance of personal fulfillment. That's because we were taught its importance by the Declaration of Independence: there Jefferson lists "the pursuit of happiness" as a right whose truth is self-evident. In our culture, you see, the values reflected in FIRES are the bottom line. So we won't tolerate and can't understand a diversity that questions those assumptions.

I used to find the abortion debate puzzling, and I still often don't understand arguments between pro-life and pro-choice people. That's a dangerous thing to admit in a rights-based society because it makes me a bad guy to both sides.

However, over the years it has become clear to me that the abortion culture grows out of deeply sanctioned social views on freedom and the pursuit of happiness. Practically speaking, the argument goes something like this: "Screwing is fulfilling; I am free; therefore I will screw whenever the pursuit of happiness beckons. The consequences of screwing (pregnancy) aren't fulfilling for some people (especially when they're young, unmarried, and female); people are free; therefore those who don't feel like being pregnant must be allowed to abort their babies on demand."

I see no flaws in this argument. It's watertight. The arguments the justices of the Supreme Court used to legalize abortion may have been absurd, but better arguments are available. Abortion is the inevitable outcome of the American Dream. If you prohibit abortion, how are people to feel free and fulfilled? The only way you could prohibit abortion is to repeal the Declaration of Independence, the United States Constitution, the Bill of Rights, the American Dream, and the culture they produced and grew out of.

And repealing them is something churches need to hasten to do in their own life together. The abortion argument may be valid, but its premises are wicked. We must stand against them. Not on the grounds that they violate the rights of babies, but on the grounds that the whole argument is desperately selfish.

Perhaps the next time you're invited to pro-life rally, you should agree to go providing they let you speak against freedom and fulfillment. Probably most people there won't understand what you say, but maybe someone will get a glimpse of the Light.

Self-immolation vs. self-sacrifice

The tragedy here—or one of them—is that the whole FIRES worldview is based on a silly mistake. It assumes that happiness is the sort of thing that can be successfully pursued, that fulfillment correlates with things like pleasure and freedom. However, I would have thought that what's self-evident is that people find happiness not when they're pursuing it but precisely when they forget themselves and pursue something larger than themselves.

It's known as the hedonistic paradox. Pleasure and happiness are the sorts of thing that sneak up on you; you only find them when you're not looking for them. As soon as you start worrying about them or even noticing them, they're gone. Contentment comes only to those who have stopped trying to fulfill the ever-changing desires of their dictatorial wills.

Jesus puts it succinctly: "If any want to become my followers, let them deny themselves and take up their cross and follow me. For those who want to save their life will lose it, and those who lose their life for my sake will find it. For what will it profit them if they gain the whole world but forfeit their life? Or what will they give in return for their life?" (Matt 16:24–26; see also 10:39; Mark 8:35–36; Luke 17:33; John 12:24–26). Life and joy come from the pursuit of the cross, not from the pursuit of happiness.

Now it's more than important to understand that following Jesus is filled with happiness and fulfillment. Our faith is not a dreary duty, but a joyous life. This leads some people to talk about Christian hedonism—and they're right.[10] However, by definition, if you're following Jesus with one eye on self-fulfillment and in hopes of finding pleasure, you won't find them. Joy is the consequence of following Jesus no matter what the cost, not the motive for making small sacrifices in the hope they'll pay big.

Jesus tells us we have a choice. We can pursue our right to happiness, which brings misery and self-immolation. Or we can pursue self-sacrifice for the sake of the cross. Which happens to be the path to joy.

Victims, resentment, and joy

Western culture probably has fewer people who are victimized by oppressors than past cultures, and many of the oppressed are oppressed less.[11] That's largely to the credit

---

10. See John Piper, *Desiring God*.

11. This is less true if you include those the West oppresses outside our culture, in the Global South.

of FIRES. Nonetheless, we probably have more people than ever who feel victimized. That, too, is because of FIRES. It's odd, and also sad.

But it's easily explained. FIRES encourages us to notice when our rights are violated and to fight for those rights. So naturally rights are respected more than they used to be. African Americans can stay in any motel they can afford, and women can vote and get a wider variety of jobs. We have a long way to go, but FIRES has dealt with a lot of oppression.

But it has also turned us into a society of victims. It's quite natural. As people come to see how victimized they are or were, they get angry, often just as the oppression is finally being dealt with. Anger at oppression is appropriate, but if it then comes to rule our lives, it robs us of our joy. This often hasn't been noticed by FIRES-based psychologies, which tend to encourage people to dwell on past injustices, real and imagined. They do this in the name of honesty, and they're right that abuses must not be swept under the rug. But honesty doesn't require obsessive preoccupation with past wrongs. Besides, it's the opposite of the way of Christ. Instead of nurturing his resentment, Christ took on the sins of his oppressors, and we should follow in his steps.

Furthermore, taking on being a victim encourages us to waste ourselves on resentment of things past rather than focusing on things present. And the things present are the only ones we can do much about. Why not forget about past oppression while following Jesus and calling others to do the same? One of the startling things for me as a pastor has been observing how formerly abused people don't grow much or serve well until their past seems less important to them.

To put it differently, being a victim messes with being part of the body of Christ. Becoming part of a group has to do with developing a common identity. So if your identity is in being a victim, you can only truly join groups of victims. If you talk mostly about how you were victimized, you not only become touchy and boringly repetitive, but you have no time to talk about the good things Jesus is doing. How do you then become part of the people of praise on which listening to others is built?

FINDING A NEW CENTER

So we need help imagining ourselves into better alternatives. Many years ago, I read in some popular magazine that ours is the first society in history where people are encouraged to think of themselves first. Always before people were encouraged to think first of their tribe or nation. This of course was said as praise of our culture: we are the first people with enough sense to realize that the good of the individual is more important than the good of the group.

Whether this is historically accurate, I'm not learned enough to say. But it fits what I do know. That's not to say that previous people always did think of the good of the group first; but they thought they should. They believed, whether they acted on

---

For example, a key reason for hunger in the third world is that their ruling elites ship their food to the West.

it or not, that the good of the group was more important than their own pleasure or happiness.

That's the alternative we need to try to imagine ourselves into. It's difficult because our minds immediately fill with images of people who have turned into angry prunes while sacrificing themselves for the group. I've met people who were so duty bound that they'd lost all joy in life, but what does that have to do with seeking the good of others? Duty is a terrible motivator and brings more misery than release.[12] And it's not what I'm advocating. I'm advocating being motivated by love, the love of God and of the body of Christ. I'm talking about doing it for the love of the whole rather than out of morbid duty.

Our movies and books set up a choice. On the one hand are dour religious people so far out of touch with their feelings that they remove the bell from their churches. On the other hand are joyfully hedonistic, rambunctious, freely self-expressive secularists, who focus on sex and fun.

I object. Not so much to the focus on sex as to the fake choice. We don't have to choose between morbid fundamentalism and relaxed, self-expressive hedonism. Not because there's a third choice our culture ignores, but because neither choice exists. I dare say there are morbid fundamentalists who pretend sex doesn't happen, but I was raised in fundamentalism, and I'm not sure I ever met one. This group, if it exists, isn't large enough to fight.

Equally few in number are joyful, self-expressive hedonists. I spent some years trying to make myself comfortable in that imaginary world, and I never met anyone in it who was notably happy. They were always struggling to find pleasure and happiness, which was always just beyond their grasp or ended a few months after they moved in with their latest flame. They spent their time in analysis, smoking marijuana, and being angry that their parents hadn't taught them to be more self-expressive.

Baloney. Do you really think that Hollywood hedonists or sixties dropouts are any happier than dour fundamentalists or constipated stockbrokers? The pursuit of happiness produces people like Woody Allen, not people like Tinkerbell. It perhaps made sense to pursue that paradigm in the sixties (I thought it did then anyway), but by now you have to be stupid to entertain the notion that self-expression leads to any place but Hell (on earth).

Happiness comes from losing yourself in something—preferably in something larger than yourself, preferably in God, preferably in our loving God.

In my experience, that love does not produce prunes and Pharisees. If you sacrifice for the sake of your kids, does that turn you into a prune? If you do it out of duty, maybe. But if you do it out of love? My experience is that sacrifice then brings joy.

Let me give a trivial, if incriminating, illustration. When I'm writing, it irritates me if I'm interrupted. If someone asks me to drive her somewhere, I say no. But from

---

12. It may be a necessary stage, but it's not meant to be more than that.

time to time, my daughter asks me to drive her to work. I almost always do it without a thought, even if I'm writing. And the same goes for my wife.

That's because I love them. Serving those you love is fun. My problem is that I don't love those other people. And people you don't love are irritating no matter what they do. A sobering thought. What I'm advocating here isn't being more dutiful but more loving. That's great joy. I've never known a person to be miserable who loved well.

Love more people, put more people first, love the whole group. It will bring great joy. But FIRES kills.

Now I realize that some psychologist will object that to have any sort of mental health, we need to be able to say no. And he'd suggest that as a dominant white male, I have so little trouble saying no that I don't understand the problem. There's probably something to that. And he'd argue that I probably have a responsible daughter. If she were always interrupting me, I'd get frustrated with her too. And there's something to that as well.

But I'm still not impressed with this individualistic analysis. People who know they're loved don't need to keep asking for things. So if someone keeps interrupting you, love her better. Soon she'll be able to leave you alone.

Besides, if you're in a body that's functioning, this problem isn't yours alone. Someone else can do the job that would have interrupted you—if what you're doing is genuinely more important than the interruption. And someone else can tell others to stop bugging you—if that's what needs to happen. Let the body decide. Those are the sorts of alternatives we need to learn to imagine.

Aristotle

Aristotle gave one of the classic statements of what it's like to live corporately. I explain this not to persuade you to be an Aristotelian, but because as a pre-modern person, Aristotle was still able to imagine something other than FIRES.

For Aristotle, the city you lived in was the organizing point of life, not the individual. The task of individuals was to accept a role in their city and fulfill it well. Each person had a role, and of course the roles interacted with and depended on one another. So a ruler couldn't rule well unless the city's soldiers fought well, and they couldn't fight well unless the blacksmith made weapons well, and the blacksmith couldn't smith well unless the farmers grew enough food, and on and on until the role of each person in the city was described. Here the individual was not the organizing point.

To modern and postmodern people, this seems to sacrifice the individual. It looks like individuals can't express their deepest being but have to fit in, be less themselves. But what happens to individuals in our society who can't sort out what their deepest being is? It's a standard problem since modernity. Those people then have no purpose, nothing to do. So they get depressed. They then go to a psychologist who tells them they need to stop letting their role be dictated to them by society. They need to stop being so dutiful and repressed and start following their bliss. Oddly enough, this therapy rarely helps.

Those psychologists have it precisely wrong—and almost have to in our individualistic culture. Surely meaning comes from having a role in a larger, meaningful whole. Psychologists are puzzled that depression and youth suicide are increasing so rapidly. I'll tell you why. It's because individualism is bearing its fruit. We no longer have a recognized larger whole, and what whole we have no longer seems worth being part of. Consequently, young people no longer have a way of finding meaning; in fact, they no longer have a meaning to find. The puzzle is why so few people kill themselves. (It may be lack of courage.)

What psychologists need to be able to do (and can't in our culture) is point people to something bigger than themselves that they can serve. Then depressed people could stop focusing on their depressed little selves and get on with their lives, even if they don't feel great. Do you have any idea how depressing it is for a depressed person to try to find meaning in being fulfilled? Do you have any idea how depressing it is for a depressed person to start analyzing herself when her self is feeling rotten?

It's a vicious cycle from which an individualistic culture has little escape. If we got hold of Aristotle's city, half the psychological problems in our culture would disappear.[13] The lostness and depression and anomie would evaporate if our culture gave us meaningful roles in something larger than ourselves. That's what church is.

Now, there's a problem with the Aristotle example. Aristotle gave people roles in an unjust larger whole. Half the population was slaves and half was women, and both were disenfranchised. Furthermore, the roles even of male citizens were hierarchical and partly hereditary. So Aristotle's solution to depression and loss of meaning had terrible costs. But what if your larger whole were the people of God? And the people of God weren't racist and sexist? And what if that empowered them to be who God meant them to be?

Perhaps the psychologists in our society who can help most with depression are those who are part of such churches and can point people to a whole worth serving.[14] Of course, to do that churches will have to ask people to make church the organizing principle of their lives, and to do that churches will have to be a lot more than Sunday-morning affairs. If a church is mostly Sunday meetings, only the performers have roles, and being a member can't give your life meaning.

Is a person lacking in self-esteem? Don't tell her to focus on building herself up; have her become part of a church that needs her and in which she can do something worthwhile. Then she'll have self-esteem. Or is it that she will forget about that quest?

---

13. Of course, some depression is physiological. I'm not denying that, though it is interesting how much more common depression is now in Western culture than before or in other cultures.

14. Others can of course prescribe medication, which is extremely important.

PURPOSE AND MEANING

To put it differently, ethics and behavior are much less puzzling if you exchange the individualistic paradigm for a corporate paradigm. Aristotle's version of this was unjust, but that's not essential to corporate paradigms.[15] Corporate paradigms allow ethics and life to be purposive. To go back to Aristotle, a good knife is one that fulfills its purpose—its purpose of cutting well. Similarly, a good person is one who fulfills her purpose well. That's why we're always asking, "What am I for? What's this all about?"

However, what's the purpose of the individual? An individualistic culture allows few responses to this question, and none of them are good. (Its natural answer is self-fulfillment, which is self-defeating.) But for a corporate culture, like church is meant to be, the answer is straightforward and concrete. If you want to know a person's purpose in a body, you just find out what she can do to serve the body. Doing that is her purpose. She is then a good person if she does that well, just as a knife is a good knife if it cuts well.

Of course, in a culture with a basic commitment to personal fulfillment (and all the rest of FIRES), this will seem disturbing, maybe even outrageous. But it's not like individualism is turning out great. Take rule-based individualism, so common in the church. In that model you're a good person if you don't do certain things and you do your duty. Now, that is depressing. Psychologists who object to that are right. But that's not the model here. I'm proposing a model in which you have a purpose in life (much better than a duty). I'm proposing a model in which you are seized by a vision larger than yourself, or rather a model in which you are seized by God for a vision so large you lose yourself in the joy of living it out.

Let's do it. Then we'll find out what fulfillment is.

---

15. It is, however, the way the paradigm is most likely to go wrong.

FIVE

Counterfeit Plans of Salvation (Personal Identity, Affinity Groups, and Nationalism)

In the American paradigm the individual is important, and the group is not. However, human beings know better. We were created by God, and down deep we need to belong. We know it. Or at least, we act on it. So people join groups or emphasize those they're naturally part of: family, nation, ethnic group, country club, gang, church, the Marines, Little League, sorority, law firm.[1] These groups are substitute churches with their own plans of salvation.

To a large extent, we learn who we are from our church or substitute church. Or rather, we become something as we find a role in a group. We get our personal identity from whatever group we identify with, from the closest thing to a church that we're part of. That's how we learn our way of life and how we get a sense of purpose.

That's why kids are so desperate to belong; otherwise, they don't know who they are or how they're supposed to act. Human beings rarely get their values by study or by thinking things through. We catch them, rather like we catch colds, from groups we're part of. And this is not a mysterious process: we catch values by accepting the roles that groups give us. I suggest that roles and values and personal identity are almost the same thing.

Which shows the strength and weakness of our need to belong. Everything good and everything bad can be seen (often magnified) in the groups we belong to. If we're part of good groups, we grow. If we're part of bad groups, we shrivel. And by and large, the available groups leave something to be desired. We wind up joining groups where we get bad roles and therefore bad values and bad identities. Youth gangs and the Marines and sororities are not the best groups to join. So strong, good churches are important.

---

1. Americans are joining less than they used to. See Robert Putnam, *Bowling Alone*. This makes the family their group more and more, which is probably more pressure than the family can take.

AFFINITY GROUPS

Let's look at two sorts of groups. I will call them thin groups and dense groups. Perhaps because of our stress on individualism, many groups today are thin—oddly thin, oddly insubstantial. They don't have enough density or intensity to give us the meaning we need to feel that life is worth living. These groups you might call affinity groups. Groups of people who are alike, usually in some quite limited respect. We join groups of people who run the 5K or who own Airstream trailers or who use Macs.

So, for example, I belong to the Dolphins South End Club (DSE). It's a running club (our motto is, "Start slowly and taper off"). There I get to know people who run 5 or 10K seriously. I can get coaching there, and we sponsor races every weekend that someone else doesn't. I enjoy those people, and I enjoy their activities. They're like me. They're mostly white, well-educated, trim, active, goal-oriented, environmentally-conscious, and aging rapidly. Like me.

For me, belonging to DSE may be fine because I don't often confuse running with salvation or DSE with my church. But I worry for some of the others. Running just isn't substantial enough or broad enough to give real purpose. Why do these people work so hard at running? Do they study *Runners World* as if it were the Bible? (You see, we don't really live up to our motto. Few of us ever taper off—at least before the finish line.) The roles DSE offers are things like organizing the next race or mailing out the newsletter or being the fastest runner in your age group; the conversations we have are mostly about training regimes and sports doctors. Those sorts of things don't make a life or give a sense of importance.

In my case, I have a life elsewhere, a diverse people who give me a sense of purpose. But if you ask the others why they run, most of them say something about their health or living longer. Which is true for me too. But good health or a long life isn't much of a goal by itself. You have to have a life before it's worth having a long one. What's the point of good health without a King to die for?

This sort of club is too thin to give purpose, meaningful roles, or an ethic. The coaches can help me run better, but they can't give me a reason to run or a reason to bother with a long life. And the goal of beating my PR (personal record, 20:44 for 5K) isn't enough. Not nearly enough.

NEIGHBORHOODS AND AFFINITY GROUPS

Oddly, urban neighborhoods are also increasingly thin groups. When we moved into the Mission District of San Francisco, we tried hard to work in our neighborhood and get to know our neighbors. We didn't do well. That was partly because we were too introverted, but it was substantially because our neighbors weren't interested. We were the only ones in the neighborhood who thought it would be nice to know our neighbors. The others didn't know each other because this was no neighborhood. Not that our neighbors were friendless or lived anonymously, but their lives weren't organized around where their house was. Their friends and family were scattered all over the Bay area.

Our Chinese next-door neighbors have people over all the time, Chinese friends and relatives who arrive by car. Our retired Latino next-door neighbor is out a lot. Either he's taking his granddaughter two neighborhoods away to school another neighborhood away, or he's in Mexico City where one son has moved back. Our neighbors over the back fence sit on their sun deck and talk to friends whom I never see in the neighborhood except as they arrive at our neighbors'.

Today's urban people don't get to know their neighbors; they get to know their affinity groups. It doesn't matter where the others live, providing they're like me and have interests in common with me. So I get to know people dog walking. This is done best at Fort Funston, clear across town, where everyone who really loves their dogs takes them to walk. There I know I am with dog lovers, with people like me. (If only San Francisco had a club for basset hound owners!)

At Fort Funston you can also hang glide. So there you can also get to know the affinity group of hang gliders—providing hang gliding interests you. Your affinity group could be wine tasters, people who dress well, stamp collectors, skiers, people into SM—almost anything people get into.

So contemporary people (especially if they have some money or education) get much of their identity from these thin groups. But people in affinity groups are too much alike. And the groups have such surface needs and narrow visions that they don't give their members meaningful roles or much sense of meaning. No wonder depression has become such a serious problem. Your dog isn't enough to live for, nor is wine tasting. And if your self-esteem depends on your hang-gliding ability . . . .

Aristotle's city was different. It had a wide range of people, with a wide range of needs, with the potential for a broad vision (of serving one another, to switch to Christian language). And old-fashioned neighborhoods were like that to some degree. When someone was sick or needed a job, you could help. Which was a role worth having.

Families are getting thin too. It used to be that most people married and had their kids in the area where they were born. So your uncle lived across the road, and you went to school with your second cousin once removed. This was a large group with real needs that gave all its members real roles. But to go back to our neighbors in San Francisco, only one of our six immediate, adult neighbors was even born in the United States, let alone in San Francisco. So they don't live among extended family the way people used to. The Chinese family has live-in grandparents, but I'll bet the number and depth of connections are nothing like they were before they came to the United States.

Ghettoes used to have density. Despite the wickedness of segregation, African American communities used to at least be economically integrated. The doctors lived with the people on welfare, who lived with the teachers, who lived with the factory workers. I'm not advocating a return to segregation, but all African Americans of whatever economic standing used to be in the same pickle together. This gave people natural roles.

Today African American neighborhoods tend to be not only racially segregated but also economically segregated; middle-class African Americans move to middle class neighborhoods (spelled white) as soon as they can. Which you can't blame them for. But it leaves the old neighborhood so thin, so purposeless. African American doctors then mostly relate to those in their affinity groups, which may well be white doctors, who may well live in yet another neighborhood. The groups left for poor African American kids tend to be gangs.

Churches have followed the same route as neighborhoods and include narrower and narrower bands of people. When I was a kid in a town of a few hundred, the town doctor, the farmers, the factory workers, and the grocer all came to my father's church. They didn't have much choice. It meant that the doctor knew when the widow's kids were sick and didn't worry much about her paying him. And when the doctor's wife was sick, the widow sent dinner over.

It's not that I'm waxing nostalgic about the good old days. But whatever the benefits of modernity are with its penicillin and computers, church is harder to do. Today people will drive miles to find a church made up of people like them.[2] Churches have become collections of affinity groups, of people of the same class and interests, with few roles to assign other than passing the collection plate. How then can church give us a meaningful role, a sense of purpose, an ethic? How then do we reflect light out to the world?

Without our noticing, our culture has helped us forget what game we're playing. Is this a church, or is it a counterfeit?

Just a touch of hate at Rome

My moral is obvious. Human beings need denser groups to join, or they wither like plants left in the refrigerator for a week. Since we don't have many dense churches and since affinity groups are too thin, people create counterfeits that have some density. They create law practices, youth gangs, the Marines, service groups, the KKK, the Nazis.

Let's start with obviously negative groups, like gangs. They make the kids feel important, they give them roles, and they fill their time. They ask a lot and give a lot. Their members have a reason to live, meaningful roles, commitment, and—people to hate. The same for the Marines, the KKK, the Nazis.

One of the crucial functions of groups is to define who's in and who's out. This is probably true of most all groups (including affinity groups), but it can become destructively true for dense groups. They define who their members are superior to and who's dangerous. This feels great (to the insiders). Often, dense groups give their members

---

2. I'm not denying that churches have long had a class orientation, but it was harder when transportation was more difficult. See H. Richard Niebuhr, *The Social Sources of Denominationalism*, esp. 21–25.

people to hate. This feels even better. These folks finally have something to live for—hating and resenting enemies. That makes people feel important. They have a personal identity.

Notice this dynamic in nationalism. Since the affinity groups we join are thin, people are at a loss for how to live. Nothing they do feels important. They don't care about much because nothing in their lives amounts to much. Then their country goes to war. Naturally, it's against an evil power led by a monster. We have to fight to protect the world's agreed-on values (democracy, FIRES). We have someone to hate. It's invigorating. Right away, there's an upsurge in patriotism, in the president's popularity, and in new recruits for the Marines. More people watch the war on TV than watch the Super Bowl. Finally, we have a purpose. Something to die for, and therefore something to live for. Something to feel deeply about.

As a nation, as a vast collection of affinity groups, we finally achieve some density. We become one people, with roles. We can go to war, buy bonds, become a welder in the Naval Yard. We have a purpose large enough and compelling enough to draw us together despite conflicting preferences and colliding dislikes. We are drawn together in hating the enemy. Diverse people can come together and feel superior. Whites, blacks, men, women, the poor, the rich—we can all agree to hate Hitler or Saddam Hussein.

This is a counterfeit.

The alternate church of nationalism is founded on hate, and churches of Jesus Christ are founded on love. Unfortunately, the counterfeit is easier to pull off. Hate seems to come naturally. It's something larger than ourselves that we readily sell out to. That's why *Jesus Christ Superstar* has Simon the Zealot advise Jesus concerning the crowds in Jerusalem to "keep them yelling their devotion, / But add just a touch of hate at Rome."[3] Simon felt that otherwise Jesus would fail.

He was more or less right.

I once gave a lecture defending just war theory to a college ROTC. I told them that the catch was that to fight justly you have to refuse to be whipped up into hating gooks or Huns. You have to love your enemy. If you are to go to war Christianly, you have to shoot weeping. The commandant was on his feet almost before I was done, assuring me with heat that under those conditions, war was impossible.

He was more or less right too.

And the same is true for nationalism. If we don't license ourselves to feel superior to people from other countries, if we don't manufacture enemies to hate, little or nothing will be left of nationalism. And the same for the KKK, the Marines, youth gangs, and the Nazis. We then lose the density we need.

---

3. Rice, "Simon."

FAMILY

The family is a much better counterfeit. It's based on love. It gives important and meaningful roles. Adults who goofed off in high school often work hard to care for or earn a living for their kids. That's a role young people can understand better than diagramming sentences. As the kids grow and begin going off to school or to work, the family gets together at the dinner table to love one another, debrief, regroup, remind each other of the family's values. There they rejoice together in each other's successes and cry together over losses.

This is how the God who created the universe meant life to be. A loving, committed group of people who know each other and serve each other, who live and love among each other. That's why he first chose a biological family as his people, and then transposed that to churches that live as families. This is a group with density, a group with love (ideally).

But human beings are fallen, and it hasn't always worked well. Adultery, child abuse, divorce, busyness that leaves us too distracted to attend to one another, more concern for success than for warmth, warmth that turns into lifelong domination, misunderstanding, or hatred.

The late nineteenth-century invention of the nuclear family has made it harder. (Of course, there's some gain: it's now easier to escape abusive or frozen families.) With nuclear families of four or so, the scale is too small to make people feel the grandness of God's plan. Though the vision is much better than most affinity groups, it's limited compared to an extended family, not to mention compared to the kingdom of God.

Put differently, the nuclear family is too small to give everyone roles in all periods of life. What's a housewife supposed to do when the kids grow up? The feminist answer of career is one of the saddest things known. And my main concern isn't leaving kids in daycare. It's that career didn't work for men. Why would it work for women? We need to be part of a larger whole that has a meaningful goal. Leaving an empty nest for a high-pressure law firm is of limited value.

Part of the problem is our individualism. Adults are supposed to take care of themselves, crazy and impossible as that may be. So middle-aged people no longer feel responsible to care for their parents, and grandparents no longer feel responsible to care for their grandchildren. This leaves us all isolated, roleless, stripped of loving relationships: grandparents in old-folks homes, grandchildren in daycare, and parents at the marriage counselor. (Not a coincidence.) We are simultaneously stripped both of our relationships and our roles. And we get depressed.

Part of this is an inevitable result of the change from an agrarian culture to an industrial culture to an information and service culture. There is no practical way for most of us to move back to our extended families. (In my case, every member of my family would have to move, and where would count as "back"?) And it's hard to know what the role of children is in an industrial society, let alone in a post-industrial society. On the farm we worked as soon as we stopped being afraid of the rooster. We had something to do with our lives. Today's parents often fight to let their children be children, but playing rarely makes anyone happy, and going to school somehow doesn't cut it.

I don't know what to do about much of that. But God in his astonishing wisdom has given us an answer that works surprisingly well across cultures. It's the church. (Surprise, surprise.) If our extended family is scattered, we join the new extended family of God where in slightly different forms all the old (God-ordained) roles reappear. There are kids for the grandparents to love and care for; there are elderly people for the middle-aged to adopt. And there are elders for the young marrieds to learn their roles from.

That's the kind of density and love we need to make a go of life. But it requires a commitment, an openness to intimacy, an excitement at servanthood, an ability to laugh at the surrounding world. And it requires the power of Jesus.

ALLEGIANCE AND PLANS OF SALVATION

Another way of looking at all this is in terms of allegiance. Groups offer something to be loyal to. In thin groups, it will be something like DSE's promise of long life or dog walkers' promise of joy in dogs. Those allegiances aren't big enough to be effective in saving people; so denser groups offer bigger allegiances that feel more like they're worth serving. Law firms offer money and career, status and power. The Nazis offered the Aryan race focused in Hitler. Nuclear families swear allegiance to their children. U.S. nationalism offers the nation focused in Thomas Jefferson, the Revolutionary War, the Constitution, and carefully selected stories of a "glorious" past.

A group's allegiance reveals its plan of salvation. You are saved by running, by taking care of your dog, by serving Hitler and the Aryan race, by having successful children, by being a good American and dwelling on the stories of your past. It can be anything: emotion before a great painting (art museums are especially busy on Sundays), having a good wine cellar, dressing well, getting rich. The bigger it is the better, or it wears thin.

The problem with these plans of salvation is clear when they're too small or too hate-filled. But the Bible suggests that only God merits our allegiance. Giving allegiance even to good things, like biological family, is idolatry: "Whoever comes to me and does not hate father and mother, wife and children, brothers and sisters, yes, and even life itself, cannot be my disciple" (Luke 14:26–27). From Abraham to James Hudson Taylor,[4] God has been calling us away from our biological families to God and the family of God.

Anything else is too small. What do you do if you idolize your son, and he fails you? More important, what does he do? What do you do if you idolize nuclear family, and you can't pull one off? After all, few of us do.

---

4. A missionary who left his family to serve God in China.

I'm not suggesting that the Bible wants us to abandon spouses or children, but that family works better when God and his people are first, when the family is part of a larger whole. It keeps things in a healthier perspective. Putting your family on center stage where God belongs is almost as destructive as putting your ego there. The nuclear family makes many of its true believers miserable while setting them up to fail.

Because salvation cannot be found there—whatever some may say about family values.[5]

NATIONALISMS

What's true for family allegiance is even more true for ethnic and national allegiances. Don't misunderstand me. There's a place for some loyalty to country, race, gender, or whatever, but it has to be a loyalty subservient to the kingdom of God. Jesus comes before Thomas Jefferson, Malcolm X, or Gloria Steinem. Way before. And your local church comes before other African Americans, white Americans, or women.

In our age of cultural diversity, it's striking how little attention the Bible pays to our little cultural categories. It determinedly divides the world into two groups: the children of light and the children of darkness, followers of Jesus and followers of the only other power. In the Bible any other distinction is insignificant by comparison. When other groups are mentioned in the New Testament, it's often to emphasize their unimportance. "There is no longer Jew or Greek, there is no longer slave or free, there is no longer male and female; for all of you are one in Christ Jesus" (Gal 3:28; see also Col 3:11; 1 Cor 12:13; Rom 3:29; Eph 2:11–22; 3:6).

I have a vague sense of how hollow this is when advocated by a dominant, white American male. That identity is probably as central to me as it is invisible to me. It's easy for me to tell African Americans or white women that they need to give up those identities; it will make it easier for me to get things done the way white males do them. It feeds my will to power.

But that doesn't change the truth of it. Something pretty close to that is just what the New Testament says, whatever color or gender I may be. And whatever our identity outside Christ may be, the whole New Testament calls us to forget it and recognize that it's an alien identity foreign to the people of God. Not that we are to become a nothing in a vacuum and not that we are to be integrated into some dominant group, but we get a new identity in a new group. An identity in Christ and his people.

> Come to [Jesus], a living stone, though rejected by mortals yet chosen and precious in God's sight, and like living stones, let yourselves be built into a spiritual house, to be a holy priesthood, to offer spiritual sacrifices acceptable to God through Jesus Christ. For it stands in scripture: "See, I am laying in Zion a stone, a cornerstone chosen and precious; and whoever believes in him will not be put to shame." To you then who believe, he is precious; but for those who do not

5. For a more nuanced and extended discussion of this topic, see Rodney Clapp, *Families at the Crossroads*, esp. 67–88.

believe, "The stone that the builders rejected has become the very head of the corner," and "A stone that makes them stumble, and a rock that makes them fall." They stumble because they disobey the word, as they were destined to do. But you are a chosen race, a royal priesthood, a holy nation, God's own people, in order that you may proclaim the mighty acts of him who called you out of darkness into his marvelous light. Once you were not a people, but now you are God's people; once you had not received mercy, but now you have received mercy. Beloved, I urge you as aliens and exiles to abstain from the desires of the flesh that wage war against the soul. (1 Pet 2:4–11)

The New Testament was written at a time when ethnic identities were at least as important as they are today. People measured themselves over against the hated Romans; Jews especially did this. But in the midst of this intense and legitimate Jewish nationalism, a primary point of New Testament writers is that ethnicity stuff is of no importance. Christians are aliens in a new land, who aren't to find their importance in their race or how they've been unjustly treated. Instead, they're to feel at least a little ill at ease whenever they aren't with the people of God:

> By faith Abraham obeyed when he was called to set out for a place that he was to receive as an inheritance; and he set out, not knowing where he was going. By faith he stayed for a time in the land he had been promised, as in a foreign land, living in tents, as did Isaac and Jacob, who were heirs with him of the same promise. For he looked forward to the city that has foundations, whose architect and builder is God. . . . Therefore from one person, and this one as good as dead, descendants were born, "as many as the stars of heaven and as the innumerable grains of sand by the seashore." All of these . . . confessed that they were strangers and foreigners on the earth, for people who speak in this way make it clear that they are seeking a homeland. If they had been thinking of the land that they had left behind, they would have had opportunity to return. But as it is, they desire a better country, that is, a heavenly one. Therefore God is not ashamed to be called their God; indeed, he has prepared a city for them. (Heb 11:8–10, 12–16)

To make it clearer where our allegiance lies, we at Church of the Sojourners are fond of saying that we're neither Republicans nor Democrats, but monarchists. Jesus is king.[6] Not feeling at home in the presence of Mayor Willie Brown (as with the mayors before him), we await another city.

At Church of the Sojourners, most of us don't say the Pledge of Allegiance to the Flag or stand for the National Anthem, and a few of us refuse to vote. (Hence our name.) These are of course merely symbolic indicators of loyalty, of no importance in themselves. More important perhaps is that on the Fourth of July we don't celebrate our nation. Instead we have a celebration of Yahweh's Kingdom. We party and pig out half the day in honor of the true king.

6. Church of the Sojourners is the church community in which John lived when he wrote this book, and in which he eventually died.

THE NEW PLAN OF SALVATION

In some way (it doesn't have to be our way), all Christians must find ways to distance themselves from allegiances to all groups except the church. That doesn't mean that women need to pretend that men don't oppress them, and it certainly doesn't mean that African Americans need to be tolerant of white supremacy.

It means that the people of God have a different way of dealing with oppressors. We invite them into the church, into our family. There they will be transformed into our friends. Not easily and not cheaply. But by forgiveness, by our accepting the pain of their sin against us.

So Paul doesn't take slavery on by denouncing it the way Elijah might have. Instead, in one of the slyest lines ever written, he tells slave masters, "Masters, treat your slaves justly and fairly, for you know that you also have a Master in heaven." (Col 4:1). Talk about aggressive, transforming nonviolence!

That same way of challenging injustice is found in Paul's shortest letter. His friend, Philemon, owned a slave named Onesimus. Onesimus ran away and somehow got together with Paul and became a Christian. (I'd like to think he came to Paul because he knew Paul was a kind man, even if from the oppressor class.) Then Paul does something unthinkable to us. He sends Onesimus back to his master with a letter. This is risky because Philemon has the authority to kill Onesimus. But once again Paul is sly. He tells Philemon he could command him to let Onesimus off completely, but instead, "I would rather appeal to you on the basis of love" (Phlm 9a). For love, not duty, is the basis of Christian transformation. Paul wants Philemon's transformation to be voluntary, not forced (14). He goes on, in intimate, affectionate terms:

> I, Paul, do this as an old man, and now also as a prisoner of Christ Jesus. I am appealing to you for my child, Onesimus, whose father I have become during my imprisonment. . . . I am sending him, that is, my own heart, back to you. . . . Perhaps this is the reason he was separated from you for a while, so that you might have him back forever, no longer as a slave but more than a slave, a beloved brother—especially to me but how much more to you, both in the flesh and in the Lord. So if you consider me your partner, welcome him as you would welcome me. If he has wronged you in any way, or owes you anything, charge that to my account. I, Paul, am writing this with my own hand: I will repay it. I say nothing about your owing me even your own self. (9b–10, 12, 15–19)

Historically, theologians have often read these passages as justifying slavery. Too bad they can't read.

Naturally this is unintelligible to the world. It's virtually unintelligible to us. Forgiveness is fine if someone hurts your feelings, but forgive a slave master or the murderer of your daughter? Even if they're not sorry? This calling is costly.

But it's the only way the world will see the light we hope to reflect. In this day of Tutsis and Hutus, Serbs and Croats, white supremacists, male chauvinists, and anti-

Semites, we have to do better than feminism and black nationalism and Americanism. We have to move forward into loving our enemies and forgiving them.

I suspect that all dense groups easily become principalities and powers. That's what's scary about Nazis and nationalists of all stripes. Their belief in their own superiority and their touch of hate gives them a power that goes beyond reason. It's no answer to reply with an opposing group that adds a touch of hate in the cultural wars. That's to fight the devil with demons.

On average, of course, churches haven't been all that different. We too feel superior to outsiders. But we must instead become a people of love. That's our mission and the heart of our calling.

SIX

Vocation (Why Your Job Is Not Your Calling)

I suspect that the single most important thing distracting faithful people from being the church is our culture's views on jobs and vocation. We get so busy with our jobs that we have little time left over for being the people of God. And much of the problem grows out of the Reformation.

THE HISTORIC POSITIONS

The standard Roman Catholic position in the Middle Ages was that God calls people only to jobs in the church. That is, the only vocation is to be a priest, nun, or brother. Not that other jobs are illegitimate, but they aren't vocations and therefore they're second-rate. (Some fundamentalists hold a parallel position, at least implicitly: their ideal is full-time Christian service—preaching, teaching in a Christian school, being a missionary.)

The Reformers reacted to the Catholic position by saying that since God created the whole universe, all legitimate work is God's work. Being a farmer or soldier is just as good as being clergy, just as much a calling of God. The only question is whether you're trying to do God's will, whether you're caring for God's creation. Within this perspective, the work you do can be a primary avenue for serving God and transforming the world.

By contrast, Anabaptists taught that our only calling is to be disciples of Christ in a local church. We're not called to be shoemakers, farmers, doctors, or even professional clergy; we're called to be fully functioning members of the body of Christ. Of course, Christians have to earn a living, but we are not called to particular trades, careers, or jobs. So Christians should choose those jobs that will best let them serve the body of Christ (where the body of Christ is understood as local churches). Our actual employment is of limited importance.[1]

---

1. The best statement of this position comes not from Anabaptists, but oddly enough from the World Council of Churches: Alan Richardson, *A Biblical Doctrine of Work*.

CALLING IN THE BIBLE

Which view of vocation are we to take? The Anabaptist argument is that in the New Testament, "calling" or "vocation"[2] doesn't refer to employment but to what we are to be spiritually. We are called, for example, to "eternal life" (1 Tim 6:12), "into the fellowship of his son" (1 Cor 1:9), "out of darkness into his marvelous light" (1 Pet 2:9), not "to impurity but in holiness" (1 Thess 4:7). God "called us with a holy calling" (2 Tim 1:9), and "Those whom he predestined, he also called, and those whom he called, he also justified" (Rom 8:30).

Nowhere in the Bible is anyone called to a trade or job outside the church: Paul was called to be an apostle (Rom 1:1; 1 Cor 1:1) and he and Barnabas were called to be missionaries (Acts 13:2–3).[3] Meanwhile, the Bible records that Paul was a tentmaker (Acts 18:3), but nowhere does it say or imply that Paul was called to be a tentmaker.

1 Corinthians 7:20 is the one passage that uses vocation to include jobs, and it includes jobs only implicitly: "Let each of you remain in the condition [calling] in which you were called." The surrounding verses are about circumcision, marriage, and slavery, and Paul is telling the Corinthians that they need not be too concerned about such things. Whatever they were doing when they were saved (called) is fine. Including slavery. Such things are no big deal. Paul isn't talking specifically about jobs, but the principle would presumably apply to jobs. So in this one place calling includes jobs. However, notice that jobs aren't important: "Whatever job you have, keep it. They're no big deal."

OTHER BIBLICAL WORDS ABOUT VOCATION

Of course, though the Bible doesn't use the word we translate "call" in relation to standard jobs, it might use some other word for the same meaning. It might use a word like *sent, ordained, placed, set apart, anointed,* or *chosen.* Such words would convey God's special choice of a job for a person. However, a study of such words gives the same conclusion. In the Bible people aren't set apart for jobs except in the church.

For example, in the New Testament those *sent* by God are entrusted with the gospel to the circumcised or the uncircumcised (Gal 2:7–8) "to bring about the obedience of faith" (Rom 1:5) and things of that sort; they are never sent to be blacksmiths or doctors. Nowhere in the New Testament is anyone sent to take up a trade or job outside the church.

---

2. *klesis* or *kaleo* also often mean "call" as in "call no one your father" (Matt 23:9), or they mean "name" as in "They were going to name him Zacharias" (Luke 1:59). They can also mean "invite" as in "When you are invited by someone to a wedding . . ." (Luke 14:8). These clearly do not refer to employment.

3. Acts also says that Paul and his party concluded they were called to preach the gospel in Macedonia (16:10).

And the same thing is true no matter what word you trace. No one is ever said to have anything remotely resembling a vocation to be a farm laborer, craftsman, tax collector, doctor, or shepherd. Occasionally people are told to give up such work (Matt 4:18–22; 9:9; Luke 5:27–28) but never, ever, to take it up.

The same sort of thing is true of the Old Testament. Of course, then people were not called to a special mission in the church; they were called to a special mission to God's people, Israel. Isaiah, Ezekiel, and Amos, for example, were "sent" on missions for God, not as soldiers or cartwrights—but as prophets to God's people (Isa 6:8–9; Ezek 2:3; Amos 7:14–15).[4] God chose Aaron as a priest (Exod 28:1), but no one was ever chosen to be a tiller of the field.

Bezaleel and Aholiab may be the one example of God's calling people to an earthly trade: God chose them as craftsmen. But it was for his tabernacle (Exod 31:1–11; 35:30–35). They were not called to craft just anything, but to craft God's tabernacle, a special mission to God's people. They were given these abilities "that they may make all that I have commanded you."

Another possible exception is kings and rulers in the Old Testament. There, many, many people were chosen as kings and deliverers and judges, usually of Israel. For example, God sent Moses to deliver the people of Israel (Exod 3:10), and he had Samuel anoint Saul as king (1 Sam 9:16). In our present situation, those are occupations outside the church, but at that time Israel was a theocracy, and so the rulers were leading the people of God: perhaps their role had some similarity to that of an apostle or bishop in the New Testament. At least, being king or judge of Israel can be seen as an office of the people of God. (And by the way, this is not just a rationalization. For reasons independent of vocation, we need to be clear about the continuity between the children of Israel and the church.) In any case, we can properly point out that while David was anointed king, he was never anointed shepherd.

So with the possible exception of theocratic politics, nowhere does Scripture indicate or imply that God calls people to any career, craft, job, or means of earning a living.

The role of Scripture

To argue that we aren't called to our jobs and professions on the grounds that the Bible doesn't mention such a thing may seem like simple-minded biblicism. It sounds like arguing that we shouldn't use musical instruments in church because the New Testament doesn't mention their use back then. I suspect that many Reformation thinkers would grant the Anabaptist exegesis without granting their conclusion. As Lee Ryken so aptly put it, Christians must learn to "think Christianly" about all of life, even those parts not dealt with in detail in Scripture.[5] I mean, we scarcely require a specific scriptural

---

4. Jonah is one example of someone sent as a prophet outside Israel (Jon 1:2). I suppose he had the office of evangelist?

5. See, for example, Leland Ryken, *The Liberated Imagination*.

mandate for medical research before we are willing to conclude that spending money on medical research is more Christian than spending it on biological warfare.

To do less is to slide into simple-minded fundamentalism, and the next thing you know people will be arguing that we shouldn't have separate Sunday school classes because 1 Corinthians 14 teaches that no more than one person should speak in church at a time.

So in Reformation and Roman Catholic thought, enormous intellectual structures are built on ideas like Creation and Fall, and applications are made to contemporary times even if Scripture makes no parallel applications. So the argument runs: work in general was instituted by God at creation, and therefore we can talk of particular jobs and professions today as being vocations.

But we should be careful what we consider thinking Christianly. I suggest that thinking Christianly will be easier if we use biblical language. If we start using terms that have no reasonable parallels in Scripture, we may often be sliding into thinking un-Christianly. As George Orwell suggested in *1984*, language and thought are closely related.[6]

Charles Hodge (a conservative, nineteenth-century Calvinist theologian) made the same point, interestingly enough in relation to vocation. He argues that "Words and thoughts are so intimately related that to change the former, is to modify, more or less seriously, the latter."[7] He says flatly that vocation is "the act of the Spirit by which men are brought into saving union with Christ."[8]

At issue here is basic hermeneutics. Some people believe that by immersing themselves in the horizon of Scripture and in the horizon of their culture,[9] they will be able to make applications of Scripture to their culture; they can do that with reasonable confidence, even in areas that Scripture doesn't specifically address. In the fourth century, these people were comfortable stating the relationship of Jesus and the Father and the Spirit in terms of Greek categories like substance and person. They also introduced a Platonic distinction between spirit and body. Soon they began talking about clergy and laity, purgatory, the importance of Mary,[10] and attending church. In the sixteenth century they were comfortable stating our relationship to our trades and professions as a calling of God. And in the twentieth century, some of them are comfortable talking about the Fall in terms of loss of self-esteem, some about biblical authority in terms of a philosophical view of inerrancy, and others about God in terms of being and time.

---

6. For a scholarly introduction to the discussion of the role of language, see Anthony C. Thiselton, *The Two Horizons*, 133–39.

7. Hodge, *Systematic Theology*, 639.

8. Ibid.

9. I am here using the terminology of Thistleton. I only hope I can think of a biblical parallel to that language!

10. This isn't an anti-Catholic statement. The arguments for a Catholic view of Mary are better than Protestants usually realize.

Whether such extra-biblical language introduces extra-biblical thought patterns is tricky. Since we all necessarily use modern and postmodern language (and thought categories), it may be radically incoherent to suggest using only biblical language. (Is the notion of a thought category itself a biblical category?)

Perhaps I am misstating my case. I at least need to be precise enough to say that the language we use needs to be a translation into our language of the languages in which the Bible was written. But it would be better to say that we should enter biblical thought patterns as best we can and then translate them as faithfully as possible for people today, doing our best not to introduce and baptize ideas that are extra-biblical. And that, I suggest, excludes calling normal jobs "vocations" in the Reformation sense of that word.

THE CHURCH IS PRIMARY AND EVERYTHING ELSE TERTIARY

The Reformation view of vocation seems to me to be a case study on why we should try to conform even our language to Scripture. It might seem that if the Reformation view is wrong, it's no big deal. But I suggest that this mistake has dealt a body blow to the church of Jesus Christ. It's much of the reason why Christians take standard jobs so seriously that they give them higher priority than church. When Christians have a chance to improve their job situation by moving, they generally do so with hardly a thought—and that is only the part of the slip that shows. By now when Jesus calls people to leave their nets to fish for human beings, the answer is ready made: "Hey, that's what I'm already doing as an engineer."

Nonetheless, I understand that to most educated Protestants, my view sounds oddly benighted. The idea of a vocation outside the church is basic in the thought of many of us, and to deny it seems like a return to the thought of the Dark Ages, like a collapse into the old sacred/secular dichotomy.

But I suggest that at issue here is the nature of church itself. The Anabaptists and the Reformers have a fundamentally different view of the church, and where they differ over vocation, the difference grows out of conflicting views of church and only indirectly out of conflicting views of jobs.

To sort out who is right about the nature of church is the point of this whole book. But let me say this much. If the primary way people are meant to do God's work today is through local churches (as I have been arguing), then taking secular jobs seriously will distract us from our main task. Everything except church is secondary, or maybe even tertiary—career, family, politics, financial aid to the poor, learning, creating great music, inventing a cure for AIDS, personal holiness, whatever. Then church is 95 percent of what God plans for us to do; everything else combined is only 5 percent, so to speak.[11] So in the view I'm spelling out, people are doing God's work in direct proportion to their faithfulness in using their gifts in a local church. And insofar as they are

---

11. Of course, from an Anabaptist perspective all that Christians do is part of the local church. We take church around with us 100 percent of the time, including to the factory or office.

not doing that, they are not doing God's work. So those who are not part of a local church can scarcely be doing anything substantial for God.

In this view the primary way to influence society is to call people into some church and nurture them and ourselves into increasing maturity. So the primary way to fight oppression is to call the oppressed and the oppressor to repent and become part of the church. Demonstrations against oppression have a place, but primarily as a way of calling oppressed and oppressor into the church. The way to transform political structures is not primarily by lobbying, but by inviting people into some church (that is, evangelism). Lobbying has a place, but primarily as a way of calling people into the church. That's why Paul didn't attack slavery as an institution. He didn't consider it acceptable, but he believed that the way to do away with slavery was by getting as many people as possible into church and understanding that their master is in heaven.

The Reformation view, by contrast, is that the church universal and invisible is one of many ways God intends us to do his work. It is the most important way, but business, family, politics, financial aid to poor non-Christians, learning—all are significant in their own right. The church is 55 percent of God's plan for people, so to speak, but the rest combined is nearly as important. If people are Christian, then they're automatically part of the church universal, and if they are pursuing their employment with integrity and to the best of their ability, then they are to that extent making a substantial contribution to the kingdom.

Christians are, of course, intended to be part of a local church, but failure to do so isn't fatal. And moving to a new place for something as important as work makes sense, even if that place has no good churches. While evangelism and calling people into church are crucial ways of influencing society, other things also have considerable value in and of themselves. So demonstrations, lobbying, aid to the poor are invaluable in and of themselves, whether they result in anyone becoming part of a church or not.

Playing football vs. playing a violin

One issue here is usually discussed in terms of whether the church is invisible and universal or whether it's always visible and local. I don't believe that's a useful way of putting it. I find it more useful to ask if being a Christian apart from some local church is like playing a violin by yourself or like being a quarterback by yourself.

If you play the violin by yourself, you will be unable to play much violin music as intended because the majority of violin music is for more than one instrument; it's intended for orchestras, quartets, and so on. Nonetheless, *some* violin music is intended as solo music, and much of the rest can be adapted as solo music. So solo violin music is by no means a contradiction. That's the position of the Reformation on being a Christian by yourself: it's not ideal, but it's not too bad, and it's certainly not a contradiction.

By contrast, what would it mean to be a quarterback by yourself? To be a quarterback requires a team to quarterback. If no one is there to catch your passes, no one to hand off to, then you aren't a quarterback. Being a quarterback by yourself is a logical impossibility. And that, it seems to me, is what being a Christian without a church is like. To use Paul's language, it's like trying to be a hand without the rest of the body; the idea is incoherent.

BEING A DOCTOR VS. DRIVING A TAXI

For the Reformation your employment is meant to be a major way of serving God. Whether it intersects with a church or not, it's something sacred. People who believe that would be unlikely to give up a successful career to become full-time overseers in their local church, and they would think careers in politics or medicine are considerably more significant than driving a taxi.

But from an Anabaptist perspective, employment is of no great significance; it's not a calling of God, but a way to put food on the table, like Paul's tentmaking. A physicist might well be *called* to give up her career if her gifts were seen to be at overseeing the local church. She might end up driving a taxi at night if that facilitated her oversight. If this seems bizarre, it may merely show our skewed priorities. This makes more sense if you believe that all important problems are at bottom spiritual, and that church is the center of spirituality. Then your role in church is more important than any job outside church, no matter how "important" the outside job may seem.

I suppose my claim is that being a good president of the United States will have less impact than being a properly-functioning member of a local body of Christ. Since people's role in church far outweighs their role in any job, you won't seriously consider moving across country for a job, though you would if it helped some local church. You move for the sake of the church, not for the sake of a job or for career advancement.

CHOOSING BETWEEN PARADIGMS

How do we choose between these two paradigms of church and vocation? No prooftext tells which paradigm is correct; no single passage states the Anabaptist position concisely. It's more a matter of noting what things are emphasized in the New Testament and what things are not. Using that approach, a global picture emerges of the centrality of church and the relative unimportance of *everything* else.

Part of that picture comes from what I've already argued in this chapter: the enormous biblical emphasis on our spiritual calling and the complete silence on callings to particular jobs outside the people of God. A parallel point is the failure of Paul and the Apostles to lobby for political change or to agitate for Israel's independence from Rome. Instead, they were preoccupied with church planting and church nurturing. (Read Acts and the Epistles.)

In fact, *everything*, no matter what it is, plays second fiddle to church planting and church nurturing. Learning (1 Cor 13:2), voluntary poverty (1 Cor 13:3), happiness

(Matt 5:4), even marriage and family (Luke 14:26; 1 Cor 7:7–9) are distinctly second string in the New Testament. In short, career advancement, a college education, sexual adjustedness, even watching the Super Bowl, are scarcely mentioned in the Bible as things Christians do or need to do.

The main argument, however, is an argument from silence. Most of the good things in life, things we take seriously, whether it's great art or good cooking, medical breakthroughs or politicians with integrity, Joe Montana or Joe Di Maggio, are simply ignored in the New Testament. They're not praised; they're not condemned; they're ignored. For Scripture, they aren't on the horizon. Not because they're bad, but because more important things push them out.

And what pushes them out is church. You see this in the book of Acts. It's the record of how Jesus' followers responded to his life and message: they responded by starting and caring for churches. That's what the New Testament emphasizes—to the point that everything else is Mickey Mouse. The Catholics were right that there's something second rate about secular jobs.[12] In fact, there's something second rate about everything outside church.

In fact, everything else is tertiary.

The church corporate

To put it differently, the New Testament is about the church. It gives no other suggestions on how to transform the world. For example, the Epistles aren't about abstract theology or individual ethics or about how to relate to those outside the church. They're about how the members of a church are to live as a group—how they are to be the church. The letters are about their lives together. When outsiders are in view, it's primarily about calling them, too, into the church.

The letters are not telling hands or stomachs how to behave as isolated individuals but as parts of the body and for the good of the body. Addressing an individual hand would make no sense because by itself it would be unable to do much; in fact, it would be deaf, not to mention lifeless. Similarly, it would make no sense to tell a lone Christian Jew to live at peace with Gentiles in the church; a person has to be part of a church to get so far as to disobey that command. So a command to be at peace is not mostly a command about inner psychological rest, but about relations with other members of the church. And a command not to gossip is included not because gossip in general is intrinsically bad (though it is), but because gossip eats away at relationships in the church.

To put it more concretely, are the Epistles about the private, personal, spiritual state of individual Christians with limited reference to other church members? Are they about relations with those outside church apart from the need to win them? Are they meaningful to "Christians" who aren't part of a local church?

---

12. The Catholic and Anabaptist positions are remarkably similar except they mean something different by church.

Many passages can be read either way, especially if read in isolation. But most can be more easily read to the community. Consider 1 Corinthians: it starts with how to avoid divisions, goes on to how to deal with serious sin in the midst of the church, what to do when members disagree in a way that might lead to court, whether members should marry each other, how not to handle the Lord's Supper, how speaking in tongues has limited value because it doesn't serve others, the centrality of loving one another, etc. With the possible exception of chapter 15, the book simply *is* about the interrelations of church members. Chapter 8, which is about eating food offered to idols, might seem at first glance to be about how to relate to the world, but that is the least of Paul's concerns there. His concern is not about making a *brother* or *sister* stumble (1 Cor 8:13).

The same sort of thing can be argued equally easily for the intensely practical books of 2 Corinthians, 2 Thessalonians, 1 and 2 Timothy, and Titus. Ephesians is a much more theological book, but it's a theology of church; so obviously it's about being church.

Galatians and Romans might seem to be harder problems. They're surely about the nature of justification, the role of the individual's circumcision, and so on. The way they're traditionally read addresses Christians outside a church as much as those inside. But Bible students are increasingly aware that Romans and Galatians are teaching that because we are justified by grace, Jews and Gentiles can live together in reconciliation in the church.[13]

The other Pauline books (Colossians, Philippians, and 1 Thessalonians) could perhaps be read in either way. But even they give clues that make it seem that they're primarily addressing members' relations to each other. Colossians, for example, says to "let the peace of Christ rule in your hearts" (3:15). That can easily be read as a private, internal sense of well-being. But the verse goes on to specify that the peace is the peace "to which you were called *in the one body*"—in other words, the peace of reconciliation with one another. And the next verse tells us to "teach and admonish," not anyone and everyone, but "one another." Why does the corporateness of such verses tend to get lost?

The same sort of thing happens a few verses earlier. The people at Colossae are told to put away "anger, wrath, malice, slander, and abusive language" (3:8). That would apply to those outside church just as much as those inside. However, the context makes that unlikely. The very next verse doesn't simply say, "Do not lie"; it says, "Do not lie to *one another*" (3:9). The passage then goes on with one of the great verses on racial, religious, and class unity within the church. And a few verses later, they are to "bear with *one another* and . . . forgive *each other*" (3:13). The passages that specify whether they're talking about how to treat everyone or how to treat each other specify that it's how to treat each other. So if we read the passages in context, doesn't it seem likely that those that don't specify are also intended to refer to how we treat each other?

13. For careful arguments of this position, see John Howard Yoder, *The Politics of Jesus*, 215–32 and R. David Kaylor, *Paul's Covenant Community*.

Now obviously I don't mean that Paul thinks it would be OK to lie to those outside the church. It's just that that's rarely in view for him. Such things scarcely enter Paul's mind. He's talking about how church members are to treat each other because that's a topic of such overwhelming importance to him that it pushes everything else out.

That's no different from a book on how to become a millionaire. If the book is any good, it focuses on making lots of money, and any reference to how to treat people will be from the perspective of how to make money. The book will not prohibit gossip, unless of course gossip gets in the way of making money. Making money pushes all else out. And with Paul, church pushes all else out.

I've been talking so long about church that the connection with vocation has probably been forgotten. The connection is that our vocation is to be the church; our employment is mostly a way to keep body and soul together as we do that, and so jobs shouldn't be graced with so elevated a term as *vocation*.

THE NATURE OF THE CHURCH

But how could anyone think that being church is such a big deal? How much time does it take to be an usher? Church is only a few hours a week. What are you supposed to do when no meeting is in process?

Such questions suggest that we don't know what church is. Church is more than a building or the meetings in the building, and working in church is more than ushering or teaching Sunday school or attending weekly meetings of the session. Church is lying awake at night trying to figure out how to help your brothers and sisters in your church grow into "the measure of the stature of the fullness of Christ" (Eph 4:13). It means eating and drinking and breathing ways to encourage others in your church in their walks as Christians.

But why is that so important? How could someone drive a taxi at a few dollars an hour for the sake of their church if they had the potential as a physicist to earn enough to give thousands? Can this be given a rational explanation, or must it be accepted by faith with the suspicion that its advocates have relapsed into a heartless fundamentalism? Concern for the soul and not the body?

The explanation is what this book is about. What the world needs more than anything else is reconciliation. At the heart of all our problems is broken relationships; symptomatic of those broken relationships are racism, war, child abuse, ecological degradation, drug addiction, oppression of the weak, divorce, abandonment of the elderly, indifference to the poor, and on, and on, and on. What the world needs is a sign that reconciled relationships are possible. It needs church to be a beacon of light for the world, a counterculture, a contrast society.[14]

And that's what it's all about. The church is a sign that reconciliation is possible. That's not abstract theology, but concrete relationships: blacks, whites, and browns,

14. See Lohfink, *Jesus and Community*, 63ff.

women and men, ignorant and educated working together in peace. It means people working closely together in church without ruling patterns of hatred or coldness or grudges or cliques.

The claim is that our living as reconciled churches will do the hungry more good than living out a vocation in relief and development or in banking or in politics. Jesus tells us, "By this everyone will know that you are my disciples, if you have love for *one another*" (John 13:35). Christ prays for our oneness "that the world may believe" (John 17:21, repeated in v. 23). According to Paul, the church racially reconciled is how the principalities and powers will come to know the wisdom of God (Eph 3:8–11). If the principalities and powers are, among other things, political structures and leaders, then this is nearly a proof-text for political change coming through churches reconciled more than through churches lobbying.

We don't accept this way of changing the world because the Reformation gave us an inadequate view of church. We see church mostly as people hearing the Word taught at worship services. We don't see churches as Jesus did, as reconciled families, which are therefore a compellingly attractive witness transforming the world—not through jobs and vocations, but through unity.

WHAT IS OUR WORK?

So what is our work? First, our most important work is living in reconciliation with our sisters and brothers in a church and lying awake at night trying to figure out how to help others do the same. Second, we should take whatever paid or unpaid employment will do most to help our brothers and sisters live in unity.[15]

From this it follows that many of us will be freed to work less than full time. Ideally, we're so devoted to our brothers and sisters and those who may become our brothers and sisters that our material concerns will be rather minimal, and we will therefore be free to spend little time earning money. That, I suggest, is the primary reason why Jesus and the New Testament are so concerned about money. They want us to be free from serving money so it won't take our time and energy away from serving the people of God.

To look at it differently, we'll choose work that pays as much as possible so that we can spend minimum time and energy at work and maximum time and energy with our brothers and sisters. If I can get $100 an hour as a lawyer or $5 an hour as a delivery boy, I will (other things being equal) choose the job as a lawyer. Then I can work fewer hours or give more money to God's people. Or perhaps I'll work full time, and my large income will allow me to share money with my brothers and sisters so they won't have to work as much.

15. I will focus on paid employment, but the principles apply equally to unpaid employment like painting the house, washing dishes, volunteering at the local hospital, demonstrating against U. S. military policy. They all are to be judged primarily by their effect on the church and calling others into the church.

But many professional careers present real problems. Some careers tend to demand heart and soul and therefore get in the way of a person's role in the church. So Christians with professional careers need to hold them loosely. And that in itself rules out some careers. After all, those serious about the church won't be available at work for repeated fifty-hour weeks; we won't be available to move at the behest of our career; we won't be available for travel that has us away from our church so much that being reconciled scarcely means anything. The point is simply that our minds and hearts won't be on our career (they'll be on our church), and so our attention will wander from work. And some careers and professional jobs just won't tolerate that.

Whereas being a delivery boy doesn't require as much concentration.[16]

In addition, it may be (other things being equal) that the people in a church should try to have jobs together whenever possible—preferably in a business which they control themselves. This is done by the Bruderhof and the Amish, for example. However, this criterion is about the nurturing role of church and therefore ignores the evangelistic role of the church. So it needs to be moderated with a sense of the importance of calling others into churches. Anything less leads to a separatism that is contrary to the spirit and practice of Paul and Jesus. They were in the marketplace calling people into the kingdom.

Finally, our idea of what's practical needs to change. The impact of jobs is less than we've imagined. The good that a doctor or lawyer can do as doctor or lawyer is not that much. Not that it's nothing, but if all problems are at heart spiritual and the solution to them is a reconciled church, then finding a cure for AIDS has limited value. The real need is to end promiscuity and drug addiction, and those are spiritual problems in the domain of church and not in the domain of medical research. We can do more about AIDS by getting victims into a reconciled church than by medical advances.

The primary good a doctor can do is not to give medicine but to be a light attracting broken patients into the reconciled church of Christ. A janitor in a doctor's office might do more good than the doctor if his life and words called people into the church. The world doesn't need more doctors a tenth as much as it needs more reconciled churches that will attract the world into the church. Nonetheless, being a doctor is something a Christian might be especially likely to do, not just because of the medical good you can do but also because of the way a doctor is in contact with people in trouble who therefore might be more open to becoming part of a church.

However, let me hasten to add that, other things being equal, responsible Christians will choose jobs that have the greatest potential in and of themselves for doing good. Discovering a cure for AIDS will not bring in the kingdom, but neither will being a delivery boy. So if a woman might do something toward curing AIDS and the work won't distract her from church, then by all means she should work on AIDS. But notice that church tends to push this out.

---

16. I use "delivery boy" because that is a job I held myself a few years ago. In my opinion, this criterion should override the previous one of doing the work that pays best. That is, if a person is making a lot as a lawyer but that job is taking over his or her life, then he or she should quit.

Nonetheless, helping the world isn't nothing. Middle-class Christians can often choose jobs that serve the suffering world. More and more of us should be found caring for the elderly and tending the sick and relieving the poor and inventing less polluting ways of living and teaching kids about the wonder and beauty of God's creation and the wonder and beauty of the creations of artists. (The Reformers were right; we do live in God's creation and should be taking care of it with our work and our lives.) So fewer and fewer of us should be found in meaningless or exploitative jobs and more and more of us in the helping professions—as long as we stay clear that the help they offer isn't much.

Oh, and while you're at it, choose a job you like—if that's practical.

But the main point is that our vocation is to live as a reconciled people.

SEVEN

Ministry: Being the Church for the World (Ministry and Evangelism by Being United)

I went to college in the early sixties and was distraught by the way evangelicals generally opposed the civil rights movement. I saw it as parallel to the German church's behavior during the Nazi era. So my first year out of college, I joined my mom and dad teaching at the Baptist School of the Bible, a fundamentalist, African-American school in Cleveland. And I spent the next twenty years fighting for Christians to work for justice for the oppressed and the hurting.

After my dad had worked for the school for a couple of years (mostly fundraising in white fundamentalist churches), he concluded that racism wasn't a black problem but a white problem. He wasn't needed mostly in the Bible school or anywhere else among African Americans; he was needed in white fundamentalist churches (among his own) where the sin of racism was deeply rooted. That's when Mom and I helped him start *The Other Side* to campaign for fundamentalists to open their hearts and doors to African Americans.

As the war in Vietnam began to heat up, I was working on a PhD at Northwestern and teaching philosophy at Wheaton College. From my point of view, evangelicals were once again on the wrong side, and I began to devote much of my time (and much of the space in *The Other Side*) to opposing the war. I was profoundly distressed that "biblical" people were indifferent (at best) to both racism and violence, not to mention poverty. It seemed clear that many of the "Christians" I knew would have sat back in the 1930s and let the Nazis come to power (and some would have joined them).

So I devoted my life to trying to get evangelicals involved in peace and justice ministries (and if not evangelicals, then whoever else would listen). Every church I spoke at, I campaigned for justice and challenged people to get more involved serving the poor and oppressed. Naturally, invitations to evangelical churches grew scarce. (This wasn't entirely their fault: I was pretty self-righteous!) And the five or six fundamentalist readers of *The Other Side* soon canceled their subscriptions.

A NEW PARADIGM

That decades-long process was so confusing that I questioned most everything: the existence of God, orthodox theology, whether a decent person could be evangelical, and (surprisingly) my own notion of ministry. As the years went by, I focused more and more on whether I was right about ministry. One time I was on a panel at the Evangelical Press Association, and I said that if evangelicals would take as clear a stand against torture as we did against pornography, torture would cease for thousands of people. The Kissingers of the world would then have to behave in Chile and Palestine.

A man in back asked me if I saw any sign that New Testament churches took such stands against Roman injustice. I didn't, but instead of saying so, I asked him if he saw any sign that the New Testament church took stands against pornography in the Roman Empire.

He nailed me.

"Certainly not," he said. "They opposed sin and injustice in the church, not in the Empire. They would've opposed pornography in their churches, but I don't see them denouncing the emperor's sexual sin. The only justice ministry I see in the New Testament is evangelism and church planting. They called pagans to decide on Jesus, repent of all their sins (including both injustice and sexual immorality), and become part of a church. I see no sign that they tried to get Romans to clean up any part of their act apart from Jesus. They were calling people to discipleship in the body of Christ, nothing else."[1]

I don't know whether he was a card-carrying fundamentalist or an old-fashioned Anabaptist, but for months I'd suspected something like what he was saying. It dawned on me that I hadn't moved as far from my fundamentalist roots as I thought. I was either going to have to basically revise my views on ministry or abandon the Bible.

It was a tough call. What was the point of evangelism and church planting if it made people into heartless evangelicals? The Bible and "orthodox" theology hadn't helped "biblical" people much; maybe I should just dump all that. For perhaps a year, I consciously moved in that direction. I grew a new appreciation for Bultmann and liberation theology.

I didn't like political conservatives, and I thought I was right. (By the way, never try to have a ministry among people you don't like.) I much preferred the company of people with my political views. After I was with folks from the peace and justice movement, I would regularly say to myself, "Those are my people." And when I was with conservative evangelicals, I'd say, "Those aren't my people; what am I doing here?"

---

1. I don't actually remember his words. These are too like the ones I use now to be what he actually said, but this is the impact his words made on me.

War at home

So for a couple of years I moved in and out of abandoning orthodoxy, of joining those who say that it doesn't matter much what you believe as long as you care about peace and justice. But in the end I went the other way. I've come to believe that biblical theology has the only answers for those desiring peace and justice.

However, Bible study wasn't what turned me back to orthodoxy. What turned me back was the level of conflict in the peace and justice movement. It gradually dawned on me that we peace and justice types were no better than those evangelicals I despised. We fought as much as the fundamentalist sectarians I was raised among. (That's actually who we were, just a slightly different incarnation.) Besides, our marriages weren't great. (I read somewhere that divorce rates correlate positively with political liberalism!) And by then, the kids of the peace and justice movement were growing up, and they were at least as troubled as the children of evangelicals. I began to suspect a basic lack of righteousness among us.

I'd been saying for a long time that the Greek word for "righteousness" was the word for "justice"—that for New Testament people justice and righteousness weren't two ideas but one. I had been telling evangelicals that if they were truly righteous, they'd also be just. Then it dawned on me that the shoe was just as much on the other foot. Justice is also unattainable without righteousness—the two are one. (For a simple illustration, think about young men who abandon their women and babies who then often get caught in a lifelong cycle of poverty and injustice.)

I'd been saying, "If you want righteousness, pursue justice." Which is true. But another slogan is also true: "If you want justice, pursue righteousness." It began to dawn on me that what you need to emphasize depends on who you're talking to. It depends on which half of the seamless garment people have hold of.

Another way to put it is that I'd been seized long before by the love and unity taught in Ephesians 4 and John 17 (I'd been seized by God?), and to settle for perpetual conflict in the peace movement would have been to settle for too little, for death. I had to find a people who were at peace with one another, who lived in loving unity.

Tragically, I saw no sign that those of us with a passion for peace and justice (Christian or otherwise) were living that passion out in our personal lives. Nor did I see it among those few evangelicals I was still comfortable with—those with ministries among the poor. Far from the unity of John 17, they, too, fought endlessly. And equally far from Ephesians 4, they weren't mature adults growing into the fullness of the stature of Christ. We were infants fighting over who had the purest vision and over who controlled our tiny organizations. That might have been tolerable—if I'd seen any sign that we were even in a process of growing up.

But I didn't. The average peace and justice leader and the average leader of ministries to the poor had ego needs the size of a movie star or a fundamentalist evangelist. I began to think we were all playing tiddlywinks on the infield.

Or was I being too demanding and sectarian again? Was I asking too much, asking that people be perfect? Probably, but I was pretty sure it was more than that. I was pretty sure that neither of the peoples I lived among (evangelicals and peace and justice folk) were playing the right game. But where were the people who were playing the right game?

A PEOPLE WHO LOVE EACH OTHER

Fortunately, about the time I was reaching total despair and cynicism, I found a tiny example of such a people: the Church of the Servant King in Gardena, California. They weren't playing the game very well in my opinion, but they were playing it. Lots of dropped flies and too many bean balls, but they weren't playing tiddlywinks.[2]

The new vision that I was getting from my reading of the New Testament and from Church of the Servant King was just as concerned about peace and justice as my old vision, and it was just as concerned about evangelism as the fundamentalist vision, but it was a new way of working for both. (New for me, that is. It's actually an old way. It dates back at least to the Anabaptists of the 1500s, and if I'm right, to the time of the Hebrews and of the New Testament.)

You work for justice by calling yourself and everyone else to trust God, repent of their sins, and become part of his people. Meanwhile, among God's people you begin to learn to live in peace and justice: you serve suffering humanity mostly by your life and words reflecting the light into the surrounding darkness. And by inviting the oppressed to move in with you. You try to become a demonstration plot for the kingdom of God, an advance colony of the coming peaceable kingdom, so that the world may believe. In this way, you evangelize *and* work for peace and justice.

The theory is that we love one another so the world can know that we are Jesus' disciples. Seeing and experiencing our love for each other, people will feel at home (perhaps for the first time) and will choose to join the people of God. This is especially true if they live with us. On the other side of mutual love—and only on the other side of mutual love—is there justice or righteousness, peace or love. Everything else is Band-Aids.

That at least is my present theory—and I believe it's the theory of the whole Bible. Not all the external ministry stuff I used to preach.

DOES MINISTRY EVEN WORK?

I was driven away from the ministry model by a second thing as well. It didn't work. I had abandoned standard evangelicalism mostly because it didn't work. I had conclud-

---

2. John ended up having serious reservations about the direction Church of the Servant King Gardena took in later years.

ed decades before that "getting saved" and joining an evangelical church left people as racist and insensitive to the poor as before.

But I wasn't seeing much happen as the result of social ministry outside the people of God. "You will know them by their fruits" (Matt 7:20). I was unimpressed by the fruits both of the peace and justice movement and of the evangelical ministry movement.

Church of the Sojourners used to be the primary sponsors of a law center serving undocumented people. We began to ask, "How much have we done if we help a Salvadoran get a green card and work her way into the middle class of the United States?" Soon she'll move to the suburbs and become a patriotic citizen of the United States, as racist and insensitive as the rest of the culture. Have we crossed sea and land for a single convert and made her twice as much a child of hell as she was before (Matt 23:15)?

What benefit is there if we fight for affirmative action to get more minorities into law school if it means that after they graduate they make so much money they sell their souls? What benefit is there if we stop abortion and keep all those babies alive to be raised in homes where they learn abandonment, promiscuity, and divorce?

Not nothing. If we accomplish those things, we've done something worthwhile. But that's a whole lot less than the vision of Jesus and Paul and Isaiah. Were we dispensing Band-Aids?

Suppose you're a doctor serving the poor. A man comes in who's been shot in a dispute over drugs. You operate, and he lives. He goes back out on the street—to deal more drugs, to shoot or be shot. How much have you done? No more than if you helped him take Jesus as his personal savior, and he stayed on the street and never became part of a church.

So I began to wonder how much we were even helping the poor and oppressed, and how much we were ensuring our sense of superiority over all those unenlightened conservatives?

Besides, it had long been pretty clear to me that a surprising number of ministries were ego farms for their leaders. Were we playing the same ego and control games as everyone else, only in different and often smaller ponds?

Combining two approaches

The obvious solution is to combine the evangelical and "ministry" approaches. When the guy gets shot in a drug fight, you try to evangelize him. You talk to him about Jesus and try to fix his soul as well as his body.

That makes sense. Maybe each side has half the gospel, and we need to combine the two. And I'm encouraged that I read that sort of combination more and more in both *Christianity Today* and *Christian Century*. But I no longer find that analysis sufficient. Instead of combining the two, we must find a third way.

Both leave our voracious egos and control needs firmly at the center. We have to die to ourselves so that Christ can live in us. Then we have to call others to do the same. We have to call oppressors to die to themselves so Christ can live in them, and we have to call the oppressed to die to themselves so Christ can live in them. That's our ministry, and that's our evangelism. And that's how we combine the two. We combine them into a ministry of evangelizing people into dying to themselves so Christ can live in them. Anything less is a Band-Aid.

What has a woman gained if she becomes a United States citizen and her ego is still alive and well? If it's still in charge, she'll just invent new forms of injustice and misery with which to oppress herself and others. Those oriented to social ministries seem to have remarkably little sense (in their ministries especially) that the real problems of our world are spiritual problems—things like selfishness, the drive for power, disunity, the hope that meaning can be found in money. And until those things are addressed, we haven't done much. And the only way to address them is by following Jesus and calling others to do the same.

And what has that same woman gained if in the process of becoming a United States citizen, she also invites Jesus into her heart? That isn't much use either if she then joins First Church and her racism and insensitivity to others remain intact. Somehow she has to come to understand that the only way she can invite Jesus into her heart is by agreeing to join him in letting God kill off her ego among the people of God.

The fundamental human problems, the fundamental causes of violence, injustice, and misery are spiritual problems, and those problems can only be addressed spiritually. That doesn't mean everything else is completely useless. If you want to know what good it does to end a war without getting at its spiritual causes, just ask the people having napalm dropped on them. Nonetheless, those few who understand the ultimate source of people dropping napalm on one another need to devote themselves to addressing the real causes. Let good, secular people who don't know the deeper level dispense the crucial Band-Aids.

We need to be calling people into a costly but gracious discipleship in which we are decreasing and Jesus is increasing. And into a discipleship that isn't an instantaneous, private transaction with Jesus. It's a continuing process that involves the people of God having a life *together* in which they can encourage and challenge each other.

So at Church of the Sojourners, instead of going out to minister to oppressed people, we've started asking a few to come be among us and experience life in the body of Christ. For example, we've stopped serving in emergency shelters and begun having someone who needs housing live with us for a couple of weeks. Then if they're interested in becoming disciples, they may stay for years; a few have become members.

I wish I could report that we have had a substantial impact on emergency housing needs in San Francisco, but of course we haven't. Nor can I report hundreds saved. But a tiny handful have stayed on and become serious followers of Christ in our church. But for that to happen, the people of God have to have a life together that they can share with those in need. Which is all of us.

That is, new disciples need to join a body—a united body, if you'll pardon the tautology. But first they have to be able to find some united bodies. And they don't grow on trees.

A UNITED BODY

The importance of a united body is another way of talking about the weakness of combining justice ministry with personal evangelism. Neither is aimed at becoming a united body, a body whose members love one another deeply. You see, both have been profoundly shaped by FIRES. And in the confines of the FIRES worldview, you can have only the most limited view of justice, righteousness, and salvation. In that worldview, you can't even talk about death to ego; in fact, in that worldview you help people by strengthening their egos. So evangelism becomes impossible, as does dealing with the roots of injustice. To put it more obnoxiously, the only grounds for a swollen ego better than a belief in my personal rights is a belief that I have a personal relationship with God. (Which of course doesn't make either false, just misfocused.)

So evangelicals focus on a personal relationship with Jesus that is so individualistic that we have little place for living as a body where the parts take on each other's pain and poverty. Jesus and Paul must be surprised that we think we're resisting our culture and pointing people toward the New Testament. A personal relationship with Jesus is no replacement for joining his body, and such individualism destroys even if it's in the name of Jesus.

Then there's the peace and justice folk. We emphasize individualistic rights till all possibility of community is destroyed. Groups who have been influenced by us become so paranoid that their rights might be violated that they can't work even with the groups closest to them. So peace activists can't work with blacks, can't work with Latinos, can't work with feminists, can't work with peace activists. Rights are no replacement for love, and individualism destroys whether it's from the left or the right.

We need to grasp that "leading people to Jesus" without taking them into the family of God is like a mother abandoning a newborn in a public bathroom. And so is helping poor people join the middle class without helping them become disciples of Jesus. (Perhaps we need a constitutional amendment criminalizing both.) And joining First Church doesn't help much, especially if it supports the U. S. military machine and teaches its people to be more disturbed by poor people on welfare than by capitalists who keep raiding the U. S. treasury.

More to the point, if our egos are alive and well, we can't become part of Christ's body (or any other body we don't dominate). And peace is then impossible. Because peace isn't the cessation of violence but life among a people you love and care for and who love and care for you. That is, peace is life in a body—unintelligible as that may be in FIRES. And we become part of a body, we become one with others, by dying and letting Christ live our lives, not by learning to be assertive or by increasing our self-esteem. Nor do we become one with others by throwing off our oppressors or by having a private, personal relationship with Jesus.

Every spiritual leader in the history of the world has known this. But tragically, it's an obscure point to political theorists, psychologists, and most church leaders. Which is why Jesus is deeper than Jefferson, Freud, and Pat Robertson combined. (Not that they're wrong exactly; they just missed the point, all of them.)

Which makes ancient Jews almost the only people worth reading on peace and justice or evangelism. If you want to understand either of them, read people like Jesus or Isaiah.

Isaiah

I used to be drawn to Isaiah because of his emphasis on justice. I remember saying that the only thing Isaiah condemns more than injustice is failure to trust Yahweh. Now I wonder whether I heard what I was saying. I proceeded to preach on injustice, not on trusting God. But trusting God is more basic than justice. It's the basis for justice.

At least, that's what Isaiah says. His central concern isn't justice, but Yahweh. He cares deeply about justice, but he's not Marx (though he influenced Marx). He's not Marx because he sees injustice growing out of Israel's failure to trust their loving God: "The ox knows its owner, and the donkey its master's crib; but Israel does not know, my people do not understand" (Isa 1:3). It would never occur to Isaiah to get the government working better any way other than calling it to return to Yahweh. Isaiah knew in advance that any reform that didn't include following God would fail to produce justice—as Marxism regularly has.

Isaiah called the children of Israel to leave pagan gods and return to the one who had cared for them like a vineyard. "My beloved had a vineyard on a very fertile hill. He dug it and cleared it of stones, and planted it with choice vines; he built a watchtower in the midst of it, and hewed out a wine vat in it; he expected it to yield grapes, but it yielded wild grapes" (Isa 5:1–2). The only possible solution is for the people of Israel to love Yahweh and stop trusting themselves, stop trusting military alliances, stop trusting foreign gods. It would never have crossed Isaiah's mind to separate justice from Yahweh.

It shouldn't cross our minds either. It is bizarre for Christians to put much stock in any legislation to improve, say, the situation of the poor apart from the poor and their oppressors turning to God in repentance and trust.

That's probably offensive to the left. (We've moved from freedom of religion to the idea that your religious beliefs don't have much influence on your politics.) But what Isaiah says is equally offensive to the right. Notice that his call was to the nation of Israel, to his people as a whole, not to individuals. (At this point, Marx was true to his Jewish roots and understood Isaiah corporately, which is ahead of both evangelicals and liberals.)

Of course, Isaiah doesn't talk about dying to self. But how about this passage? "O LORD, be gracious to us; we wait for you. Be our arm every morning, our salvation in the time of trouble" (Isa 33:2). If that's not dying to yourself, what is? He's telling the children of Israel to stop trusting themselves and to let God do the work. Or as Paul puts it, "I have been crucified with Christ; and it is no longer I who live, but it is Christ who lives in me. And the life I now live in the flesh I live by faith in the Son of God, who loved me and gave himself for me" (Gal 2:19b–20). Substitute Yahweh for Christ, and Paul is giving a great summary of Isaiah.

That's especially true if you add Isaiah's servant passages and ones like this: "For thus said the Lord GOD, the Holy One of Israel: In returning and rest you shall be saved; in quietness and in trust shall be your strength. But you refused and said, 'No! We will flee upon horses'" (Isa 30:15–16a). Isaiah is telling them that they won't get peace with Assyria by military might or anything they can do; they have to die to themselves and trust God.

He's talking into a situation equivalent to a developing nation being eaten by the United States, and what does he tell them? Organize to oppose their oppressors? No, he tells them to repent, die to themselves, and trust God.

Not exactly what peace and justice folks tell the developing world. And not exactly what the right tells Americans.

THE IMPLICATIONS OF THIS VISION

OK, so Isaiah's vision is for people to rely on God, give up on themselves, and live as a body. Some version of this is the driving vision of almost every part of the Bible. The heart of human beings is rotten, in rebellion against God, out for its own pleasure and power. This leads to violence, poverty, racism, and every other sort of oppression. The only possible solution is for people to repent, trust their loving God, and begin living as part of God's people. Omit any part of that, and our lives will be mangled along with the lives of those we're serving.

Anything else, no matter how well intended, is ineffectual. That includes every form of ministry that isn't driven by this vision. So personalistic evangelism that gets people to say a prayer and leaves them sitting on a park bench is ineffectual. As are soup kitchens, congressional reform movements, and anti-war rallies. Though all that is fine if driven by a vision to call people out of their egos to a loving God who gives life among his people.

Within that vision, most any ministry is good, as long as the people involved in it are clear. So for Christians the driving vision of anti-war rallies and soup kitchens must be calling people to repent and become loving as God is loving. And the driving vision of any sort of personal evangelism must be to call people beyond their personal concerns into a corporate (as well as individual) relationship with God.

My own position on this is more extreme than what I just said. I suspect that any ministry that isn't calling people pretty directly to repentance and into God's loving people is a distraction. The form of a ministry tends to become the end, to reshape what we set out to do. So mass evangelism, soup kitchens, anti-war rallies, daily vacation Bible schools—these good things tend to become ends in themselves, distractions from basic heart issues. They become bunny trails leading away from the paradigm of discipleship among God's people. This leaves the people of God so unattended to, so uncared for, that we have no light to project out so a fallen world can see the way home.

That, I suspect, is why Isaiah and the rest of the leaders in the Old Testament and New Testament spent so little time organizing and institutionalizing ministries and lobbying heathen governments.[3] They kept it simple. They called for a return to God and for specific repentance and not for much else. They didn't have much by way of detailed plans to reform the government or even to feed the hungry. Their plan was for the people of God to become righteous together, solving the world's problems by drawing them into their midst.

And I suspect that that should be our only plan too. I know my position is extreme, but perhaps it at least merits consideration.

GETTING DISTRACTED BY THE WORLD'S METHODS

What happens is something like this. We develop a proper passion for the world's hurting people. We look around for ways to help. Not being terribly creative, we copy what we see being done around us. That often means joining some secular political movement or at least adopting its methods. In Latin America it often means becoming a Christian Marxist. (This is one oxymoron I don't care for.) In the United States it often means joining the Christian right. (Another oxymoron I don't care for.) In short, we try most everything except following the strategy of the New Testament. Why not try being formed into the body of Christ, the way the New Testament suggests, and inviting seekers to move in with us?

It's often said that Marxism is a Christian heresy. That's true. Marxism has (or should I say had?) some deeply Christian concerns—but without grasping the heart of Yahweh. Marx was rightly moved by Isaiah's denunciations of injustice, but he then made up his own solutions. The same, I suggest, is true of the Christian Coalition, and almost everything else that doesn't focus on church planting—whether it's massive programs to feed the world's hungry or law centers for undocumented people. We need body life, not programs.

Throughout history, one tragedy of the church has been getting its concerns wrong. (This has, understandably, driven many serious people into the arms of Marx and other confused people.) But a comparable tragedy is churches that have good concerns but adopt unbiblical means to deal with those concerns. (I now believe I was in

---

3. Some of my distress with "ministry" is with institutionalized ministries. They're oddly prone to becoming tools of their leaders' egos or to becoming fundraising machines that lose their ministry vision. But I don't want to be naive: anything we do quickly becomes institutionalized, including live-in churches. That's unavoidable. But I still wonder if social ministries need to be kept on a smaller scale.

that category for the twenty years of my "ministry" career.) This doesn't apply just to social justice concerns, but to all sorts of ways we respond to our culture. Faced with sexual abuse, economics, psychology, conflict resolution, small groups functions, or education, we adopt the world's methods rather than the Bible's.[4] We get concerned about oppression and instead of applying the gospel, we apply FIRES. We get concerned about someone's psychological pain, and instead of applying the gospel, we add a counseling center to our church that applies the latest pop psychology.

Now I'm not suggesting that our forms and methods have to look exactly like those in the New Testament. As I'll try to show in the next chapter, we need to figure out the function and develop forms that accomplish the same sort of thing. But instead we go off and do our own thing, without seriously grappling with methods and means and forms. At least, I did.

The problem is that our methods can distract us from our real work. For example, few things are more all-consuming than external ministries. So, like Martha, we let these good things keep us from doing the essential things. We let good things distract us from living out our real calling of dying to self and living for Christ and his body. Then there's no body life, nothing to invite troubled people into. So our ministries end up as only ministries instead of being way stations toward joining the people of God.

Two kingdoms

It's a sort of two-kingdom theory: you don't call people to do the kingdom of the world less sinfully. You call them to abandon the kingdom of this world and become part of the kingdom of God's beloved son, where peace and justice are growing. And that's not just high-sounding words. Becoming part of the kingdom of God's beloved son means joining a church with a real body life. Forget reforming the world—except (and it's a huge except) to challenge the allegiance of its members. Ask people whom they serve: Jesus, or the self in all its endless incarnations—personal and institutional? Call them to turn away from all that and become part of a people of God who by their life together—personal and institutional—call the world to peace, love, and justice.

Actually, this isn't a two-kingdom theory at all. It's a one-kingdom theory. The Bible never calls the leader of darkness a king or his domain a kingdom. He is at best the prince of darkness and his domain the principality of darkness. Our mission is to rescue the slaves from the clutches of this beast, not make minor improvements in the inevitably beastly behavior of dragons. As Nat Turner and Abraham Lincoln realized, we don't need to make slavery more comfortable: we need to abolish it.

The only kingdom is the kingdom of God. Its competitors (whether racism or pornography, abortion or violence, money or status) don't deserve the name of kingdoms: they're merely rebellious principalities—dark, jealous dragons brooding on their self-destruction. You don't call sinners to serve their dragons less sinfully; you

4. This is another way of understanding most of Part II of this book.

don't call them to sin less sinfully. You call them to abandon their allegiance to a rebel principality and become part of the kingdom they've rebelled against, the kingdom of God's beloved son (Col 1:13).

Of course, part of the task is to pick up the pieces left behind as beasts careen destructively through their principalities. We need to love the victims (and the victimizers). But our basic task is to get both victims and victimizers to see that they need to serve the King, not yet another rebellious princeling.

Note, our goal is to get the victims too, to choose the true King. For no adult is just a victim. We all serve the beast in some incarnation, even if it's only ourselves. We must not sugarcoat that fact. So even if we feed and house all victims, we have done too little. For victims have not been rescued from the clutches of the beast until they have put themselves decisively into the hands of their loving king.

So whether we are putting our bodies between a beast and his victims or dispensing relief to victims, we must be clear that our primary task is to help people understand whom they serve. Our justice ministry is to get people to decide about Jesus. If their allegiance is still to Beelzebub, getting them to behave more morally is of limited value. So if Nazis are rising to power, we mostly need to call them to repent and serve Jesus. Let others do the lesser task of working for their political defeat. As the Nazis rose to power, Barth had it right when he traveled around preaching a simple sermon, "Jesus was a Jew."[5]

DIAKONIA

As I was trying to sort all this stuff out, I did a study on the New Testament words for "ministry." The main cluster of words is around *diakonia*. Etymologically, these words probably mean running errands (note, not walking errands!). The basic idea became any sort of literal serving, as in waiting on tables or doing other menial tasks for others. The New Testament uses it that way fairly often. So, for example, the Gospels talk about Peter's mother-in-law serving Jesus or an angel serving Jesus.

But one of the unique and wonderful things about the New Testament is the way it moves serving to the heart of ethics. So when the disciples argue about which of them will be greatest in the kingdom, Jesus says, "Whoever wants to be first must be last of all and servant of all" (Mark 9:35).

Treating serving as an ideal is foreign to Greek thought. For Greeks, the ideal was to fulfill your potential, and in the hierarchy of potentials ruling was near the top. The Hebrews weren't all that different. Although traces of servanthood as an ideal can be found in the Hebrew Bible (Isaiah's servant songs), first-century Judaism had little notion of serving the poor beyond being fair and giving them alms.

So Jesus wasn't overstating his case when he said, "You know that the rulers of the Gentiles lord it over them, and their great ones are tyrants over them. It will not be so

5. See, for example, "Sermon on Romans 15:5–13," in Karl Barth, *The German Church Conflict*, 22–25.

among you; but whoever wishes to be great among you must be your servant, and whoever wishes to be first among you must be your slave" (Matt 20:25–27). In other words, Jesus didn't come as a warrior king, but as the servant of his people (Phil 2:1–18). And he showed this graphically by washing his disciples' feet (John 13).

Progressives naturally use this notion as a paradigm for our relationship to everyone. And I guess they're right. But in the midst of this study, I discovered something striking and disturbing. The New Testament doesn't use *diakonia* that way. When *diakonia* is used of Christians serving the poor, it's never referring to social service outside the people of God. To be more precise: of the eighty-nine times that the word-family is used in the New Testament, where you can tell who is being served, only ten refer to serving the poor, and every time it's poor Christians.

In Acts 6 Jewish-Christian widows raised abroad felt they weren't being fed as well as native-born Jewish-Christian widows. So the church appointed deacons (servants) to take over waiting on tables and distributing food fairly. In other words, the deacons took care of poor Christians, not of poor people generally.

So although progressive Christians like me often use "ministry" to mean social service outside the people of God, the New Testament itself never uses it that way as far as we can tell. In fact, it often uses "ministry" to refer to things that aren't social service at all. In the New Testament "ministry" refers to using whatever gifts God has given us for Christ's body. It's something like the various "ministers" in a large church, only not limited to clergy (minister of music, of visitation, of youth). So Paul uses these words to describe the full range of ways we are to be serving in our churches. The Bible has no notion of ministry apart from serving the people of God. (At least, none connected to *diakonia*.)

Perhaps "ministry" is another word we should use more biblically. If we use it to refer to things that the Bible doesn't use it for, we give them a false authority, a pseudo-biblical authority. And that leads us to give them more importance than the Bible does.

THE LIGHT OF THE WORLD

Now, I'm not so silly as to think this word usage proves much. New Testament Christians may have had all sorts of social ministries without happening to use the word *diakonia*. Or our situation may be different. (We may be enough larger to be able to do more, for instance, and it must make some difference that we live in a democracy.)

But I suggest that this word usage is a clue to the structure of New Testament thought. For example, in the last few years it has come to be generally recognized that the Epistles are crammed with concrete concern for the poor. But because we don't have the clue that the Bible focuses on the people of God, we insist on reading them as how to relate to everyone, outside the church and in. But the plain fact is that the concern for the poor in the Epistles is concern for the poor in churches.

So Paul's major collection for the poor was not for Jerusalem in general; it was for the church in Jerusalem, for the saints (2 Cor 8:4; Rom 15:26). And the same sort of thing is true of the famous command to give to the poor in 1 John: "How does God's love abide in anyone who has the world's goods and sees a brother or sister in need and yet refuses help?" (1 John 3:17). And James' famous saying about not neglecting the poor is: "If a *brother* or *sister* is naked and lacks daily food . . ." (Jas 2:15).

Again, the same is true of Jesus' story of the sheep and the goats. We've somehow transmogrified it into meaning that anytime we feed a hungry person, we're feeding Jesus. But that's just not what the text says. It says, "As you did it to one of the least of these who are *members of my family* [literally, my brothers], you did it to me" (Matt 25:40).

Our task is to live out together a lifetime of discipleship to Jesus in peace and love while calling others to join us. We do this by our words and by our love for each other. "By this everyone will know that you are my disciples, if you have love for one another" (John 13:35).

I've probably said this too often, but here's how people will be evangelized: by our love for each other. Not by our service to the poor and oppressed, but by our love for each other. Not even by our love for the people we're trying to evangelize or serve, but by our love for each other.

I've probably said this too often, too, but in our world people don't seem to be able to live together in peace, let alone in love. Marriages break up, parents fight with their adult kids, non-profits split weekly, political parties have more internal wars than Baptists. The world needs a demonstration that life together in peace and reconciliation is possible.

The world has seen oppressed people band together and throw off their oppressors. We've even seen evil empires crumble under their own weight. Such things are rare and heartening events. But we know they can happen. The question is whether after the oppressed no longer have the oppressor to hate, no longer have the oppressor to unify them, can they then live with each other in peace? That would take a miracle. Especially if a few of the oppressors joined in.

So Jesus basically tells his disciples, "If you stay together and love each other over the years, everyone will know they've seen a miracle. Then they'll know that God, the very God of the universe, is working among you" (see 13:34–35, and John 17:20–23). The peace and justice movement doesn't do that. Law partners don't do it. Couples usually don't do it well. So if anyone does do it, people will flock to them to learn the secret (Isa 2:2–3). People need to see body life.

But if you don't love each other, you'll have all the evangelistic appeal of used spaghetti. So don't bother to serve outsiders while you're fighting and while you're failing to serve one another.

Maybe it's no accident that in Matthew when Jesus told his disciples how to be great he didn't tell them, "Whoever wishes to be great among you must be a servant." He told them instead, "Whoever wishes to be great among you must be *your* servant."[6]

6. This is true in Matthew 20:26 and Mark 10:43 . It's not true of Luke 22:25–27. I suspect that it's implicit in the context there: they're competing with each other, and so the serving may be meant to be

It was a very particular teaching: you are to serve each other. The general teaching may be true, but Jesus was saying more than that. He was saying something more specific, more costly, more rewarding—and much more explosive evangelistically.

It's relatively easy to learn to be a servant generally, a servant of people you see every once in a while. But the real test is whether over a long period of time you can keep serving the people you live with. After a hard day at the office, can you come home and serve your spouse or roommate? After a bad morning with the kids, can you go to work and serve the people you work with every day? That's what we are to do with each other in the family of Christ.

It's called reflecting light to the world.

The social ministry of Jesus

A while after discovering the New Testament idea of ministry, I ran into two more discoveries. They're in *Jesus and Community* by Gerhard Lohfink. I've rarely been so irritated by a book. I already practically agreed with his conclusion, but nonetheless he put it so baldly that I just hated it. I suspect I knew I was fighting for my life as an advocate of ministry to outsiders.

The big arguments against what I'm saying are that the Old Testament is full of pleas for justice and the Gospels are full of social ministry to people who aren't disciples. I'd already figured out that while Old Testament prophets talked about justice, what they did was more like evangelism. And they were working among the people of God, not trying to get heathen to behave better without serving Yahweh. The one prophet who went to the Gentiles (Jonah) was engaged in evangelism straight up, not social ministry at all.

Then came my next discovery, or rather Lohfink's. He forced me to conclude that something similar was true for Jesus. He did a lot of social ministry—among the people of God. He worked among Jews, not among Greeks or Romans. And when the Syro-Phoenician woman approached him to heal her daughter, what does he say? "Let the children be fed first, for it is not fair to take the children's food and throw it to the dogs" (Mark 7:27). He proceeds to heal the child, but he's clear that his primary ministry is to the children of God.[7]

I fought this hard. Then a test occurred to me. How did his disciples understand his ministry? Did they follow him by specializing in healing ministries among unbelievers, or not? Once I'd formulated the question, the answer was disturbingly obvious. The disciples followed Jesus by evangelizing, starting churches, and caring for believers. From Acts on there's nothing that can be understood as outside ministry (except evangelism, of course). There's not a single illustration of an organized social ministry in either the Old Testament or the Epistles.

---

of each other too. However, the different wording may illustrate that while biblical teaching is mostly particularly to the people of God, it applies secondarily to the world.

7. Lohfink, *Jesus and Community*, 7–29.

So probably I'd been misunderstanding the ministry of Jesus. (Now I realize that this argument isn't completely decisive. I can respect people who reject it. But I suspect that honest people who live with this for a while will come to take it seriously.)

LOVING ONE ANOTHER

I wasn't even close to recovering from my irritation at Lohfink when I collided with another discovery of his. He points out that the New Testament doesn't say much about our loving unbelievers. Its focus is on loving one another. He calls this the best kept secret in New Testament studies.[8] The jerk.

What's worse, he had a footnote listing all the relevant passages, and his case seemed pretty sound. With my handy-dandy computer program, I printed out all his verses and some others in a vain attempt to recover my identity—but to no avail. The case may not be quite as overwhelming as he thinks, but it's overwhelming enough. We're told to love our enemies (many of whom are presumably outside the faith). And the story of the good Samaritan makes it clear that we're to love all sorts of people we think of as outsiders. But without a doubt, the New Testament focus is on loving our brothers and sisters in Christ—by a huge margin.

By now it seems obvious to me. We're to love everyone. We're to forgive everyone. That's a key way we're different from others. But even more important is that we love our brothers and sisters. That's how the world will know that we're living the truth. That's how we can work for justice.

Don't misunderstand me. Of course, "whenever we have an opportunity, let us work for the good of all." But don't forget the other part either: "especially for those of the family of faith" (Gal 6:10).

I've probably said it too many times, but once again the point is the same. All sorts of evidence from all sorts of places point in the same direction. Our task is to follow Jesus by becoming part of his body. As we love one another, we will reflect light to the world, and some will stop serving their favorite dragon and join us in the body of Christ. Our task is to become holy people, righteous and just, those who love our brothers and sisters. That's our ministry, our evangelism, our vocation, our way of working for justice.

THE MINISTRY OF THE CHURCH

I was cornered by these arguments and after a struggle of only ten or twelve years, I gave way. I had the exegesis, I had the philosophy, all I needed now was a slogan. I got it some years later at a church retreat. In a discussion our visiting speaker, Bob Appleby, said that the ministry of the church is to be the church for the world. (A phrase I've already used in this book.)

---

8. Ibid., 110ff.

That says it all. Occasionally folks tell me I don't believe in ministry anymore. Now I know what to say. I say, "I do too believe in ministry. We just disagree on what ministry is. The ministry of the church is to be the church. To live in such a way that we know each other intimately and, despite that, still love each other. We do this not for our own comfort, but for the world. So that we can lessen injustice. And we also invite troubled people to live among us, see our lives, and be discipled. So the world may believe.

The ministry of the church is to be the church for the world.

Perhaps the only ministry.

PART THREE

Reflections on Doing Church in America
(Church Structures)

EIGHT

Form and Function (Different Tree, Same Monkeys)

By now it's pretty clear that I'm concerned about the form of churches. And it might sound like I'm getting ready to say that if only we got the form of our churches right, the kingdom would arrive and we would quickly grow into the full stature of Christ.

Well, I may be stupid, but I'm not that stupid. Forms guarantee nothing: when we rely on forms, we've begun playing tiddlywinks. Be clear. If we move to a different tree, we'll still be the same monkeys. What counts is changed hearts among the people of God. The Holy Spirit can use the worst forms, and human beings can ruin the best forms. Besides, every age and society may need different forms in which to do church. Which is probably part of the reason the New Testament gives so few details on the shape of the church (or on anything else). You do church however works best in your situation.

Forms aren't the issue; function is. We don't have to copy the forms of New Testament churches; what we need to copy is their function(s).[1] That is, we need to sort out what churches in the New Testament were about and invent forms that help the same sorts of things happen in our cultural situation. What I'm complaining about isn't that today's churches fail to copy the form of New Testament churches. No, I'm complaining that our forms aren't good at supporting the functions God gave his people.[2]

---

1. This isn't just a principle for determining the shape of the church; it's a basic principle of hermeneutics. This is the tragedy of fundamentalists. Early in this century, they were among the few people who took Scripture seriously. Many of them took courageous and prophetic stands against the religion of the age, but all too often they tried to enforce the forms of the New Testament while failing themselves to find the heart of Jesus.

"Form and function" is, of course, metaphorical language borrowed from architecture and other sorts of design. It may not be entirely clear in theology and ethics, but I hope it helps us see things anew. "Ends and means" is more traditional language, but it has had a controversial life I'd rather avoid.

2. Arnold Stoetzel of Catholic Integrated Community pointed out to me that some functions of churches might legitimately change in different cultures and times. He suggests that the changes in the office of bishop were in some respects legitimate as more and more people became Christian over larger and larger areas. This makes sense to me, and so perhaps I'd make my point better by talking about essential functions.

In any case, what I'm after here is that the essential function of every church member is to share the gift that God made her or him to be. That function doesn't change over time, though the form for sharing it may.

On the other hand, Del Birkey suggested to me that we do need to keep even the forms of the

However, although forms aren't the heart of the matter, not all forms are equal. Form and function are related: some forms do better at supporting the functions of church. Form should follow function. For example, Judy (my wife) and I love dried roses. We used to pin them to the closet door in our bedroom. Unfortunately, the closet door was near my side of the bed, and when I get up in the morning I tend to stumble around. You can fill in the rest. Dried roses pinned to the closet door didn't do much toward the function of supporting a staggering man or of soothing the soul of a raging beast. And after a few encounters, neither did they do much aesthetically.

What I'm suggesting, of course, is that since Constantine, the forms of churches have been rather like dried roses put where people bump into them. Which has made it harder to do church well, which has made it harder to grow into the stature of Christ.

Churches haven't done quite as badly as the roses because Constantine's forms fit with certain functions of the church. For example, proclamation of the Word can be done with a large group in a large building. Worship can be done well in a huge cathedral. In those respects, form follows function. Constantine's forms also work for some kinds of teaching and prophecy.

Even in those respects, however, his forms have weaknesses: they encourage passivity and an entertainment model, not to mention the professionalizing of clergy and of musicians along with the dominance of economics (buildings and performers are expensive). These are problems, but any form has its weaknesses: some people may be able to use Constantine's forms without being eaten by them. (Those whose balance is better than mine at 6:00 AM can have roses on their closet door.)

But large gatherings alone do not make a people. Even less do they make a family or a team. And even less a body. And neither do large buildings. If one of your forms is a thousand people in a big building, you must create other forms (of equal or greater importance) that support family and intimacy and commitment. You must create additional forms in which "every part" can be a gift to every other part and in which all the parts tend to become interdependent. You must find ways to do church in which peoples' lives overlap extensively. Otherwise there will be parts of church that you won't do well. You won't learn to play baseball well if your primary training is listening to inspirational lectures (though inspirational lectures have their place).

And these forms we create can't be an afterthought or secondary. Smaller groups of some sort have to be at the very heart of church. They can't just be a way to get people involved so they'll keep attending the main meetings. And the smaller groups can't serve the preaching or the building: rather the preaching and the building must serve the smaller groups, must grow out of their needs.

---

church. The fact that only house churches appear in the New Testament means that we too must have house churches. He makes the interesting point that this form is completely cross-cultural. As culture changes, the house changes, and so the culture makes the changes in form necessary for it to be culturally relevant.

Otherwise, form and function are reversed, and we find ourselves playing tiddly-winks. And then few churches will grow into the fullness of the measure of the stature of Christ.

FAMILY

I'm making strong claims about the function of the church in the New Testament. Insofar as I've argued it, I've mostly used Paul's picture of the church as a body. That picture appears in Ephesians, 1 Corinthians 12, and Romans 12, so by itself, this is a strong argument. Our churches need to take forms that support our functioning as a body.

But the evidence for the importance of these sorts of things is much stronger than those few passages. It comes from all directions in Scripture.

One direction is that the most frequent picture of the church in the New Testament is family. That is what the New Testament means by calling God "father" roughly 250 times and what it means by referring to other Christians as "brothers" sixty-five times. The children of God are our new family. That's part of what is involved in being born again.

So when Jesus' mother and brothers came to get him thinking he was nuts, he said, "Who are my mother and my brothers? . . . Whoever does the will of God is my brother and sister and mother" (Mark 3:33, 35; compare Matt 12:46–50). For Christians, our most important family isn't our biological family but the family of God. So "whoever comes to me and does not hate father and mother, wife and children, brothers and sisters, yes, and even life itself, cannot be my disciple" (Luke 14:26; compare Matt 10:37–38).

The theme of family goes back to the Old Testament. God's first people were a literal, biological family: they were the children of Abraham, Isaac, and Jacob (Israel). So throughout the Bible they are constantly called "the children of Israel" or "Israelites" or just "Israel"—all of which were the name of a family, of their patriarch. When they are called by other names, it's often the name of one of Israel's sons or grandsons especially Judah or Ephraim, family names again. And Jews also talk regularly about Abraham as their father.

But the point isn't only that family was God's strategy in both the Old and New Testaments. It is that we today are the successors of the Israelites. Or rather, the church has joined the children of Israel. We are to carry on with the same strategy God gave them because we have been added to them. The word the earliest Christians used for church (*ekklesia*) is the word the Greek Old Testament uses for the gathered assembly of Israel.[3] That's who the early church thought they were.

The central point of Romans, Galatians, and Ephesians is that by God's grace Gentiles have been grafted into Israel. God has made both groups into one. (Sometimes

---

3. See, for example, Exod 12:6; Deut 23:1–3; 1 Chr 28:8.

we're told that their point is grace, which is true, but then that's the point of almost every passage of Scripture. So the question becomes what any particular passage is telling us about grace. And these three books are telling us that by grace God has added believing Gentiles to Israel.) Along with believing Jews, we are the new Israel.[4] So promises to Israel are also promises to us: Israel is a light to the nations; the church is a light to the nations. God's covenant with Abraham and his descendants is also his covenant with us.[5] So you can hear the references to Israel when the very Jewish Peter writes to a church:

> You are a chosen race, a royal priesthood, a holy nation, God's own people, in order that you may proclaim the mighty acts of him who called you out of darkness into his marvelous light. Once you were not a people, but now you are God's people. (1 Pet 2:9–10b)

FAMILY AND FORM

So from Genesis to Revelation family is what the people of God are. Our present question then is, what forms for the church support the functions of family? For most of us I suspect, family is a pretty empty metaphor in relation to church. But as often as the metaphor is used in the Bible, it's not likely that it's mere rhetoric. Those of us who talk about the authority of Scripture must find ways to embody this metaphor.

So what is the function of family? Families propagate themselves, they provide love and respect, good ones nurture each other, they provide discipline (especially for younger members), they're the basic economic unit, they find ways to support members economically who can't do it themselves (with little attention to the economic "worth" of the individual), and they have deep loyalties to each other that include equally deep obligations. Ideally, family is the main place we get a sense of identity and "belonging," a place we can return to with few questions asked when we screw up or have been screwed over.

Families in cultures outside the West usually differ from ours, first, by doing these things even more (more loyalty, more discipline, more identity, more economic sharing) and, second, by including more relatives than the nuclear family. For example, a Guatemalan who used to be in our church seemed to send half his meager income to his family back home, and that family included great aunts and second cousins once removed. Something like that is what Paul and Jesus would have meant by family.

How do you go about "doing" family in that sense? What forms will encourage that sort of family to develop healthily? Well, what forms do healthy families take? You don't have to be a rocket scientist to figure that out. Families carry out their functions by forms like eating together, living together, working together, giving to each other in times of need. Even in modern Western cultures, families typically want to be together

---

4. Rom 2:28–29; 9:6–8; 11:17–24; Eph 2:8–19. My opinion is that unbelieving Jews still have a special place in God's plan, but this isn't the place to discuss that.

5. Gen 12:3; Isa 9:2; 42:6; 60:3; 62:1; Matt 5:14–16; Acts 13:47; Eph 5:8; Phil 2:15.

in times of celebration and mourning, and they care for each other in sickness and stress.

To what extent does your church have forms like that? We do pretty well with short-term sickness and trouble. Meals get delivered, the pastor visits, money is given. I don't belittle all that. But it's a pale image of family, especially the intense, extended family of biblical cultures.[6]

Do you know what happens when a barn burns in an Amish community? The church has a barn raising. No insurance company, no government hand out, not even much self-reliance. The Amish depend on God through their brothers and sisters.

Odd, isn't it? Or are we the ones who are odd? And does our oddness, our forgetfulness of our church family, help account for our churches being spiritual midgets?

Then there are celebrations. We do fairly well at weddings. But we've lost rites of passage. (Which is too bad: teenage sex is a bad substitute.) Then there's Thanksgiving: we all go to Grandma's. (Who is it that we're thanking?) And Christmas—ever notice the different people at church on Christmas? Everyone goes home. Which isn't bad. But it makes it clear that church isn't home.

One recent weekend at Church of the Sojourners, Dale Gish and Debbie Mateer got married. We took the whole weekend at it. A weekend of work, partying, games, preparing food, telling stories from the past, sharing thoughts for the future. Sixty people stayed for two nights at a Quaker retreat center in the redwoods. It was so different from twenty minutes of going to church, and then off to the country club for a dance. We drew together in intimacy, love, and commitment. Dale and Debbie were not alone in the commitments they made to each other.

Two days later in Jackson, Mississippi, our friend Spencer Perkins died. He was forty-three and left a wife, three children, his parents, and Antioch, the community he pastored. They took the next week burying him. Five hundred people came from all over the United States. Many of us thought we had come to comfort the bereaved, but we found that we came to be comforted, to be bereaved together, to cry together. His church fed everyone, brought scores of people from the airport. You could hardly take a step without someone asking if he or she could do anything for you. It was a terrible time, but with the people of God rallied around it was also a wonderful time, a growing time. So different from half an hour at a funeral home with a handful of people.

That's the sort of thing it means to be the family of God.

---

6. I'm told I'm idealizing family in this section. That's true. When the Bible calls us to be family, it's calling us to be an ideal family (in fact, *the* ideal family). At the same time, in the midst of our failures as family, one of the key aspects of a family (especially an ideal one) is how much grace they extend to each other. Like the prodigal son, you can come home again. That is, even ideal families miss the ideal regularly and are called to keep forgiving each other. This is a particularly important aspect of family as it is of church.

EATING WITH YOUR FAMILY

Then there's eating together. How much do folks eat together in your church? I suspect that frequency of eating together is one of the best indicators of the health of a biological family. And I wonder if that's not also true of church families.

Maybe poverty should be calculated by whether we have enough to eat plus whether we have enough people to eat it with plus whether we connect with those we eat it with. You're poor if you have too little food, eat alone, or are lonely with those around you. And your church is poor unless you're connecting with your brothers and sisters while eating with them regularly.

Did you ever notice how extravagant eating is in the Bible? They sacrificed animals to atone for sin and gave some to the priests to eat. And do you remember what they did with the rest? They ate it. Together. They feasted on it. With their extended families. They were celebrating the forgiveness of their sins. By eating, together. That's what they did on every holy day (holiday): they feasted together, celebrating their God. How often do the people of God do that together where you do church?

In the Gospels there's hardly a chapter that doesn't talk about eating (abundantly). Jesus came—eating. With almost everyone. Pharisees, poor people, publicans, sinners. That's how he showed who he accepted. (Almost everyone.) It looks like he didn't do much except tell parables, heal people, and eat. The Pharisees didn't like it, but he kept doing it anyway. He was living out a parable: the parable of the extravagant banquet of the coming kingdom. Which the Bible talks about a lot. Too bad we don't live out that parable more, eating with everyone who will eat with us.

Then the night before Jesus was killed, guess what he did? Yeah, he ate. With his disciples. And told us to remember him that way. So we eat tiny, tasteless wafers together and drink tiny cups of grape juice separately. Every month or so. Then we go "home." Odd, don't you think?

Now, eating together won't guarantee that we love each other any more than any other form will. But not eating together will make it harder: what better way to feel the texture of each others' lives than eating together? What better way to love each other intelligently and help each other grow into the full stature of Christ?

Want to grow into the fullness of Christ? Feast with your local church. Experience abundance.

EVANGELISM

With my talk of church as family, it may sound as if I think the church should be turned inward. I may sound like an escapist or a culture denier with my back turned on the world. But I don't believe that's what I'm saying. I believe I'm offering a different model of how to turn toward the world. And I hope it's a better model. We turn toward the world by inviting them to eat with our extended family, to join with us in our lives. That's what Jesus did. He ate with people. He feasted with them. He entered their lives and let them enter his. I suspect that that should be the central ministry of every church.

Eating with people. Feasting with people.

This solves certain problems. Many of us are uncomfortable with evangelism in the park when we get people to ask Jesus into their heart and leave them sleeping on a park bench. It's another matter, however, to invite someone in the park to join your family. You can invite them to "come and see" if this is the sort of family they want to become part of. They may see love and choose to let you take responsibility for them while they take responsibility for you. This is getting saved to a depth almost forgotten by modern people.

This also gets us out of the box of having to choose between transforming the world's cultures and withdrawing while hoping an apocalypse will explode them.[7] Instead, at dinner we invite people into a new culture, the culture of God's family. Together we embody the best of the world's culture in the people of God while mostly embodying our Lord himself. We become a contrast culture[8] that we invite people into.

That's a good way to be light to the world. And it's how cultures get transformed.

One way we do that at Church of the Sojourners is to provide emergency housing. We don't have a separate building for emergency housing. We invite people in trouble to live in our homes, to join our families. If they seem reasonably responsive, we ask them to stay for months that sometimes turn into years that occasionally result in solid members.

That sort of thing is hard to do if you live as small nuclear families, but our members live together as extended families in large houses. One or two more who are more troubled than average aren't that big a deal.

And it illustrates a central principle of evangelism and ministry. You win people to what you win them with.[9] So if you evangelize people in a huge rally, you have won them to coming to large meetings. Not much else. If you minister to them in a soup kitchen, they will have some idea that they should give people food. If you also preach to them, then they'll try to preach to others. But is that whole enough? As Christians, our calling is larger and wholer. It's the largest, wholest calling of all. Our calling is introducing people to God's extended family.

That brings the deepest discipleship, the deepest transformation, the most content and style to rebirth.

And remember with this calling to introduce others to wholeness, the medium is the message. Much of it anyway.

---

7. See H. Richard Niebuhr, *Christ and Culture*.

8. Gerhard Lohfink, *Jesus and Community*, 121–32.

9. I learned this phrase (not to mention half the rest of this book) from Rich Read, pastor of Church of the Servant King in Gardena, California.

A DIFFERENT PARADIGM

The trouble is, when we start thinking about forms for the church we naturally tend to get trapped in what we have experienced, perhaps especially in childhood. For most of us this means that the form of the church revolves around steepled buildings and clergy and sermons. I hope I've made it clear that these forms aren't wrong in themselves. I hope I've made it equally clear that neither are they adequate. Those of us who accept the authority of Scripture for our daily lives have no choice but to find forms for the church that support our functions as families and bodies.

This is intimidating and sounds like it could only be done by terribly gifted, creative people. And in a way, that's true—as long as we're clear that we all are terribly gifted by the Holy Spirit.

Besides, within limits, average people know how to do it in the world. Sororities know how to do it. The Elks know how to do it. The Marines know how to do it. Some coffeehouses know how to do it. With the help of the Holy Spirit, Christians can figure this out too. We just need to be clear that we're doing something which in some respects is more like what sororities do than like what churches normally do.

Of course, there are limits to sororities as a model for doing church (as there are to a mustard seed as a model for the kingdom). The exclusiveness and worldliness of sororities should give us pause, but who else parties as much as Jesus did? And using the Marines as a model for doing church does not extend to their violence and manipulation of recruits, but who does a better job at creating action groups where individuals are well trained for specific tasks that serve the group no matter the cost? Perhaps the Bible's military language is no accident.

We can also take the clues the Bible gives us, which are pretty obvious. For example, the metaphor of family suggests forms obvious enough that you don't have to be a genius to figure them out. Eat together. Party together. Take holidays together. Mourn together. Help each other when in need. Discipline each other. Give each other money. Move near each other. (Maybe into the same house.) Start businesses together.

That's how preaching and teaching and evangelism come to life. That's how you grow into the full stature of Christ. That's what it means for the kingdom to start to arrive in our midst.

What's so hard about that?

KURT VONNEGUT

Oddly enough, Kurt Vonnegut understands the similarity between church and extended family better than most theologians. Commenting on his response to a letter from a man who had spent much of his life in prison and was about to be released, he says:

> I, Honorary President of the American Humanist Association, wrote back today, "Join a church." I said this because what such a grown-up waif needs more than anything is something like a family.

I couldn't recommend Humanism for such a person. I wouldn't do so for the vast majority of the population.[10]

Here are some of his other reflections on church and family:

> *Playboy*: Is there any religion you consider superior to any other?
>
> *Vonnegut*: Alcoholics Anonymous. Alcoholics Anonymous gives you an extended family that's very close to an actual brotherhood, because everybody has endured the same catastrophe. . . . They talk about real troubles, which aren't spoken about in church, as a rule. . . .
>
> This is a lonesome society that's been fragmented by the factory system. People have to move from here to there as jobs move, as prosperity leaves one area and appears somewhere else. People don't live in communities permanently anymore. But they should: Communities are very comforting to human beings.[11]
>
> We are chemically engineered to live in folk societies [where all sorts of things are treated as personal], just as fish are chemically engineered to live in water—and there aren't any folk societies for us anymore.
>
> . . . Sigmund Freud admitted that he did not know what women wanted. I know what they want. . . . They want to live in folk societies, wherein everyone is a friendly relative, and no act or object is without holiness. Chemicals make them want that. Chemicals make us all want that.
>
> If we become increasingly apathetic in modern times—well, so do fish on river banks, after a little while. Our children often come to resemble apathetic fish—except that fish can't play guitars. And what do many of our children do? They attempt to form folk societies, which they call "communes." They fail. The generation gap is an argument between those who believe folk societies are possible and those who know they aren't.
>
> Older persons form clubs and corporations and the like. Those who form them pretend to be interested in this or that narrow aspect of life. Members of the Lions Club pretend to be interested in the cure and prevention of diseases of the eye. They are in fact lonesome Neanderthals, obeying the First Law of Life, which is this: "Human beings become increasingly contented as they approach the simpleminded, brotherly conditions of a folk society."[12]

I would only suggest that no golden age of folk societies ever existed. But the New Testament promises us that we can move in that direction and commands us to do it. We will feel that something is missing until we do.

COMMON WORK

I've largely omitted one of the main things about family: it is the basic economic unit. That is, families generally share their money with each other with limited concern about who earned it. So wage earners generally share their money with children and

10. Vonnegut, *Timequake*, 74.

11. Vonnegut, *Wampeters*, 240–41. Of course, it depends on the community whether they are comforting. Some communities are tyrannical, though perhaps not as many as postmodern people imagine.

12. Ibid., 178–79.

any who stayed home to keep house. Even in postmodern societies, spouses generally have joint bank accounts, and family members who are sick or handicapped are supported. This economic sharing in the family seems to be even more true in earlier cultures and those outside the West; they also have a more extended notion of who they share with.

I don't mean to paint an idyllic picture. It's not unusual for male wage earners to keep much of the money to themselves, spouses sometimes have separate bank accounts, and children with handicaps may be treated badly. Nonetheless, at least until recently, families held most things in common. Most cultures assume that children's wages or labor belonged to the family. Only as families become relatively affluent is it possible for young people not to pay for their room and board, and only in wealthy families or those living in "welfare" states is it possible for the elderly not to live with and be supported by their children or other relatives.

Recently, Judy and I visited some old farmhouses in Bavaria. Grandparents and maiden aunts often had separate rooms; they also had clear, economically useful roles on the farm, as did quite small children. Industrial society has tended to minimize these useful roles, and mobility has tended to separate us geographically from families of birth. The result has been increased personal freedom, but also the welfare state, impersonal homes for the elderly, isolation for singles, and an extended (rather useless) adolescence.

I would hate to go back to "the good old days" when the elderly died younger and maiden aunts had no independence. However, exchanging extended family for extended adolescence has not been without cost. It seems likely that whatever new forms the church needs to develop, some of these economic functions of family need to be included.

That sort of consideration has led some churches to have common purses, common work, and clearer roles for children, singles, and elders. Whether the biblical picture of family should be applied that literally to the family of God may be debatable, but there are powerful, practical, and humane reasons to do so.

I will discuss forms to support such functions later, but I'm confident personally that the biblical view of church as family includes more than the kind of support you get from eating together. That is too easy to turn into pietism, into a pursuit of holiness that is mostly inward. And in America (especially in California south of the Golden Gate Bridge), it is too easy for it to turn into nothing more than psychological and emotional support.

Of course, that's not nothing. Most of us could do with a lot more emotional support than we get. But the gospel is deeper and wider than that. It's not to be reduced to the pursuit of intimacy in weekend encounter groups or even in long-term, committed support groups. If we exchange preaching services for support groups, we are merely exchanging one fragment of the gospel for another, one sort of sacred/secular dichotomy for another. We need to be clear that being the church will deeply affect the whole range of life: labor, business, education, art, music, medicine, childrearing.

God is concerned with intimacy and personal piety but not just with them. And the economics of the family of God is part of that. Faithful brothers and sisters will find ways to share economically with one another—ways that look more like Guatemalan or Chinese extended families than like couples with separate bank accounts.

Each other

I've based most of what I've said on biblical metaphors. Which is a little troubling to modern people, with our literal minds. A more literal indicator of the function of church is the number of New Testament passages that use "each other" ("one another" in some translations, including the NRSV).[13] Sixty-two times in 55 verses we're told things like: wash each other's feet, encourage each other, be kind to each other, love each other (sixteen times), don't envy each other.[14] What does that mean unless our lives overlap in something like the way I'm suggesting?

Many of these verses are strikingly concrete: "Practice hospitality ungrudgingly to one another" (1 Pet 4:9). "Welcome one another" (Rom. 15:7). "Outdo one another in showing honor" (Rom 12:10). "Confess your sins to each other" (Jas 5:16). "Bear one another's burdens" (Gal 6:2).

Like growing into the full stature of Christ, these verses assume that we live our lives together. If we work together or live on the same street or eat together four times a week or watch each other's kids or make music together, then these verses make sense. But if we mostly see the back of each other's heads on Sunday morning, they seem odd. And they have little application.

So how do we read verses like Ephesians 4:32: "[B]e kind to one another, tender-hearted, forgiving one another, as God in Christ has forgiven you"? I suspect we imagine that they're universal ethical principles. And they probably do reflect something universal. However, they aren't saying, "Be kind and tenderhearted to all those you meet." That's a good thing to do, but it's not what these verses say. No, they're talking about Christians together. They're saying, "Be kind and tender and forgiving to your brothers and sisters in Christ."

To do that, you have to be around each other a lot. Not just in meetings, and not just in support groups. I hope that doesn't seem too odd.

13. I first became aware of these passages thirty years ago or so when our pastor, John Bettler, preached a series of sermons on them. We were then members of Bethel Presbyterian Church in Wheaton, Illinois.

14. Mark 9:50; John 13:14, 34–35; 15:12, 17; Rom 1:11–12 ; 12:5, 10, 16; 13:8; 14:13, 19; 15:5–7, 14; 16:16; 1 Cor 11:33; 12:25; Gal 5:13–15; 6:2; Eph 4:2, 25, 32; 5:21; Phil 2:3; Col 3:9, 13; 1 Thess 3:12; 4:9, 18; 5:11, 15; 2 Thess1:3–4; Tit 3:3; Heb 10:24–5; Jas 4:11; 5:9, 16; 1 Pet 1:22; 4:8–9; 5:5; 1 John 1:7; 3:11, 23; 4:7–8, 11–12; 2 John 5.

Part Three: Reflections on Doing Church in America

THE HUMAN HEART AND SECULAR MODERNITY

I've been writing as if the reason it's hard to connect with others is mostly the church's fault, but that's far from the whole story. In the first place, the basic problems lie deep in the human heart and reappear in every culture. Nonetheless, the fallenness of our hearts expresses itself in somewhat different ways in different cultures. Every culture creates its own structures that produce destructive ways of life that individuals can scarcely fight on their own.

So the problems are rarely just in my heart and rarely just the result of the church's forms. For example, the very structures of modernity and postmodernity undermine the sorts of things I'm talking about. They fracture our lives so deeply that they make it almost impossible for us to connect deeply with one another. It's hard enough to get a nuclear family to eat together four times a week, let alone the members of a church.

We live one place, commute to work in another place, drive the kids out of the neighborhood for school, and then drive in a different direction to church. The people we encounter in these different places scarcely overlap. Matt is in the school play, Hannah is in the band, Dad has to fly to Mississippi on business, and Mom has her law career to think of. Then to top it all off, every ten years we move a thousand miles to a new place where we know no one and no one knows us. If no one knows us, how can anyone speak the truth to us in love? And if we know no one, how can we speak the truth to anyone in love?

Our little church in San Francisco may be extreme, but out of thirty-four people, none of the adults was born in the city limits, and only a few were born within a hundred miles. About a third were born out of state, and three in different countries. I'm probably extreme, but I was born in Kansas, moved to Ohio, and then I went away to high school in New York, college in England, and graduate school in Illinois; then I took a job in Pennsylvania, and when I had a mid-life crisis we moved to Oregon, and when that didn't work, to California.[15]

It's tempting to just accept this situation. The transience of our human connections isn't desirable, but it just is our culture. Maybe a commuter church is what you need in a commuter culture. We can't and shouldn't try to return to a Mediterranean culture of the first century. There's no point fighting morally neutral cultural forms. Instead, we need to find forms relevant to our cultural situation.

But I suggest that these forms aren't morally neutral. The forms of church and the forms of society combine to make a lethal cocktail that we can and must stop drinking. If we are to be obedient to the wonderful and enormous vision of Jesus, we must restructure our lives so that growth is possible. This is a revolutionary call, but it has

15. To be precise I have lived in McPherson, Wichita, Salina, and Manhattan, Kansas; Breesport and Stony Brook, New York; Malvern, Oxford, and London, England; Ashland and Cleveland, Ohio; St. Louis, Missouri; Arlington Heights and Wheaton, Illinois; Ruschlikon, Switzerland; Horsham and Philadelphia, Pennsylvania; Louisville, Kentucky; Dexter, Oregon; and Gardena and San Francisco, California. So far.

the promise that together we will grow into the fullness of the stature of Christ. It promises that together with Christ as our head, our churches will be the light of the (mangled) world.

Let's restructure our lives and our churches so that it's possible for us to love our brothers and sisters and be loved by them so that they can speak the truth to us and we can speak the truth to them. Then we're playing the game that will help us grow together into the fullness of the stature of Christ.

If not for ourselves, then for the world. Which needs Light so badly.

NINE

Some Models for Doing Church (Smaller Groups)

What if you believe church should be the sort of place where people's lives connect more? What should you do, practically? Well, one way to go is toward smaller groups. One of the most encouraging things I know is the spread of small groups in today's churches. Apparently many Christians feel the incompleteness of church as performance; they want something with more intimacy and participation. This may seem like a contemporary movement, but it goes back a long way:

> In the beginning shortly after he created man, God created small groups. God did not populate his world with self-sufficient individuals. Because it wasn't good for man to be alone, God created families. And God worked through family groupings and other forms of small groups to accomplish his purpose.[1]

Sociologists distinguish between primary and secondary groups. A primary group is small enough for its members to have face-to-face contact and some intimacy. This enables the individual to develop loyalty and to experience social identification. A secondary group is larger, more formal, and more impersonal—like a stockholders' meeting. Its members usually have some impersonal focus and may not even know much about each other. If the church is to do its job, it must either be a primary group (a small group) or be made up of such groups (have small groups that all its members belong to).

The movement to do this is crystallized in Ray Stedman's phrase "body life."[2] He led Peninsula Bible Church (PBC) in Palo Alto, California to become, in his own words, "a church of small groups."[3] Beginning in 1948 with five families who met for Christian fellowship, PBC has grown to include some 2,000 members. But over the past fifty years they have continued to structure their body life around small groups in which every member is called to use her gifts for ministry. The pastor teaches and

1. J. Long, "And God Created Small Groups," *His Magazine*, (March 1988) 6, quoted in Del Birkey, "House," 63.

2. The full text of Ray Stedman's book, *Body Life*, is available online at www.pbc.org/ray/library/series/10274.

3. See especially chapter 12 of *Body Life*.

equips the saints for ministry at PBC. But the ministers are all the people who make up the body.

A very different approach is to keep your church small, to divide whenever you get over a hundred or so members. This is sometimes called a "hive" model. Naturally, this hasn't been a wildly popular approach (it limits pastors' salaries and prestige), but it produces a less anonymous church. Westminster Presbyterian Church in Huntsville, Alabama, has done this through most of its history. Its pastor, Paul Alexander, just happens to be my brother. His denomination once proposed aiming for one hundred churches with 2000 members by the year 2000. He proposed instead 2000 churches with 100 members. Somehow his proposal never reached the floor of synod.

Yet another approach is house churches. House churches meet in homes and divide when they outgrow their living rooms. Some have divided half a dozen times. They have at most one or two staff people serving a whole cluster of house churches, and they thereby do wonderfully at avoiding the clergy/laity distinction. Which also means they do especially well at avoiding meetings that are professionally run performances. It also cuts down dramatically on the cost of buildings and salaries.

A favorite such cluster for me is Summit Fellowships in Portland, Oregon, staffed by Dan and Jody Mayhew. Their clusters meet together as a whole once a month. Summit has been especially noteworthy for succeeding at reaching out to gays and lesbians and people with green hair and rings in their noses.

House Churches

Robert and Julia Banks have become spokespersons for the house church movement: he is professor of the ministry of the laity at Fuller Theological Seminary, and together they help sponsor house church gatherings in different parts of the country. They have started clusters of house churches in Australia and are now involved in a cluster around Pasadena, California. His book, *Paul's Idea of Community*, is a must for those willing to do serious reading.

I won't write much about this model because I have little experience of it, but my opinion is that it is as good a form as those I will give more emphasis to. At their worst, house churches can be commuter churches that have lost the sense of the cost of discipleship and that shelter individualists who need to have every gift themselves. But every form can be perverted. At their best, house churches help people to connect with each other deeply enough that they naturally begin to lay down their lives for one another and the gifts the Spirit has given them naturally begin to surface. If you have a house church in your neighborhood, check it out.

INDEPENDENT SMALL GROUPS

But millions of us don't have churches nearby of any of the sorts I'm describing. What should you do if you don't? Or what should you do if you're committed to a large, standard church that doesn't have small groups? Well, you might decide to try as an individual to broaden and deepen your social connections there. (If you never get beyond this, you'll still have done a lot.) You might start by inviting people from church over for dinner. If you already do that, do it more. A lot more. See if anyone will agree to come for dinner every week, twice a week. Spend part of the time together studying the Bible. Find out who's serious about following Jesus.

And don't just invite people like you or people who can invite you back. This isn't a collection of natural buddies but a ragtag group of Jesus' disciples. (One of the original disciples may have been a political revolutionary, and another was a traitor employed by the enemy. Apart from Jesus they wouldn't have been on speaking terms. Small groups—and churches—should be more like that and less like collections of similar people.)

Out of such efforts a small group might grow—not mostly to talk about how you felt that week, but to find ways to embody the Word in your lives through Bible study and prayer. Go together to workdays at church or at a soup kitchen. Together invite street people to dinner. Throw parties at your church. Vacation together. Strategize to see if people in your small group can move into the same neighborhood, get jobs together, find a regular mission together, or start a business together. And you might ask your pastor if your small group could lead a Sunday school class on different models of doing church.

Judy and I did this thirty years ago at Bethel Presbyterian Church in Wheaton, Illinois.[4] It was a good time, and we recommend it. However, we hit two problems—problems we have hit in one way or another in every church we've been part of since. The first was that we were all too busy. I, for example, was married, teaching college, helping raise a child with a handicap, editing a magazine, writing a dissertation, and being faculty adviser to an activist student government. (It was during the Vietnam war—in a college where the president was a retired navy officer!) Oh, and Judy and I like to travel.

This sort of small group won't go far toward helping people become a genuine extended family unless its members radically simplify their lifestyles. (The same is true for house churches.) We must make a fundamental commitment in which following Jesus in this new family is the first priority of every person. But that sort of commitment is foreign both to the secular and the church cultures we're part of: we give that sort of priority only to self. However, unless we're willing to take revolutionary steps to reverse that, changing the forms for church won't produce the extravagant changes Paul assumes in Ephesians. Our experience is that growth is roughly proportionate to

4. The other members of this group were April and Bob Carlson, Ebeth and Lane Dennis, Bob and Dawn Webber, and all our children.

commitment—or at least limited by our level of commitment. We have to chop other things out of our lives to have the time and energy to grow.

The second problem I'll call the problem of unity, though the problem of authority would work as well. You see, some of the elders in our church in Wheaton were uncomfortable with what we were doing. That won't always be true (Vineyards and Calvary Chapels, for example, actively encourage intense home groups), but it will often be true. Thirty years ago, I had little sympathy with the nervousness of those elders, but as I've become an elder myself, I've come to suspect I was wrong. It wasn't clear which was our church, which was our authority: the small group or Bethel Presbyterian. Were we giving authority to the pastor and elders and congregation,[5] or were we following a divisive vision disconnected from our church? (Being divisive didn't bother me at all in those days; I thought I was Amos.) It was clear that we were saying, at least implicitly, "The Reformation didn't go far enough. A healthy church will be a collection of small groups like us, not one big impersonal congregation like you." And while we may have been right, our spirit was often wrong and divisive. And elders need to worry about spirit. So be gentle if your small group makes some in your church nervous.

There was a final problem too. The Alexanders moved. Thousands of miles away. And so did another family. Which was the end of that (before we knew what fruit the group might bear in our church). That's the first problem again: lack of practical commitment to being Christ's family when something more attractive beckons.

It's typical.

CORPORATE SMALL GROUPS

One irony about independent small groups like ours is that they're trying to be more corporate by being critical and independent of the existing church and its leadership. Besides, independent small groups are generally led by rugged individualists, and how likely are rugged individualists to function corporately? (The medium is the message, and so is the messenger.)

So from my perspective, for small groups to have half a chance of making their point, they need to be a corporate, church-wide strategy. If small groups are the strategy of only a few individuals without the support of the corporate leadership (not to mention the rest of the congregation), the small groups will suffer from the profound contradictions of individualism within a body.

In any case, getting small groups going is something that churches can choose to do corporately—and often do. If your church doesn't want to pursue small groups, you might do best to go someplace where they do. Your pastor may appreciate your leaving. It's divisive to stay. And it shouldn't be that hard to find such a place: churches with small groups have been common for decades.

5. I realize this way of putting it will seem odd to most American individualists. It would have seemed odd to me too at that time.

One way churches can organize small groups effectively is by dividing their people up by neighborhoods and assigning each group a church elder. Since group members then live near one another, their lives overlap more easily than otherwise. And having a church elder as leader helps solve the problem of unity with the larger church.

However, these groups are still limited by the commitment of their members, just like independent small groups. The kids have to have ballet lessons, and each family takes their vacation at a different time. And just when people are getting to know each other well enough to speak the truth in love, someone (the elder as likely as not) moves. So folks rarely get to the point where they talk honestly about a full range of tough issues. Consequently, in these small groups deep spiritual growth happens less than it might. There's not enough commitment to make Ephesians practical.

Grace Fellowship Community Church in San Francisco deals with the commitment issue up front. They have membership classes that last six months in which they make it clear that the first priority of every member is to be the church. Not career, not family, not parachurch ministry. Joining isn't like joining an art museum—for the privileges. Rather, it's accepting the responsibilities of life in a new extended family. You're free not to join, but if you join, you're committing yourself to be at all meetings, including the meetings of your small group. And each year they clear the membership rolls of people who don't attend. They aren't fierce about it, but if you aren't around much, soon you're not a member. This has the delightful result that when Sunday morning rolls around, attendance exceeds membership.[6] More to the point, it increases the chance of "each part working properly."

Grace Fellowship has also done well in dealing with a second problem of small groups. In some churches, the goal of small group is intimacy and intense personal encounters. Bob Appleby (the former pastor) insists, however, that intimacy is not the goal. It's the by-product. An important by-product—often a measure of whether much is happening even—but still not the goal.

Church of the Savior

An even more drastic story can be told of one of America's most famous churches, the Church of the Savior in Washington, DC. They have such high membership standards that the first book about them was entitled, *Call to Commitment*.[7] Their small groups are called mission groups (or used to be) and have a specific ministry—anything from maintaining the church's library to rehabilitating apartment buildings for the poor. Attendance is non-negotiable. They have moved on from *Call to Commitment* to a more communal style, but that early book is still one of the best introductions to church in a different key.

6. They have about two hundred members and three hundred in attendance. This may seem like a small thing, but it's unusual.

7. Elizabeth O'Connor, *Call to Commitment*.

This is vital. The problem is that, like everything else, small groups tend to be fundamentally shaped by the culture in which they arise. The small-group movement in the church found its most influential expression in California in the sixties. At that time California had all kinds of "secular" small groups, and they emphasized spontaneous expression of feelings as if that were itself redemptive.[8] This is a worldview unto itself, and it would require a whole book to try to sort all that out.[9] But I suggest that this paradigm has more to do with Jean-Jacques Rousseau and romanticism than with Jesus, more to do with Freud and psychobabble than with the New Testament.[10]

In the church the goal of small groups must be to grow together into a body whose head is Christ. We can best do that by reflecting together biblically and concretely on our present lives. (Consequently Grace Community Fellowship Church calls their groups "discipleship groups" rather than small groups.) Their experience (and mine) is that people who are mostly concerned about expressing their deepest feelings rarely manage to put their hearts and minds into feeling what Jesus wants them to feel. Instead, they demand more and more attention for their own feelings, making individualistic feelings their god and body life merely their rhetoric.

A third problem of small groups within a church is that inertia often wins out and the church reverts to the standard model for churches in our culture. We easily succumb to our cultural busyness and laissez-faire attitudes. Then, first thing you know, the church (without noticing) stops expecting their members to put the body of Christ first. Small groups then begin to wither; they become optional social groups, auxiliaries for the lonely or the really committed. When small groups begin playing second fiddle to the worship service, the church has reverted to type.

Sunday morning meetings rarely wither; that would be culturally unacceptable! Besides, singing and preaching are fairly easy for a professional staff to perform, while the same staff is often unclear on how to nurture a body. (That's scarcely taught in seminary.) Still, it doesn't have to go that way. Church of the Savior and Grace Community Fellowship Church prove that.

Besides, small groups within a larger church have one big advantage: they look normal in our culture. People who think of church as something you go to Sunday morning may have an easier time accepting the notion of church as family if it's being done within a form they're used to. A case can be made for making Sunday morning an easy on-ramp.[11] (At least as long as that ramp leads to a freeway and not just a perpetually slow-moving parade of performances.)

---

8. A particularly horrifying example is Dick Westley, *Redemptive Intimacy* (note the title).

9. At about this time, California was originating all kinds of psychological and new age encounter groups seeking salvation by expressing their feelings. Often good movements get crucial insight into the gospel from the surrounding culture but then are also contaminated by it. In California at least, stressing intimacy, spontaneity, and expression of feelings are natural ways to distort small groups.

10. The romantic worldview is one of the main topics of my book *The Secular Squeeze*, esp. 78–110.

11. I owe this idea (including the language of easy on-ramp) to Rich Lamb of InterVarsity Christian Fellowship.

So in principle this is an attractive and powerful model. It has severe problems, but so does everything else. I suggest pursuing it, especially if you find a church of small groups (not just one with small groups) in which the members are deeply committed to life together.

The Need for Pastoral Hearts

When I talk to pastors trying to make small groups work in their churches, they don't talk about the problems I've given. They talk about the lack of elders capable of leading small groups. They say they don't have enough elders with pastoral hearts. Unfortunately, my experience suggests that this problem is huge and nearly universal: few churches have an excess of people—lay or clergy—with pastoral hearts.

But then that's not a problem just for the small group model. My observation is that this is a struggle in every model. Where are the people ready to devote themselves fully to gently shepherding the family of God? This is especially serious because God has promised us these people; they are the gifts of the Spirit.

What can the shortage mean? Either God is letting us down, or Christians aren't taking this function in the church seriously enough, aren't working hard enough at helping each other become compassionate listeners who also have some grit.

Which do you suppose it is?

TEN

Life Together (Religious Orders and Live-in Churches)

Although I'm encouraged by the popularity of small groups within standard churches, you can tell that I'm also more than a little suspicious of it. Too often, small groups mean little, and even when they do in the beginning, there's a powerful tendency for such churches to revert to standardness. Their members slip back into going to church.

Many years ago, this led Judy and me to search for a more radical model. So in July of 1973, we began to live in an intentional Christian community on Logan Street in the Germantown section of Philadelphia. By November, that community had ended in a painful explosion. Nonetheless, we were soon involved in starting another community, Jubilee Fellowship of Germantown. Why is not always clear to me (are we crazy?), but since 1973 we have always lived communally.

Intentional Christian community has so many problems that I'm no longer willing to use that language. But I'm convinced that done right (!), the people of God living together has the kind of depth and power that enables growth into the fullness of Christ. The problem is that when done wrong . . . .

LIVING TOGETHER

Through most of Christian history, various Christian groups have lived together intentionally and with major economic sharing. The church in Jerusalem seems to have done something like this (Acts 2 and 4). The church in Thessalonica may well have: they had their money in common enough for Paul to say that those who don't work, shouldn't eat (2 Thess 3:10). The Thessalonians probably at least had common meals. And the way Paul says it (almost in passing) makes you wonder whether some form of communal eating was standard in Paul's churches.

Then there are Catholic orders. It's no accident that the monastic movement started in the days of Constantine when church as family was being compromised or that Francis of Assisi recruited "brothers" instead of living out his vision alone. Nearly a million Catholic Christians live communally today as monks and nuns, using the language of brothers and sisters.

During the Reformation, Anabaptists stressed community, and one group (Hutterites, followers of Jacob Hutter) required living together. They started in Moravia and numbered 15,000 around the turn of the seventeenth century. Now, almost 500 years later, there are some 35,000 of them still doing this in the Western plains of Canada and the United States. They live in "bruderhofs" (brother houses), own farm land in common, and run businesses together.

Another group, the Amish, date back to 1693. They don't live together in big houses, but they live close enough to experience life together. They have learned to depend on each other dramatically. They don't need insurance because they cover each other. (Why don't all Christians do this?)

In 1920, Eberhard Arnold started a group in Germany that is similar to the Hutterites. They had to flee Hitler's Germany, but today that small band has grown to 2,500, mostly in the United States, but also in England, Australia, and Germany. They live in rural "hofs" of about 200 and have common work, common lunch and dinners, common child care. (Their lives are so much in common that individuals usually don't even have money!)

In 1948, other Germans who had opposed Hitler started Katholische Integrierte Gemeinde (Catholic Integrated Community) in Munich. It has around 600 full members plus hundreds of children, hundreds in the membership process, and many in a special category called "friends." It has groups throughout Germany as well as two in Tanzania, one in Italy, and fledgling groups in Austria and Hungary.

Then in the sixties and seventies, scores of "intentional Christian communities" were started in the United States and Canada. Most were made up of wild-eyed social activists (like Judy and me) or wild-eyed charismatics. We were passionate, naive young people burning the candle at both ends. Not surprisingly, most of us soon burned up and out. With the arrogance of youth and without the centuries of accumulated wisdom of Catholic and Orthodox orders, we hadn't a clue what we were doing. It's a wonder we lasted as long as we did. Still, several of these communities or their successors are around and thriving. The best known are perhaps Jesus People, USA, in Chicago and Reba Place Fellowship in Evanston, Illinois.

ADVANTAGES OF LIVING TOGETHER

These groups all live together to some degree. The big advantage of this is that it makes people's lives overlap in ways that support becoming God's extended family, in ways that support the function of sharing the gifts of the Spirit. This allows us to learn deeply from each other, to catch the values of the kingdom from each other. We have less need, for example, to keep up with the Joneses (materially) because the Joneses we know best live with us and are also committed to not being materialistic. And we have a good chance of keeping the purity and intensity of our vision in a way that those in standard churches don't. Our vision is less likely to be diluted by the world or the broader church because we have less intensive contact with them and more with each other.

Another advantage of living together is that the form itself helps deal with the lack of commitment in our secular and religious culture. Since Constantine, almost all churches have found ways to minimize the cost of discipleship: commitment isn't necessary, and even attendance is negotiable. And in the larger culture, commitment is harder and harder to find. We aren't committed to our place of work or to our town; often we aren't committed to our spouses, and sometimes not even to our children.

One of the most obvious things about Jesus is that he offered a life of promise and reward—but only to those with great commitment, only to those willing to bear the costs. The very form of standard churches since Constantine belies this. How many churches do you know where members in good standing are actually expected to follow the way of Jesus with its cross? Most churches consider it legalistic even to expect members to go to church regularly.

To put it differently, life together becomes possible among a people (and only among a people) who have gained substantial clarity of intention. It's possible only among those who are fairly clear that the only thing that matters is quietly being the servants of God and of your sisters and brothers. The cost then begins to lose its bite. Career, the lust for possessions and extramarital sex, the desire for power and glory— all must have been executed (well, at least they have to be on death row). Otherwise, we will not be able to live together in peace with Christ as our head.

So faced with a form that requires living together, Sunday-morning Christians must choose: either they repent, or they exclude themselves. This is the sort of choice with which Jesus regularly faced people.

Now, much of the rest of this book will be focused on living together. That's not because I think it's the only legitimate form for the church. It's because in the last thirty years that's the only kind of church I've experienced deeply. However, I believe that those within other forms of the church will still find these reflections appropriate to their situations. (And so will those who live together in other contexts, like marriage, family, or roommates. The principles of life together are the principles of life together, whether in common housing or not.)

Religious Orders

The largest and oldest surviving example of Christians living together is the monastic movement. From Constantine's time on, the impetus for monasticism has often paralleled the concerns of this book: distress at the spiritual collapse of "Christendom." With vows of poverty, chastity, and obedience, monks and nuns have led the way in living out the drastic teaching of Jesus. They also use a broad range of their members' gifts. Meanwhile they have pioneered in living together in peace, in rigorous prayer, in service, and in (generally) sane forms of submission.

As you'd predict from what the Bible says about the secret of spiritual growth, orders have produced an astonishing proportion of the people whom the rest of us think of as saints and spiritual guides. (Just think of Thomas à Kempis, Sister Therese of Liseaux, Bernard of Clairvaux, Thomas Merton, Mother Teresa, and whoever your favorites are.) Also predictably, these communities have repeatedly been at the heart of profound spiritual renewal in the church. (I believe that this paragraph is one of the most important in this book. Note it well.)

Langdon Gilkey's *Shantung Compound* is the story of the camp for Westerners in China when the Japanese bombed Pearl Harbor. Many of those Westerners were missionaries, Catholic and Protestant. Though Gilkey is himself a Protestant, his account of the relative spiritual depth of Catholic and Protestant missionaries is embarrassing. Embarrassing, that is, for Protestants.[1] When the toilets didn't have their plumbing connected, it was the missionaries who cleaned up, mostly the Catholic missionaries. The members of religious orders didn't complain about the crowding, but guess who did? The monks and nuns had learned to bear the cost of serving Christ and in the process had learned that it was not a cost but extravagant freedom and joy.

The Catholic Integrated Community is a fascinating example here. They're especially interesting for my purposes because they share much of the vision of this book and because, unlike actual orders, so many of their members are married with children. Moreover, they make no bones about the fact that they are working for drastic congregational and spiritual reform within Catholicism.[2]

From a Catholic point of view, they certainly aren't an order. (They allow marriage, and they don't take vows.) However, from a Protestant point of view, they're more like an order than anything else we know. Part of the genius of orders (both Roman and Orthodox, and including Catholic Integrated Community) is that they have remained in submission to the larger church even when in tension with it. Instead of starting new denominations, they have held out the call for reform from within. Tragically, Protestants have no comparable way to deal with those who call for deeper commitment. Since Luther was expelled by Rome, all sides in Protestant conflicts seem almost to assume the inevitability of division (especially in the United States). Protestants make dissenters so uncomfortable that they leave (except when it's the other way round). This leads to disunity so extensive it can be described as nothing less than the shattering of the very body of Christ—repeated shattering. And the shattering of Jesus' prayer in John 17.

Protestant "orders"

As I've said, Protestants don't usually have orders for members who want a more communal church. However, many groups within local Protestant churches remain part of their church while having "higher" standards than the church at large. I find it helpful

1. Except for Eric Liddell, who died there as a saint according to Langdon Gilkey, *Shantung Compound*, 192. Though it is clear from the context that the reference is to Eric Liddell, Gilkey calls him Eric Ridley.

2. Not surprisingly, one of the formative influences on the church I'm part of is a book by one of their members, Gerhard Lohfink. See *Jesus and Community*.

to think of these groups as religious orders if they live together and have made substantial commitments.

There are many such groups. Antioch in Jackson, Mississippi is one. They are part of Voice of Calvary Fellowship and started as a group to discuss racism. In time, they bought a big house together and all moved in. (They now live in two houses, a couple of doors apart.) Families have somewhat separate "apartments," but the whole group eats their dinners together. Every summer they vacation together. And like a Catholic order, they have a ministry together. Theirs is a ministry of racial reconciliation (they're mostly black with a few white members). Most of them work in the ministry, and most months it almost feeds them. They meet together one morning a week to pray, study the Word, and discern God's direction for their lives.

All of them belong to Voice of Calvary Fellowship, and one of them is an elder there. That means they don't have to plan worship services, Sunday School, youth group. And they can lean on the pastoral and teaching gifts of the larger Fellowship. They have the support of the pastor, though tensions occasionally arise over where their loyalties lie and over whether their energies are being diverted from the Fellowship at large.[3]

THE BIG PROBLEM

While the church I'm part of hasn't chosen this model, I find it compelling. Though I will argue otherwise, this may well be the way to go.

In my opinion, what I'm calling religious orders have one basic flaw. They normally buy into the model of going to church—at least for those not in the order. They implicitly project the message that "going to church" is fine: the church as a whole can't be asked to live as if it were the body of Christ. That's a special calling for the few with a "vocation" for it. Extensive body life is optional, a work of supererogation (super-love, beyond the call of duty) for especially dedicated Christians; it needn't be asked of the average church member.

Now of course, whether extensive body life is optional depends on what you mean by extensive. Those who say this may just be making the obvious point: not every Christian has to live in a big house with lots of other Christians. And that's true. What's more, it's important to say that loudly and clearly. However, almost the same words can also mean something disastrous: The way of Jesus and Paul is the ideal, but there's no point calling most people to it because it ain't going to happen. Being the church is a work of supererogation for saints and those with special callings; going to church is fine for normal Christians.

3. Since this writing, their primary leader (Spencer Perkins) has died, and they have disbanded.

Editor's note: In June of 2004, 60 representatives of Protestant orders and live-in churches (including former members of Antioch and members of Church of the Sojourners) met at the Rutba House in Durham, North Carolina and named 12 marks of the Spirit's common movement in their communities. Essays on the marks were later published as *Schools for Conversion: 12 Marks of a New Monasticism*, Eugene, OR: Cascade, 2005, edited by the Rutba House. For more information on new monasticism, see www.newmonasticism.org and my introduction to this book.

So, as much as I respect Protestant orders (some of my best friends, and all that!), they can easily compromise the cost of the gospel and the nature of the church. And my conviction is that when that happens, the gospel has been gutted and the promise of the normal Christian life has been minimized. At that point, community is an add-on, not at the heart of church. It's central to them, but not part of the nature of church; it's optional. By contrast, I'm arguing:

1. At the heart of normal Christian life is stopping going to church so we can become the body of Christ, the extended family of God.

2. We all need to do this, not just special disciples or those with special callings. Church as community and family is one of the central theological categories of the Bible. So we must be calling others to it. If we aren't doing it in ways that normal Christians can, we'd better find ways they can.

3. Those without a deep commitment to living as Christ's body are fated to remain spiritually stunted and to experience little of the abundance of Christ.

4. Until those with such a commitment increase, our world is fated to remain in its terrible darkness, with no way to see the light set on the hill.

I believe that going to church is such a serious problem in our time that we must find ways to stand against it. We must find ways to make it clear that church is the full-time occupation of all Christians, the only full-time occupation. Church happens on Thursday as well as Sunday, at work as well as in a particular holy building, and it has more to do with being an extended family than with watching a priest perform.

Now I'm taking a tough position here, and I mean every syllable of it. However, I need to be clear. First, when I say all Christians need to live as an extended family, I mean that they're mistaken if they don't. I don't mean that if they don't they aren't Christian or even that they aren't faithful. Similarly, I mean that churches that understand themselves mostly as putting on performances are mistaken; I don't mean they aren't churches, and I most certainly don't mean that we should depart from them. Churches that mostly have solid preaching, teaching, and public worship, are at least 50 percent churches,[4] which is quite a lot. Those of us who think we have more pieces than that may be surprised some day; we've probably got even fewer pieces and just don't know the ones we're missing. (Humility just might be one.)

Second, when I say we need to live as an extended family (and things like that), I'm talking about function, not form. The forms are optional, but the functions aren't. That is, we don't all have to live with lots of other Christians, but we are responsible to find ways to be an extended family—in deed, not just in word.

So far I've talked about several forms (small churches, house churches, small groups, and "religious orders"). They all serve the function of becoming a family. However, those aren't the only options. I suspect that they're the best ones in our culture, but I'm not sure. I don't know which to add, especially since I have little expe-

4. See my *Secular Squeeze*, 135–37.

rience of others. However, some mission groups support this function (if they don't become exclusively activist) as do having jobs together, some men's groups, some sewing circles, etc. Also, let me repeat that, other things being equal, small churches and small towns can do better than large churches and churches in cities. Body life is also encouraged in churches with strong leadership training if leadership is seen mostly as spiritual growth and almost everyone is actively recruited to lead. (InterVarsity and Navigators often do a wonderful job here; they deserve more space than this sentence. If only there were more churches with a similar vision!) Remember, what we're really after here is the gifts of the Spirit functioning more broadly and deeply. Whatever forms you create that support those functions are fine.

Nonetheless, I still hold to my obnoxious claim. Let me put it differently: it's crucial not to develop two levels of membership in the body of Christ, one that tries to live out Jesus' teaching on the cost of discipleship and another that doesn't. In principle, "orders" can avoid this problem. They then need to say (in my opinion) that the cost takes different forms for different people (we have different gifts, after all), but we all must follow Jesus with our whole being. So for example, Integrated Community is clear: not all faithful Christians have to live communally anymore than all Jews in AD 30 had to follow Jesus physically.[5] Reba Place Fellowship says something similar. However, my experience is that although orders don't have to support going to church, they almost always fudge the issue.

So I suspect that being an "order" within a less-committed church is second best. However, it's a close second. I've spelled out one big disadvantage it has, but in a sense that's hardly interesting. Every model has a big disadvantage or three.

The model I'm about to get to, the one my church has chosen, has a disadvantage or three of its own. I've already made clear what it is: too often we continue the process of fracturing the church. Some of the churches with this model are in unity with no one but themselves. We regularly come to disapprove even of groups like us or of our own members. This is more destructive than can be said.

Religious orders normally avoid this.

LIVE-IN CHURCHES

I'm a member of the Church of the Sojourners in the Latino section of San Francisco. We are tiny: eighteen full members, eight actively pursuing membership, five being discipled, perhaps half a dozen checking us out, plus five kids. We own four houses together (one of them huge) where all full members live along with most of those pursuing membership or discipleship. We are divided into households (those we live with and with whom we eat four times a week) of four to eight people. We support ourselves entirely by outside jobs: we have nurses, construction workers, computer programmers, workers with the disabled, teachers, a social worker, a mental health

5. Lohfink, *Jesus and Community*, 39–44.

worker, people in graduate school, and one in a sheltered-work situation. We have a disproportionate number of graduate degrees, but also increasing numbers who never saw the inside of a college. Practically, we hold all things in common, but not literally—partly because the bookkeeping and taxes are too complicated. Economically, this frees a lot of money for the kingdom, especially since we ask programmers to spend the same amount on themselves as those earning much less.[6]

More to the point, first, foremost, and almost exclusively, we're a church. We worship together and eat together and pray together. We try to follow our head (Jesus), and we try to love each person as they've never been loved before. These values are at the heart of our life, as is studying the Bible together (not to mention alone). We divide into small groups of four where we have a special responsibility to speak the truth in love (as we do in our households). We encourage each other a lot, and we challenge each other a lot (probably too much). We fail a lot, sin a lot, and we also see a lot of spiritual growth.

The big problem

I've already said that the big advantage of life together is that it makes Christians' lives overlap enough that they can share the gifts of the Spirit and reinforce each other's values. Unhappily, like most strengths, this one has an underside.

It's called isolation.

It's invaluable for your primary contacts to be with like-minded people, but what if your like-mindedness is distorted? (And it always will be.) As well as sharing the gifts of the Spirit, we unconsciously share and reinforce whatever works of the flesh are favored in our group. Who then calls us out of an error that is so thoroughly reinforced? Our vision will be undiluted—including the parts that are undiluted craziness.

And this isn't just a theoretical problem. It's not uncommon for live-in churches to get so far off track that they become sects, if not cults. It's less of a problem for religious orders and others with deep connections to standard churches.[7]

This is another way of stating the problem of fracturing the larger church. Many of us in live-in churches are people who got fed up (perhaps rightly?) with standard churches and have burned our bridges; as a result, we lack accountability. Almost by definition, we develop standards for our church that exclude many other churches. Then at our frequent worst, we continue the process of developing "high" standards until even other live-in churches don't measure up. As a result, we often have no outsiders we are responsible to. And as a result, when we get off track we don't have a

6. This information about the Church of the Sojourners was true as of 1999. Although the numbers have changed some, it still describes its basic life together.

7. My guess is that Jim Jones and the People's Temple were rotten from the start, but I'll always wonder if maybe they started well but got off track by too much isolation, too high an opinion of themselves, too little outside accountability. Also, see chapter 17 for a discussion of leadership.

denomination or another church to call us back. Sometimes we don't even have outside friends we listen to.

Ernst Troeltsch distinguishes between churches and sects.[8] The details don't matter here except that sects are separatist and divisive. They have little patience with traditional forms and debates, and their direction is to stay pure by avoiding contact with the world, including "worldly" churches. They quite sensibly don't want their truth and their lives diluted by compromise and worldliness—something that happens regularly with standard churches and pretty often with orders.

As you can probably tell, I have a natural affinity for sects. Why should we let truth be diluted by people playing the wrong game? I came by my sectarianism honestly: I've spent most of my adult life with communitarians who exemplify sectarianism, and I was raised in a fundamentalist denomination[9] that practiced second-degree separation. We not only didn't fellowship with liberals; we didn't fellowship with other fundamentalists who fellowshipped with liberals. (So Billy Graham was out: he had liberals on the platform during crusades. The big question was whether to fellowship with fundamentalists who fellowshipped with Billy Graham who fellowshipped with liberals. Is this third-degree separation?)

All of us are a little weird; but if you separate yourself off, who's going to challenge your weirdnesses? Just as you easily catch kingdom values in a live-in church, so you also catch each others' weirdness. As easily as catching a cold. Before long some of the members of your own group cease to measure up, and you have to purify yourselves by purging the leaven from your midst.

We have a new person among us who, every once in a while, rolls her eyes at us and says simply, "You need to get out more." This is her way of suggesting we're so ingrown there's no point explaining things to us. She's probably right.

This seems to me to call into question the very existence of independent live-in churches. We have a radical obligation to find others to whom we can be accountable, others who will let in a little air.[10] Independent churches seem to be almost a contradiction in terms, the ultimate in individualism (lived out on an institutional level).

This is why churches in the New Testament don't look independent. So at the Jerusalem Council, they dealt together with the big dispute of those decades (Acts 15). And all three of the main biblical passages on the gifts mention apostleship, which was not a gift to one local church. And Paul, John, and Peter all seem to have exercised moral authority in churches where they didn't live at that moment.

8. Ernst Troeltsch, *The Social Teachings of the Christian Church*, esp. 331–43.

9. The General Association of Regular Baptist Churches.

10. Church of the Sojourners has developed some accountability to other churches. We considered joining some denomination, but decided against it. One of the problems is finding a denomination that holds its churches accountable without stifling them. Another is deciding whether denominationalism is any improvement on being independent. Is post-denominationalism mostly a rejection of divisive denominationalism, or is it mostly a collapse into individualism that takes denominationalism to its absurdist conclusion?

The Protestant answer to the problem of divisiveness is denominationalism, which is far from ideal. While I suppose denominations are better than independence, you can certainly make a case that denominations are part of the problem rather than part of the solution. They are themselves institutions with a momentum of their own that gives people a schismatic identity other than as the people of God. Arguably, the internal solidarity they develop isn't a sign of unity but of party spirit.

The logic of what I'm saying is to become Catholic. Which I'm not likely to do, but it's hard to see how else we can achieve any institutional unity or have any sort of authority. The other possibility is post-denominationalism. Christians today increasingly make their connections with whomever they sense is of a common mind whatever their denomination. Denominations get less and less loyalty. Certainly, insofar as it's the death of denominational party spirit and party theology, that's great. But it's also partly a sign that we Westerners can't bear to be accountable or loyal to anyone. We have to have our freedom. We can respect only those as good as we imagine ourselves to be. We haven't the faintest idea what submission means in a fallen world, among a fallen people.

Another route is to find other churches who are enough like you to understand you and hold you accountable, but different enough from you to smell your crazinesses. Perhaps we need to learn to love other local churches and then mutually hold each other accountable to the gospel. This is the route that the Church of the Sojourners is pursuing.

But I have to wonder whether this isn't the very essence of sectarianism. No existing denomination measures up. None. (As the Quaker says to his wife, "Everyone is crazy except me and thee, and sometimes I wonder about thee.") So we start our own accountability groups. And cut ourselves off from the rest of the body of Christ. Perhaps instead we need to be part of fallen church structures (other than our own!). In this way we can express our solidarity with the whole people of God—warts, sins, crimes, and all.

By grace, we are saved.

CONCLUSION: COST/BENEFIT ANALYSIS AND THE HOLY SPIRIT

How do we choose between small groups, small churches, house churches, religious orders, live-in churches? If Scripture is authoritative and not just a rabbit's foot to carry around, we must be moving towards being a family, towards relatively small groups who know each other deeply enough and broadly enough to speak the truth in love.

It is perhaps less important which way we choose than that we choose. Then we are on the road and the Holy Spirit can point us in the direction God wants. Then we are seekers, and God will find us whether we find God or not. The Bible says, "Seek and you will find" (Matt 7:7); it doesn't say, "Sit around till you get the truth all figured out and then act."

So choose we must. We must choose forms that support the functions of becoming the Spirit-filled body of Christ. We must choose forms that will deepen our social connections, our honesty, love, and submission to an ever-widening range of the children of God. And each of the forms we've looked at has strengths and weaknesses. So the choice isn't straightforward. But that's a good thing. It helps us not get too attached to our forms.

And it helps make it clear that the right forms won't themselves turn a church into a functioning part of the body of Christ. Only the Holy Spirit can make motley human beings function as the body of Christ. And that's not rhetoric. It's a fact. It's a fact even when we forget it. The Holy Spirit will use whatever forms she chooses. (And who knows? She may not have read this book to know which forms are the best!)

Still, we're responsible to sort out what we think are the best forms available. And I'm inclined to do that by a cost/benefit analysis. That's what I've been trying to do throughout the last two chapters. I've been asking not which forms are exactly right, but which forms have the best balance of strengths and weaknesses. Modern people prefer to think in terms of true/false, good/bad. Evangelicals are perhaps especially attached to this sort of bipolar thinking. But when choosing pragmatic forms, this thinking breeds confusion and self-righteousness.

Here's a summary of my cost/benefit analysis:

The great strength of independent small groups within a standard church structure is that they require only small steps—small steps which anyone can take now. And they are steps in the right direction. The great weakness is the other side of the same coin: they ask so much less than Jesus did that often not much happens. Still, independent small groups are much better than nothing. If you're not about to leave your church and it's not open to making small groups a church-wide strategy, then start having people over for dinner.

Small groups that are the strategy of the whole church are healthier, especially when they expect commitment and see small groups as being as important as the Sunday morning service. This model also has the advantage of being an easy on-ramp in a culture where church can hardly be grasped unless it owns a steeple. The great disadvantage of this model is again the other side of its strength: often their easy on-ramps lead not to a freeway but to a slow way to nowhere. Their small groups are often (normally?) a mere adjunct to going to church. Besides, they easily fall prey to cheap intimacy and meaningless psychobabble.

Much of this is equally true of house churches. Much turns on the maturity of their leadership and the presence of people with pastoral hearts. This is even more true for them than for most forms because by definition they're so small that they have to produce an awful lot of leaders for their number of members. Still, they're an improvement on most standard churches, and that improvement is of great value when they make the cost of discipleship clear and ask real commitment of members.

What I'm calling "religious orders" can take such different forms that they're hard to evaluate as a whole. But those who choose to live together while in submission to another church have strengths limited only by their openness to the Holy Spirit. Protestant "orders" struggle more than Catholic orders because they aren't organically connected to centuries of life together. But at their best, they're growing into the fullness of Christ while being accountable to the larger body and clearly calling it to stop going to church. No one does better at helping people to clarity of intention, life together in unity, and deep commitment to following Jesus no matter the cost. Like live-in churches, their life together is broader than emotional and psychological support, so they easily include common work, economic sharing, artistic expression, etc. Unfortunately, they often sponsor the idea that community is not part of the normal Christian life, but only for those with a special calling. In the process they positively encourage others to "go to church." And at their worst, they have become so "liberal" that even going to church is optional as long as you're committed to justice. (Or in the case of one order near us, the real commitment seems to be to Carl Jung!)

Which leaves live-in churches. Their great strength is that at their occasional best their members are together growing into the fullness of Christ and thereby reflecting Christ's light out to the world. And by their very existence, they call others in the larger body of Christ to stop going to church. They're also well suited to help people toward clarity of intention and steadiness of commitment.

Their great problem is that live-in churches often have no accountability or unity outside themselves. They tend to hold themselves above others. This is an ironic incoherence for those calling for a more radical obedience to the one who prayed that we be as united with each other as Jesus with his father.

Still, the rewards of live-in churches are great. Unfortunately, the risks are also great. The question here may be how much risk you're willing to take. I'm inclined to say, "Nothing ventured, nothing gained." Maybe it's a question of personality, though I doubt it. The gospel calls us all to great risks.

Let's go for broke. The world needs people ready to take the risk of trusting God by living out another reformation.

ELEVEN

On Becoming an Apache (What It Means to Become the People of God)

Suppose a white person went to Arizona for a weekend and came back saying he'd become an Apache. He still talked the same, he still lived in the same place, he still related to nature the same way, he still talked to everyone he saw, and he didn't spend much time with Apaches. The only change you could see was that he wore buckskin Sunday mornings and went around telling people he'd become an Apache.

What would you think? I'd think it was odd. I'd suspect he hadn't joined the Apache tribe in any meaningful sense.

Now, I doubt that a white man can become an Apache at all, let alone over the weekend. But if he were to join the tribe, he'd have to learn their customs, accept their religion, master their language. He couldn't do all that in a weekend. Somewhere along the way, he'd have to spend a lot of time with Apaches.

If it's odd to think you can join a new tribe over a weekend, why don't we see that it's odd to think you can become a Christians over a weekend? The answer is obvious, of course. Becoming a Christian is by birth, and birth is rather instantaneous. Nonetheless, physical birth begins a process—a long, intense process. And I suggest that spiritual rebirth also begins a process—a process of discipleship, a process of slowly becoming part of a new tribe. To act as if it were all instantaneous is silly. You can start becoming a Christian over a weekend, but you can't begin to grasp what it means to be part of this new and strange tribe.

Biblical scholars, theologians, and Christian ethicists are increasingly emphasizing something like what I'm saying here. They argue that the Bible isn't aimed at individuals; it revolves around a people, a tribe, a family, a church, the body of Christ, whatever language they prefer. But seeing that the Bible is about a people is one thing; moving away from a culturally-instilled, private individualism is another. This is a radical paradigm shift. How do we make it real?

One step is to think of becoming a Christian as something like a white person becoming an Apache. It's not just a private transaction between you and God. It also involves a commitment to a particular local church (tribe), a church that has a culture as different from the world's as Apache culture is different from English culture. I suggest that the Bible teaches that Christians will undergo just such a transformation of practices and loyalties: a transformation as deep as the changes that would take place if you became an Apache.

Like all metaphors, this one is open to misunderstanding. Given the Western view of native Americans, it may sound like a call for exotic and pointless changes. Wearing a feather headdress, moving to a reservation to avoid contamination, or stopping speaking English, for example. But that's not the sort of direction I mean.

The direction I mean is becoming deeply committed to a particular group we live among while letting that alter our culture in spiritually relevant ways. So in Ephesians 4, Paul talks about being transformed by living as part of a body with Christ as its head. He then goes on immediately to say, "No longer live as the Gentiles live" (4:17). We're so non-tribal that we easily overlook the ethnic element he inserts. But I suggest that part of what Paul is saying here is, "Stop living as your ethnic group does; give up your old cultural practices and national loyalties." Then, a few verses later, he goes back to emphasizing the importance of our new tribe in transforming us:

> So then, putting away falsehood, let all of us speak the truth to our neighbors, for we are members of one another. Be angry but do not sin; do not let the sun go down on your anger, and do not make room for the devil. Thieves must give up stealing; rather let them labor and work honestly with their own hands, so as to have something to share with the needy. Let no evil talk come out of your mouths, but only what is useful for building up, as there is need, so that your words may give grace to those who hear. (Eph 4:25–29)

You may think that in this passage Paul is just listing general rules. If so, go back and reread it, asking yourself if he isn't instead telling the community how to grow each other up. Remember, this is the same chapter where Paul talks about local churches as bodies growing together in love by speaking the truth to each other.

Colossians 3:1–17 is similar. While the Ephesian version starts with an appeal to abandon their old culture, the Colossians version climaxes with an appeal for the new loyalties that override the old ethnic and worldly ones:

> Do not lie to one another, seeing that you have stripped off the old self with its practices and have clothed yourselves with the new self, which is being renewed in knowledge according to the image of its creator. In that renewal there is no longer Greek and Jew, circumcised and uncircumcised, barbarian, Scythian, slave and free; but Christ is all and in all! (Col 3:9–15a)

I'm sometimes told that this verse isn't meant to undermine ethnic identities, only to say that the gospel is available to all independent of ethnicity. So it doesn't mean a white person should be any less white, but that they can be saved. However, in a similar passage, Paul not only dismisses old ethnic identities but asserts that we have a new ethnic identity. We are all Jews! Jews, metaphorically, as I am using Apache metaphorically.

As many of you as were baptized into Christ have clothed yourselves with Christ. There is no longer Jew or Greek, there is no longer slave or free, there is no longer male and female; for all of you are one in Christ Jesus. And if you belong to Christ, then you are Abraham's offspring, heirs according to the promise. (Gal 3:27–29)

Now, for reasons that aren't clear to me, this will be read as saying that black Christians should adopt white culture. That is not it at all. Rather we will all take on new practices in a way that brings light to the culture we were converted from. Black people will still keep many black cultural practices, but they will also reject many black cultural practices and adapt others in Christian directions.

Of course, it isn't only a matter of changing tribes. The relational changes aren't all horizontal. New birth is crucial, as is a continuing recognition that the local body isn't just human and natural. The body of Christ is the body of Christ, not our body, and it's healthy functioning depends on our continuous submission to our head and on the Holy Spirit's continuous intervention.

But a significant part of our transformation is joining God's people. What do we think that means beyond private, individual salvation? What is the concrete significance of joining God's tribe, of becoming one member of Christ's body? I suspect we don't think about it. I suspect we use "people of God" as if it were an empty metaphor with little concrete meaning. But joining God's people is as concrete as joining a tribe of Apaches. After birthing, the process is actually rather similar, and it includes learning a basically new culture, alongside other disciples.

It's important to work consciously at learning the ways of a new tribe. (Most of us have to put our shoulder to the wheel in a highly disciplined fashion whether we're trying to learn how to speak Apache or how to read the Bible.) However, don't misunderstand me. An awful lot of becoming part of a new group is subliminal. Gaining a new, ethnic identity is only partly a decision, only partly cognitive. It's more like catching a cold than like studying the anthropology of Apaches. It's a subtle, substantially unconscious process that requires years of being with people in the other tribe. That's part of why some sort of community is essential; otherwise, talk of becoming part of a new tribe is necessarily more rhetoric than reality. You have to be with people to catch their identity just as you have to be with them to catch their colds. My guess is that that's part of why the author of Hebrews warns against "neglecting to meet together, as is the habit of some" (10:25).

I don't know how to talk about it. (Perhaps because it's so subliminal?) But becoming an Apache is partly the process of moving from talking about "they" to talking about "we." At least, the process is well on its way when new people normally refer to the group as "we."

The Marines expedite this process by deliberately disorienting new recruits. They use everything from personal insults to sleep deprivation, cutting them off from old friends and old means of orientation, putting them in intense situations with people they want them to form an identity with and be loyal to. Then they dress them all alike.

Obviously, such methods aren't open to Christians. (Their use by a church is a sign the church has become a cult). Nonetheless, part of the goal of the Marines (the part about forming a tribe) should be the goal of all local churches. And it's not going to happen well in churches whose members mainly see the back of each others' heads in rather lackadaisical meetings. Getting beyond that is the genius of mass evangelistic rallies, charismatic worship, all night youth activities, and summer camps. It also explains their severe limits. (It's why adolescents' emotional commitments made in summer camp tend to evaporate when they've been back with high school peers for a month. And fifty-year-olds aren't all that different.)

Hence the need for ongoing church community with human interconnections that go way beyond artificial situations, meetings, and cognitive lectures. We need lots of life together (day to day, not just summer camp). We need ceremonies, we need distinctive, recognized traditions, we need extravagant celebrations, we need deep friendships, we need to eat together—all without playing with the minds of those who are easily manipulated. The process of joining a tribe is the work of a lifetime.

Or perhaps I should say the grace of a lifetime.

GRACE AND WORKS—AGAIN

For here is the genius of Christianity. The peculiarity, the oxymoron. Joining the people of God is an instantaneous event, the result of being born again into a new family. As with physical birth, it's not caused by the works of the baby but by the acts of the parents. But this new person has work to do, things to learn both consciously and unconsciously.

Let's back up. It's like it would be for Apaches to let white people join their tribe despite our being the ones who destroyed their culture and most of their people. That really would be grace. By grace, Apaches would be allowing us murderers to join their tribe as God lets us rebels join his tribe—despite the devastation we've created. And it doesn't happen because we master all of God's customs and language (even on a subliminal level).

From this, some Protestants are tempted to draw the conclusion that it doesn't matter what we do. It's by grace. But this leaves us open to near complete absorption into the cultures of the world. We sense little need to master the language and customs of the new kingdom into which we've graciously been born. But that's rather like a child deciding she doesn't need to learn to walk. She's already born, so why should she bother to do anything more?

Suppose a group of Apaches decided to reconcile with Europeans. If you became an Apache that way, would you think it appropriate to do nothing more? Wouldn't you, in response to their grace, feel a desire to study Apache culture and how your people had wronged them? Having already been accepted, wouldn't you work all the harder at repenting?

At least, that's the genius of Jesus. The oxymoron that is the gospel. Accepting people as they are, and letting that acceptance help transform them/us into a new tribe. Cognitively learning the law won't do it. But having people live and be loved among a new tribe is one crucial part of the process.

CALL TO COMMITMENT

Joining a new tribe means various things. One of the most important is a serious commitment to a particular local group. Now if this were just a call for Christians to join a local church, it wouldn't be very controversial. But obviously, I'm calling for more. I'm calling for a serious, long-term commitment. And these days, that makes people nervous.

Which brings us to the modern, Western notion of church "membership." In New Testament times, churches don't seem to have had formal membership. Presumably, new Christians automatically became part of whatever church was in their town, and at first there was usually only one. At that time, becoming a Christian meant something more like the call to the rich young ruler, and it often led to persecution, occasionally even death. People usually understood the cost of discipleship: they knew they were being asked to give up all.

But our cultural situation is different. Soon after Constantine, all citizens automatically became members of their parish church. That is, the cost was taken out of being the church; suddenly you could join the people of God without fear of persecution, without giving up wealth or power or family or ego. Later, the Renaissance and Reformation produced an individualism that led to competing churches with different ways of reading the Bible, different beliefs and practices. Then modernity further multiplied the variety and number of churches by giving us mobility, cultural diversity, freedom of religion, and an anonymity unknown in towns and villages. As a result, today we have a vast range of churches.

Another difference between now and then is that our culture trains us to treat everything as a commodity; that is, we make our purchases based on attractiveness, convenience, and cost. And given our culture's emphasis on the self (its feelings, its psychology, and its freedom), we choose our purchases substantially by what they do for our egos.

All this combined naturally produces designer churches. Different strokes for different folks. So we moderns and postmoderns tend to "shop" for church. We buy one on the basis of how many of our felt needs it promises to meet compared to how little it costs. Then we move to another church if anyone offends us, if we get bored, or if another church seems more attractive.

For some of us, theological convictions matter, but other things are usually at least as important: musical taste, the academic level of the teaching, how entertaining the service is—not to mention whether the church has an abundance of people in our affinity groups (age, class, gender, race, political preference, income level, personality type). Then there's the adequacy of the youth group, of the Sunday school, the architecture, and perhaps the exercise facilities. Oh, and don't forget whether it's in the city, the suburbs, or the country.

This alters the very essence of church. Churches now compete for members in good capitalist fashion, and they compete with each other at least as much as with the world. If a preacher is boring, you have to replace her. You hardly have a choice. How else can you continue your building program? Easy parking is a must (can you imagine Jesus urging the disciples to remember to arrange for easy parking?), and the music has to be good, which means hiring a top-flight music director and organist. And remember youth leaders. It also helps for your building to be at a major intersection: "location, location, location," as they say in church-growth seminars.

In this context, preaching cheap grace makes a lot of sense. What do you think it does to people's cost/benefit analysis if the church stands for costly grace?

Now I don't know this for a fact, but I venture to guess that Christians in the catacombs weren't unduly concerned with how entertaining the pastor was or with the attractiveness of the architecture or the size of the youth group. Peoples' mere participation meant they were giving all. From the nature of their cultural situation and the message of their preachers, they understood the cost of being a church.

But in postmodern cultures, being a church member has little cost.[1] Little persecution from a diverse culture and few expectations from churches that have developed easy on-ramps for a consumer culture. Postmodern preachers are more and more like postmodern politicians whose stands are determined by polls as much as by conviction. We're left with perpetual on-ramps that lead to no contrast culture. So works are diminished as is any real sense of grace. As is our light for the world.

In this situation we need to help people do more than go to church; we need to help them really belong to the tribe of God rather than to the tribe of the empire while having church membership on the side. To put it differently, we need to help people give all. We need to find benign means to help people become Marines. Lacking readily available lions, we need to graciously help people experience ego death, to be particularly the church rather than generally the church and particularly the world.

Costly church membership

One aspect of this is finding ways to embody costly grace in our life together.

This emphasis has a long history. It can be found in Catholic and Orthodox orders throughout their stories (with their emphasis on rigorous standards and a vowed, permanent commitment). It's also found in the Donatists in the fourth century and the Anabaptists in the sixteenth century. In fact, from the Donatists on, church dissenters tended to reject automatic church membership in favor of a believers' church. In

1. We need to be clear that not all cultures today are postmodern. Afghanistan, Iran, China are not. By most accounts, more Christians are persecuted now than ever before. We need to remember that while praying for continuing toleration of us in postmodern cultures.

America, the Reformed tradition picked this up. They actually took attendance (still do in a few Christian Reformed Churches), and the elders issued tokens to certify if a person was prepared to take communion. Early Methodists emphasized this sort of thing with their class meetings where people were asked a standard set of questions about their Christian life.

In the 1960s, Church of the Savior in Washington, DC, became famous for the cost of being a member there. They actually required folks to become people of prayer and service before becoming members. This must have struck a responsive cord because Elizabeth O'Connnor's book on it, *Call to Commitment*, was a Christian bestseller.

Much of the problem is that modern people don't like commitment, and post-modern people hate it. We'll tolerate talk of commitment to Jesus as long as it's between him and me and doesn't apply to my geographical mobility, personal freedom, or much of anything else. But commitment to a particular set of human beings beyond our nuclear family[2] feels stifling to us. As a result, we don't know one another deeply and can never really learn the meaning of living as the body of Christ.

COMMITMENT—TO A CULTURE OF GRACE

Another part of our problem with commitment is that those who have understood the importance of commitment have often collapsed into an ungracious legalism. That's why the emphasis of this book is that we need to focus on God and grace, not on ourselves and our ability or inability to keep the rules. That is, the cost of discipleship needs to grow out of grace and love. We need to develop a culture of grace. A culture of love, of reconciliation, of forgiveness. For each visitor, member, and leader, we need to develop a collusion of grace.[3] We need to conspire to love people as they've never been loved before. We need to extend grace to people as they've never experienced grace before. This has to be the essence of the costly culture of any local church.

And make no mistake. This costs. It means loving people outside your affinity group; it means daily forgiving people who are sinning against you daily. (It even means daily forgiving people whom you imagine are sinning against you, which is harder and more common.) And that hurts. Giving up our resentments hurts because resentments are a large part of the identity of many of us. (Who will I feel superior to if I give up looking down on people who sin in ways I don't?) This is costly. C. S. Lewis put it perfectly, "Everyone says forgiveness is a lovely idea, until they have something to forgive."[4]

---

2. Increasing numbers of postmoderns feel stifled even by nuclear families.

3. I learned this phrase from Jack Bernard, one of the teachers at Church of the Sojourners.

4. Lewis, *Mere Christianity*, 115.

GETTING SPECIFIC THE SOJOURNERS' WAY

OK, so part of the meaning of joining a new tribe is commitment to a particular local body. And part of that is learning a new culture. Most of which is learning a heart of grace and mercy. But I've said those things *ad nauseum*.

At Church of the Sojourners, we have taken some more steps. We reflected on our lives and cultures and concluded that we needed more specifically Christian practices. We concluded we need practices (disciplines) that would help keep us from being too conformed to the world and would help us be transformed so that we have the mind of Christ. We don't think all local churches need to share our practices, but we suspect that almost all churches need to develop more practices relevant to the gospel and to their cultural situation. Our distinctive practices are part of what make us Sojourners. If other Christians wonder about joining us and aren't comfortable with our practices, we don't feel compelled to persuade them we're right. We encourage them to go to some other local body that has practices they find more helpful.

That is, we're Apaches, but we don't object to others being Iroquois or Lakota. What we object to is people thinking they're "Indians" without being part of any par-ticular tribe.[5] You can't be an Indian generically, nor should you try to be a Christian generically. If you think you're being a generic Christian, we suspect you actually wind up being a middle-class, white, male American. Or a black Baptist preacher, or a radical feminist, or whatever. To have the mind of Christ, you have to express it in a particular way with a particular body with a particular character, or you aren't expressing it.

Similarly, Church of the Savior developed specific requirements about spiritual disciplines for their members. They didn't try to persuade all churches to accept their standards, but it seemed to them that they were in a cultural situation in which prayer and biblical reflection had little meaning often even for Christians. So they asked peo-ple who wanted to join them to go through an extended novitiate where they practiced extensive spiritual disciplines.

I hope this is obvious, but the practices churches develop need to be both spiritu-ally relevant and culturally appropriate. So at Sojourners, we don't develop practices like always eating unsalted oatmeal for breakfast or dyeing our hair green (though I suppose we might consider the latter if we were in the Haight). Such things usually won't address our own spiritual issues, nor will they convey anything meaningful to the cultures around us.

The disciplines and practices Christians develop need to be things that address ways our culture(s) are seriously out of phase with the New Testament. So our practices will wind up having to do with materialism or fidelity or lust or racism—things like that. To put it crudely but in a way modern people understand, God gives us principles and intends us to apply them in different cultures. Or as I would prefer to say, God gives us stories set in particular cultural, historical, settings and intends his church to

---

5. I owe the extension of the Apache metaphor to cover other tribes and not being generically Indian to a conversation with Dale Gish and Jack Bernard of Church of the Sojourners.

discern how to embody those stories in other cultural, historical settings.[6] The stories give us functions, and we need to find specific, pragmatic forms that promote those functions. That is, our task is to develop a church culture that embodies the gospel story.[7]

COMMITMENT AND BEING A BODY

Let me be concrete. At Church of the Sojourners, as we reflected on these questions, it seemed clear that commitment was one of the things we needed to address. We live among tribes that have only the most limited sense of commitment, and consequently we have only the most limited commitment to our local church, to our tribe.

So at Church of the Sojourners, members agree that they won't leave for the sake of a job or because they like the music more elsewhere. They agree not to leave without working it out with the other members. They also agree that being the church is more important than taking vacations when you feel like it. So we normally take vacations

---

6. I suspect that talk of applying biblical principles to our culture is seriously mistaken. The Bible doesn't give us disembodied principles to apply. It gives us concrete, historical situations in which the will of God is or is not being lived out. The idea that you can have principles independent of any cultural situation sets you up for trying to be generically Indian. It makes it sound as if the Bible gives timeless generalities that float above culture and our task is to sort out present implications. This seems to me to be wrong in almost every respect.

First, we don't have one culture, perhaps especially in San Francisco. We have scores of cultures, and in important ways each one of us is part of several different and conflicting cultures. So at Sojourners we are parts of the cultures of the upper-middle class, the working class, medical personnel, teachers, the intelligentsia, the artsy, engineers, Belize, El Salvador, generation X, baby boomers, InterVarsity, etc.

Second, we're all bound to our cultures and can't just step out of them; we can't become cultureless and objective. This is most especially true of the activities of the people of God: we are ourselves a culture not identical with the other cultures around us. Misunderstanding this leads people to speak as if culture were something unitary that the church could take a stand for or against. Which is nonsense. What we must do instead is to oppose certain practices of cultures we are part of while (much more importantly) reaching together as a church toward cultural practices that better embody the gospel.

Third, a more important way of saying this is that the Bible's preferred way of speaking isn't in terms of general principles that rise above all cultures and are culturally neutral. Rather it gives us specific stories that embody the gospel story in a specific culture. Even very generalized things aren't given in a cultural vacuum: for example, Leviticus was written for an agrarian society surrounded by pagans who practiced human sacrifice and ritual homosexuality. We'll be doing something silly if we try to read Leviticus as general principles that can be read on to our cultural.

The point isn't those particular specifics but that in any given instance the Bible's texts are in some particular historical setting. To put it badly, our task is to discern the general principles within the specific applications in the Bible and then to apply them specifically to the different cultures we are part of, especially in our life together.

What I've said is the important thing to say to most Christians. But in postmodern society, we also need to be clear that with most things it's reasonably clear how to embody the Bible's specific stories. If our hearts aren't hard, knowing how to embody the Bible's specifics isn't that hard. For example, "Thou shalt not commit adultery" is reasonably clear across cultures (though it's not always perfectly clear as missionaries in polygamous societies have found). God created human beings with reasonably specific natures, and those natures aren't infinitely changeable by social construction the way the more relativistic postmoderns believe.

7. That's a primary function of binding and loosing in Matt. 16:19 and18:18.

and weekends-off at the same, pre-agreed times. That way, we're all present when important decisions are made or when important teaching is given. For the same sort of reason, members don't take jobs that require them to be on the road a lot. We need to be with our tribe enough that they know the truth about us and can tell it to us in love, and vice versa. We need a home with a there there.

These sorts of disciplines seem to us to grow naturally and almost inevitably out of our view of church and of our culture. Another discipline that seems natural to us is that members try to bring all their important decisions to the whole body. So if someone is thinking of changing jobs or having a baby or going back to school or anything that will affect the whole church, we ask them to work it out with the whole body.

The very mention of joint decision-making chokes many people. We Westerners tend to be committed to our own freedom more than to anything else. But what then can it mean to be part of a body? How are you part of a body if you're a hand and leave without working it out with the rest of the body? Or decide on your own to quit your present function and take on new ones?

To understand what this discipline means for us, you have to be clear that we don't have an internal police force. If people don't follow a joint decision, they aren't excommunicated. And I hasten to add that we've never refused anyone permission to have a baby or go back to school. However, on occasion, we do say no to things. We once advised against a particular marriage. (Our advice wasn't taken, naturally in this culture, and both spouses in the couple are still members in good standing.) And we once asked a person not to move away to go to school. (She agreed.) In any case, just talking about things together in a loving way encourages body life whether we agree or not. (However, if people consistently don't agree to otherwise unanimous views, you eventually have to ask them how they're part of a body.)

DATING AND MARRIAGE

Another way of thinking about all this is that certain practices of our culture are obviously dysfunctional. One of these is our institution of marriage. Conservative Christians tend to address this by preaching against divorce. But by the time people are thinking divorce, it's pretty late. Besides, it's obvious that many of the problems with marriage grow out of our culture's notion of romance and our dating practices.

So in our culture, marriage is based to a large extent on being in love—despite the fact that we know perfectly well that being in love is exceptionally fleeting. But with our focus on what amounts to infatuation, dating makes sense and arranged marriage seems appalling. As a result, men tend to choose their dates by their appearance, and both men and women have impossibly high standards for a lifetime partner—we want the right person. Furthermore, we generally make a marriage choice at an age and in a hormonal state that militates against being sensible. Couples then marry—and before long disillusionment sets in followed by resentment, if not divorce and a renewed search for the "perfect" partner. Or a married man falls in love with his secretary and thinks that justifies a divorce. "What can I do? I'm in love."

Another way marriages go wrong before they happen is that in our culture couples spend a lot of time alone and get sexually involved. They then marry with little thought of what's needed for a committed marriage, and pretty soon the sex is less exciting and both have failed the other in many ways. They then divorce—or resent each other for the rest of their lives.

Instead of figuring out that the whole process is silly, divorced people are likely to do the whole silliness again. And if they don't do it again themselves, they sponsor their children in doing it. I don't know how many people I've heard say they just haven't found the right person yet.

But no one can live up to our dreams.

As Christians, we need to be proactive about the institutions of the cultures around us. Why don't we pioneer new courting practices? What we pioneer won't be perfect, but it can hardly be worse than the cultural practices of the tribes around us. Naturally, outsiders will see this as legalism, but that doesn't make it so. And isn't it far less legalistic to prevent a marriage from happening than to make a couple stay together later when everyone but they knew the day they met that they were mismatched?

So at Sojourners, we work harder than average at making "appropriate matches" (though what we do is a long way from arranged marriages). We counsel potential couples extensively and ask them to let us say, "No." We also ask them to spend next to no time alone.

I don't know that we've done enough, but I suggest that most people, including non-Christians, know on some level that our culture's dating practices are silly if not actively destructive. So, though our culture's views on FIRES will raise problems, some non-Christians will be attracted by sensible alternatives. If we function as a contrast culture and invent new practices (or more likely, adapt old ones) and those practices make more marriages work, it will be light for the world.

Money

Or take another example: money. Most of us sense the absurdity of our consumer culture. What could be sillier than Barbie dolls or the latest Nikes and BMWs? And don't most of us want to be freed of caring about the status of keeping up with the Joneses? And isn't it insane to work so much we have just enough time to spend our money but not enough to enjoy it?

We all know it's a rat race. So why keep living that way?

Somehow few Christians ever manage to choose out. Generally, no matter how much the preacher preaches on economic lifestyles, we don't change much. We don't become a people whose economic culture is deeply different from the heathen tribes around us. I find that puzzling, but it has to do with the way fool's gold glitters even after we know what it is. And with the God-given difficulty of being different from those around us. And with the difficulty of inventing alternatives that aren't somehow ascetic, impractical, legalistic, or incoherent. Few of us will change our lifestyle unless we do so as a group—or rather as a people.

So let's make some choices together, as a people (where there's enough of us that we feel less compelled by the standards of outsiders). At Sojourners, we decided (among other things) to set a standard (a reasonable but arbitrary standard) for how much members would spend on themselves. But we were careful not to fight too long about how much money it would be, lest we turn it to law. (As if we could get the amount exactly right, as if that even means anything!) Most of us have found that extremely helpful.

To summarize, at Church of the Sojourners, we have a strenuous membership process. It normally takes a couple of years, and longer isn't unusual. During that time, we introduce people to a way of life hopefully focused on grace and love, but it also includes specific disciplines. Members are asked to spend no more than a certain amount of money on themselves each month (rather a lot), to own cars in common (rather few), to live in households larger than their nuclear families, to have a troubled person or two in their household (in addition to themselves!), to stay with their household either at Thanksgiving or Christmas, to attend all our meetings (three evenings a week), and to practice silence on Sunday mornings till 11:00. (And those are only the official requirements. Who knows how many unspoken ones the tribe hasn't yet articulated!)

And on a deeper level, during their novitiate, we ask people to enter the common life of the church. We give them a mentor and watch to see if they're the sort of people who are capable of being mentored. We put them in small groups to find out things like whether they know how to encourage others and whether they can be talked to about their sin, whether they know how to forgive.

And all this happens on the reservation, so to speak. They move into church housing and begin treating their household as their extended family. Then when we see that they've begun to live like Sojourners, they become members if they choose. They don't become Apaches when they've completed the paperwork but when we see that they are in fact Apaches.

But you can't exegete it

These sorts of standards seem so obvious to me that I'm startled by how regularly and strongly people react against them. It wasn't done that way in New Testament times, and you can't exegete it, they tell me.

Well, I agree that you can't exegete the details of Sojourners' disciplines. But that doesn't seem like the question. Of course, our practices are different from the New Testament's; after all, our culture is different. In New Testament times, their problems with commitment and marriage, prayer, hair length, and the role of women were different from now. So Paul naturally encouraged some practices and discouraged others, but they aren't going to be the same practices that need to be encouraged or discouraged today. Paul made his stands culturally appropriate, and we'd better do the same. If we try to read every item as legislation for all times and cultures, we'll find ourselves in peculiar messes that the world will perceive (rightly) as darkness.

So the church in Jerusalem practiced some sort of common purse (Acts 2–3, 5), but most New Testament churches don't seem to have followed that practice. That doesn't mean that the church in Jerusalem was wrong; it means that their cultural situation was different and the Holy Spirit was telling them something else. Not all Christians have to be Apaches.

And here's what the Jerusalem Council said officially to churches outside Israel: "For it has seemed good to the Holy Spirit and to us to impose on you no further burden than these essentials: that you abstain from what has been sacrificed to idols and from blood and from what is strangled and from fornication. If you keep yourselves from these, you will do well" (Acts 15:28–29). Abstain from eating blood and what is strangled? And they say that in the same clause as not fornicating? What are they talking about?

Either it's nonsense, or it's a situational way of helping Gentile and Jewish Christians live together in peace without compromising the gospel. Jews and Gentiles were in sharp conflict over all sorts of "ceremonial" things, from circumcision to eating meat that wasn't Kosher. The Council's decision was that each side should meet the other part way. Gentiles were to quit eating meat with blood in it, but they didn't have to adopt the practice of circumcision, and so on and so forth. However, Christians today feel perfectly free ignoring those practices recorded as normative in the New Testament—because the problems our culture faces are different.

And that's the way most all of us see the practices on hair length that are encouraged in 1 Corinthians 11 and on women not braiding their hair and men raising their hands when praying in 1 Timothy 2. In the Pastoral Epistles, it's obvious that they have a specific form of church government, but we aren't told enough about it to follow their practices closely. We aren't intended to. And the same for particular forms of worship and baptism and of most other things.

The Bible has many such practices, practices that were important in a particular situation but that are by no means universal regulations. We need things of the same sort, or we'll be absorbed by our culture. Which will suck the life out of us and remove our light from the world.

LEGALISM VS. A CULTURE OF COSTLY GRACE

The danger here is, of course, legalism. That's clear in the lives of those who read every cultural practice in the Bible as legislation for all times. For example, some Puritans and the Churches of Christ have insisted on singing only Psalms, often without any musical instrument. That's the only music mentioned in the Bible. And Baptists often think it's important to prove from Greek usage that baptism was by immersion. And for some at Sojourners, legalism is a common struggle: members who don't get all the details right are bad.

Part of the problem here is that our culture tends to see things in terms of law.[8] We're likely to understand morality in terms of rules, which easily deteriorates into legalism, conformity, repression, enforcement, and punishment. My opinion is that this happens rather often with Donatists, Anabaptists, serious Calvinists, fundamentalists, communitarians, and others with a sense of the cost of the Gospel. We need to be clear on the slipperiness of this slope.

But then all slopes are slippery, so far as I can tell. The solution isn't to abandon looking for cultural practices that are more Christian. It's to practice them graciously, to practice them as liberties rather than as rules. We aren't required to follow the destructive dating habits of our culture; we're free to find better ways. We aren't bound to silly spending habits where every cent we earn goes on ourselves; we have the liberty to give our money for the kingdom. We aren't bound by the practices of the surrounding cultures but can aim for the ideals of the kingdom. Together we can learn better practices, better habits, that combined begin to create a contrast culture. We aren't legalists trying to figure out the right rules so God won't be so mad at us; we're Jesus' servants freely discovering more fulfilling ways to live at peace with one another.

And the question isn't whether new people can tolerate our endless requirements but whether they want to find a way of life that will free them more deeply while reflecting light out to the world. And if some Christians don't want to do it our way, that's fine. But then they have to find another tribe somewhere that they can commit themselves to who are living the gospel out in costly ways in the midst of the tribal cultures around them.

Our task is to develop a church culture that embodies the gospel story. Let's go back to money. The New Testament is full of teaching about money, some of it specific. So the rich young ruler is told to sell his possessions. But the New Testament doesn't require this of all rich people. (See Acts 5:1–12 and 1 Tim 6:17–19.) We're almost all clear that the New Testament's teaching on money is situational. But soon, as legalists predict, situational teaching on money comes to mean little. At least, that's the way it works out in most churches.

The question is, how can we make New Testament teaching on money more than meaningless platitudes without collapsing into legalism? Part of Church of the Sojourners' answer for ourselves is to set a rather arbitrary standard on how much you can spend on yourself. Our experience is that it helps. Thousands of dollars are freed for the kingdom, for the real work of the tribe, for giving away. And some members can then work less for money and spend more time evangelizing and mentoring new Christians and each other. Joy and light can grow.

Let me put it this way. The New Testament is clear that the desire for money is a chief source of sin. Just naming it seems to do little; it leaves people trapped, striving

8. It may be that this is true of all human beings, not just our culture. Maybe human beings are natural legalists, or maybe legalism is overrepresented among religious people.

for money, and maybe feeling guilty. How about trying together to develop a tribal culture that's less materialistic? Won't that honor the authority of Scripture in a way that more materialistic Christians can't? Won't it reflect light out to the tribes of the world?

I suggest that there are certain pressure points between the tribal cultures of today's world and the tribal cultures of God.[9] Among these are marriage, money, commitment. We can denounce the world for sinning in these things while we ourselves don't decisively break with the practices that grow out of them. Which is roughly what we do. And the world isn't impressed.

Or we can reach toward a contrast culture for our own tribe. A culture where we make a reasonable effort to do things in ways that aren't so soul impoverishing. In that way we can point the world toward hope, instead of the darkness of law and rhetoric.

ON CHOOSING SPECIFIC FORMS

But we can't use any old form. We need forms in the spirit of the gospel, forms that support the functions we find in the story of Jesus and that are appropriate to the cultures around us. "Appropriate" includes being as intelligible as possible to surrounding cultures and not being unnecessarily or irrelevantly offensive. It also includes finding core sins of the surrounding cultures and creating forms that confront them well, usually by pointing in more life-giving directions.

Many Christians are offended by the suggestion that churches need to take specific cultural forms. They imagine they can be Indians generically. They forget that all churches take specific cultural forms, most of which aren't required by Scripture. This is just a fact. If we didn't take specific cultural forms, we wouldn't exist. So the question isn't whether to take cultural forms, but how well the ones we take reflect the gospel to the tribal cultures around us.

Some of this is obvious and non-controversial. We have to conduct our meetings in some language or languages. We have to meet at particular times and places and at an agreed on frequency. And even if we restrict ourselves to biblical Psalms, we still have to select music (and the music will be quite different from the Israelites'). We have to decide whether to use wine or grape juice for the Eucharist, whether to have it at every worship service, every meal together, or annually. We have to decide what combination to use of Wesley's hymns, Negro spirituals, Latino music, Bach, and choruses. Such things are pragmatic forms. A church can't be infinite: particular cultural forms have to be chosen.

9. People who think about how culture and Christianity interrelate will notice that the language of tribes is conceptually quite different from most who discuss this. Instead of talking about the culture of the world as unitary, it assumes a multiplicity of cultures at least in postmodern societies. I believe this frees us from certain confusions in the discussion of people like H. Richard Niebuhr, *Christ and Culture*. We no longer have to sort out the relationship between the culture and the church. I hope this language will free people of that sort of problem without my having to explain the intellectuals' wars over them. Something similar can be said of the language of practices and embodiment.

I suggest that all churches also take stands on the same controversial topics that Sojourners does. They take stands by their silence. And by their actual practices. For example, by their silence and conformity, most churches accept the specific economic habits of the subcultures their members came from—whatever those habits may be, however contrary they may be to the gospel. Furthermore, this results in their serving economically homogenous affinity groups, which is in gross contradiction to the spirit of the gospel. It's rather like limiting your membership to people who mostly eat cold oatmeal without salt.[10]

Similarly, by their silence and their actual practices, they take the stand that it's fine for people to choose marriage partners by their sexual attractiveness and with little consultation with others. That it's fine for members to leave their churches for the sake of their jobs. And the same for churches silently agreeing that on holidays (the real holy days?) biological family is more important than church family. To put it differently, if we don't work out our own practices on these things, we are thereby adopting cultural forms from local tribes and saying that they're OK.

It's not generally seen that churches take stands on these topics partly because the stands they take are closer to those of the tribes that surround them. Which makes their stands invisible: it's how everyone does things in their region.

These too are extra biblical. To put it mildly.

That is, each church needs to be actively trying to develop a culture that embodies the gospel. And that's not just in relation to materialism and dating. We also need to choose forms that address even more basic things like reconciliation and habits of extending grace to one another, ways to make it clear that being the church is more important than work or family. It would also include ways of witnessing about Palestine and family abuse and the Pentagon—ways that point from violence to Jesus. We need to invent such cultural forms aggressively, not apologetically.[11]

DANGERS OF CHURCH TRIBALISM

Now, I've been proposing that Christians should be more tribal and that we should do this consciously and in a way that makes us a contrast tribe. However, this sort of tribalism has real dangers.

My wife used to teach first grade. One time she mentioned that we had lived in England. One of the kids raised his hand and asked her to say something in the language they speak there. She replied that in England they speak the same language we do. The little boy said, "They don't speak it as well as we do though, do they?"

---

10. I need to be clear that we are disappointingly homogenous economically and racially at Sojourners. It seems unlikely that this is due entirely to the hardness of heart of other affinity groups.

11. We do well to also be developing high culture: things like designing furniture (as the Shakers did), sand painting (as the Navajos did), oil painting (as Medievals did), kitchens, music (Methodists, Weston Priory), or short stories.

And I've hardly ever met anyone from England who thought Americans spoke English well.

Every tribe somehow comes to believe that their practices are the right practices, the best practices. Any other practices are odd, if not wicked or sacrilegious. Other tribes are at best inferior, which has the delicious result that "we" are superior; we have the inside track with God and are the real chosen people. Of course, other people are Christians (we're terribly generous), but not like we are. Really faithful Christians would join us.

Oddly enough other tribes aren't especially fond of this stance. (At least, when others take it toward them!) They get hostile (thus proving their inferiority), and the first thing you know we have division, hatred, and war. In a tribal model, the universality of the body of Christ can get lost, and a venture meant to be light to the world turns into denominationalism.

Once again, this is a slippery slope. However, there's no other slope to be on. Postmodernists, for example, imagine themselves to be broadminded, way beyond denominationalism. And are they ever self-righteous about it. Once again, it's not like we have the choice not to be tribal; it's just a question of which tribe we're part of and whether we admit it.

We have to take an aggressive stand on this slippery slope if we're to avoid cheap grace and provide light for the world. So the question about this slippery slope becomes, How do we keep from sliding all the way down? We will slide from time to time, but how do we catch ourselves?

First, we catch ourselves by being clear that what we're pioneering are experimental, pragmatic, clumsy forms. They're influenced (we hope) by the gospel story and the Holy Spirit, but they aren't given by God. Therefore, we need to be flexible; our forms have already gone wrong (or rather we have) if they're written in stone, unchanging year after year.[12] We need to be free to grant members "waivers." So at Church of the Sojourners, our expectation that members attend all meetings flexes for people who are depressive or who fear groups.

Second, we need to refuse to spend more than five minutes a year on casuistry. What counts as spending on yourself and what as work related? Are vitamins medical or personal? How about running shoes? Or in relation to marriage, if sexual attractiveness is bad grounds for marriage, do I have to be willing to marry someone who repels me? If members need to be at all meetings, can anyone ever skip a meeting to speak to the local InterVarsity group about community? (After a reasonable amount of discussion on such topics—roughly thirty seconds—people need to be left to their sense of God's costly grace so as not to waste the body's time.)

Third, we need to be comfortable with people who refuse to join us because they don't accept our embodiments. (We mustn't write them out of the kingdom, to put it mildly.) We just need to urge them to be faithful: to find some other embodiments if

12. Church of the Sojourners has a covenant that we take pretty seriously, but to remind ourselves that it's just our ideas, we revise it every few years.

they don't like ours. What they mustn't do is get absorbed into the cultures of the world in order to avoid our legalisms.

Fourth, we've got to remember that our practices are grace, not law. If people don't live up to our high standards (!), we don't need to beat on them. We can encourage them while speaking what we believe is the truth. Jesus has already made them the best people you can imagine. Our job is to love people into becoming who Jesus has already made them.

THE WHOLE BODY OF CHRIST

Another way of putting it is that all Christians are members of the body of Christ by virtue of having been born again. And by the same token the body of Christ isn't a local church but the sum of all local churches.[13] If we're clear on that, it will help lessen arrogance even if it won't guarantee humility.

For example, at Church of the Sojourners, we need to be clear that our distinctive emphasis on the church as community, important as it may be, isn't the heart of the gospel. And Christians who disagree with us about the nature of Christian community may often understand the heart of the gospel better than we do. How about Augustine, Martin Luther, John Stott, C. S. Lewis, John Howard Yoder, *The Door*, Gustavo Gutierrez, Stanley Hauerwas, Rodney Clapp, and on and on? These folks combined provided most of what we believe, teach, and practice, but none of them understood community the way we do. So most of the important things, even about life together, we learned from Christians from other tribes. And that's true for all of us, whatever our distinctives are.

This perspective on the whole body of Christ should help keep us clear that no one (including us!) has the whole truth. We may have some pieces that many churches are missing, but then they have pieces we don't have. We just don't know which pieces they have that we're missing: so we need to be humbly and fervently searching for those pieces by reading widely and making deeper connections with other churches, communities, and Christian individuals. The question isn't whether we have huge blind spots but what those blind spots are. If we don't realize our partial blindness, we're well on our way to going completely blind.

We all have things we know we don't do well. (At least, we better.) For example, at Church of the Sojourners, it shouldn't be hard for us to be humble. We don't exactly have it all together. Despite endless rhetoric on grace, few of us are famous for the grace we extend each other. It's demonstrable that we're bad at evangelism. And we could sure use help on serving members who are mentally ill, developmentally delayed, or have been sexually abused. Besides, we're second-rate at being an interracial, cross-cultural church: a near majority of us are introverted, mildly depressive, college-educated, white yuppies who dropped out of mainstream America long before

13. However, we also need to be clear that when the New Testament uses the body metaphor, it's using it mostly of how the members of a local church live with one another.

we joined Sojourners. So we need to learn from others how to include more people from affinity groups who weren't part of our founding core.

Humility is only difficult for the self-deceived.

WHAT WE DO KNOW

So we mustn't be silly about thinking we have things right. We need to be oh so clear with ourselves and others that we're fumbling our way along, depending on the Holy Spirit to save us, doing only moderately well, and not taking our forms too seriously.

But at the same time, we must do this without giving up witnessing to the truth we believe God has given us. Self-righteousness, ethnocentrism, and imperialism are great dangers for any who believe God has led them to some truth not widely practiced. But bearing witness to the light we think we have is a responsibility we must accept. It's a dangerous responsibility, but we must do it. Otherwise we're like Jonah:

> Ninevite to Jonah: "Gosh, you're arrogant and self-righteous. What makes you think you have the truth, and we're all in the dark?"
>
> Jonah: "Yeah, I tried to explain that to God, and he sent a whale to swallow me."

On the one hand, if others start telling us we think we're doing things better than others, we need to check whether our tribalism is turning to arrogance. But on the other hand, we also need to be clear that of course we think our way of doing things is better. Otherwise, we wouldn't do them that way. So we need to feel free, for example, to call other Christians to join some particular expression of the body of Christ that's developing into a distinctive people.

We need to be in that process with sisters and brothers in Christ from all over the world. Together we all need to be creating a culture that embodies the gospel in some particular way in some particular location. (Location, location, location, as they say.) That doesn't necessarily mean we're arrogant; it can mean we're serious about living out the gospel. And otherwise, we aren't the people of God in any meaningful sense. We're just the world with religion.

Of course, faithful people don't have to choose the tribal forms we have. (Surely others can do better than we have.) But we need to be vocal that Christians aren't free to continue business as usual. We can't have no way of embodying the Sermon on the Mount or of living like we're part of a body. Yet many churches have found only very limited ways to express those things, and we need to be free to tell them that it's important for them to find more forms that embody the gospel story.

BUT I'M NOT CALLED TO THAT SORT OF LIFE

Christians in our age seem to believe that you can live lives of the sort I'm talking about only if you have a special calling. That's one of the things that Catholics, Protestants, and Orthodox all agree on. But I suggest that talk of calling is often a cop-out. You need a special calling to live closely with other Christians in exactly the same way you need a special calling to stop committing adultery. You need a special calling to live out the Sermon on the Mount in exactly the same way you need a special calling not to murder your enemies.

Living out costly grace isn't a work of supererogation but something that all Christians are called to and that all Christians can do by the grace of God. We must not fall for the notion that obedience to Jesus' teaching is not required of normal Christians, only of saints or of especially serious Christians who join an order. Otherwise, first thing you know, the Sermon on the Mount will become optional. Indeed, being a serious Christian will become optional. (In fact, it already has.) And then grace has become cheap. This mind-set has led directly to a Constantinian church where the life of the gospel is lost and Christianity has become something about the soul with limited external effects.

But we can offer hope. Living the life of the Sermon on the Mount is something that quite ordinary people can do—together. If not, the Bible and the gospel are lies.

And they aren't. They're exciting promises. In the abundance and grace of God, they'll come true now in our lives together if we choose to let them.

PART FOUR

Foundational Christian Truths and Life Together
(Theological Practicalities)

TWELVE

On Not Devouring One Another (The Love of God and the Cost of Discipleship)

There's a problem with my whole idea of church. It's all those other people. That's why Ephesians 4 isn't lived out, why we fail at the unity described in John 17, why live-in churches blow up. It's them.

Or rather, the problem is them—and me.

When people live together, the fruits of the Spirit often grow exponentially. But at least as often, annoyance, resentment, and gossip grow instead. Deep in the human heart is a great darkness. That's why almost all the seventies hippie communes (Christian and otherwise) exploded. Life together isn't possible unless the Holy Spirit intervenes and takes us beyond ourselves, giving us grace for each other and to spare. Otherwise, life together becomes a hotbed of anger and divisiveness. That's because when I live with others, they keep me from getting my way. Which makes me mad.

On the one hand, to get the fruits of the Spirit growing exponentially in our lives, we need to design our lives so they overlap. On the other hand, the more our lives overlap, the less we get our way and the more we fight. In our life together sin can grow exponentially rather than the fruits of the Spirit.

Am I involved here in an internal incoherence? Am I just full of it? That wouldn't be especially surprising, but the flaw with that explanation is that the idea of some sort of life together seems to come from Scripture. In fact, scholars are growing something like a consensus that we've been reading the New Testament too individualistically: the New Testament is best understood as teaching on how to live corporately.[1] The only thing controversial about what I'm saying is the way I'm applying it. (Or is it that I'm applying it at all?)

This raises the possibility that it's not me that's full of it, but Paul and John (not to mention Jesus). Maybe they were all mindless idealists with rosy views of the Christian life. Maybe their views must be moderated by the common sense of the merchant class.

---

1. See for example, Hays, *The Moral Vision of the New Testament*; N. T. Wright, *The New Testament and the People of God*; and John Hall Elliott, *A Home for the Homeless: A Social-Scientific Criticism of 1 Peter, Its Situation and Strategy*.

But this is a little tricky for Christians to say out loud—though it is in fact what most of us do most days. (I do, anyway.) Still, it's not what we think when we're at our best.

Which leaves another possibility: We're still missing something about the New Testament. In chapter two I suggested that what we're missing is the notion of church. But that won't do here because the problem is that the New Testament idea of church doesn't seem to work. When people's lives overlap enough for them to share the gifts of the Holy Spirit, they fight and hate.

I suggest that what we're missing besides church is the basic doctrine of the New Testament. This claim that the problem is doctrinal will come as something of a shock to those (like me) who died of boredom in seminary theology classes. But there's little to add to what they taught there. Except maybe that doctrine means more than we realized. It's supposed to take over our lives.

I have a "scientific" prediction: Christians will live together in peace to the extent that we've learned to live the basic doctrine of the New Testament. We don't need much secular psychology, we don't need much political theory (especially the Thomas Jefferson variety), and we don't need much contemporary small group theory. What we need is the doctrine of the New Testament.

So living together in peace will be directly proportional to the depth to which we, or rather the Holy Spirit, has appropriated New Testament doctrine in our daily lives. Christians who live out the basic doctrine of the New Testament will be at peace with one another, and those who don't, won't.

GOD'S LOVE

Let me make a slightly more precise prediction. (I will make parallel "predictions" later about other doctrines.) We will live together in peace to the extent that we understand the love and grace of God.

A few years ago I was teaching at the Church of the Sojourners on love. I said that although Jesus taught that loving God is the first commandment, the New Testament in fact talks more about loving each other. Someone suggested I was injecting modern, secular humanism into the Bible.

I denied it, but I promised to study the question. So the next week I used my handy Online Bible program to call up all the New Testament uses of the various Greek words related to love. Then for the next month, I neurotically classified each verse. Was it about loving God or was it about loving fellow human beings? It took many, many hours, but I'm obsessive so I didn't mind. Especially because I learned I was right—hands down. The New Testament teaches far more on loving other people than on loving God.

I also learned I had missed the point. And had been missing it for forty years. The point isn't that I'm supposed to love God. Nor is it that I'm supposed to love others. The point is that God loves me. That's the basic doctrine of the New Testament. And of the Old Testament.

Which is a whole different story than I was telling. A much better one. A story of grace.

Perhaps I was still caught in fundamentalism. Though I had changed the content, I was still comfortable with moralism. I was also reacting against the endless theoretical discussions of the fundamentalism I was raised in. You see, as a child I got tired of arguing whether Jesus healed one blind man going into Jericho or two going out. I'm not much interested in information, only in transformation.[2] And I tend to understand transformation in terms of ethics. Which easily collapses into moralism. How should I change to become more holy? (A genuinely important question.) What should I be doing to change others? (I'm especially fond of this one.)

But the afternoon I was finishing my study, I got a better understanding that the Bible isn't mostly about ethics or about how I should change others. It's about God and God's love. About the nature of reality.

Now I sort of knew that. I think they taught me that in seminary. But I hadn't understood it. Or not deeply enough.

What if a father did a good job teaching his daughter the principles she needed to live well, but he failed to convey to her that he loved her? She'd probably be so damaged she'd scarcely be able to live at all, let alone by "good" principles.

For years I'd been imagining that holiness was about my becoming good, my breaking fewer and fewer rules. But while a holy person does break fewer rules, that's not what holiness is about. It's about a relationship. Specifically, it's about God's relationship to us. And that's different from the rules. It's also different from my relationship with God. If the central fact of the universe is that God loves us, then the central point of life isn't to figure out the rules and keep them. Nor is it to become good enough that I can relate well to God. No, the central point of life is to experience and absorb God's love.

For the deepest human need is to be loved. (It's the deepest divine need too). For God is love. That's the basis of life. Only in the context of love can human beings live and thrive and grow. And only in the context of love can we learn any principles of life that matter.

That's why the Judeo-Christian story is so wonderful. It puts love right at the center of the universe. In the heart of God. Not as an afterthought, but as the core of the creator and of creation.

Which is what is so sad about all the competing stories. I don't spend much time worrying about evolution; that sort of factual, informational question tends to irritate me. But if evolution wasn't guided by the hand of a loving God, then everything is an accident. Life is about the survival of the fittest, and the only principle is that the strong win. In that world any effort to help the weak is silly; so white males might as well keep oppressing everyone else. The universe is a cold, dark place, and love is an illusion.

2. See Alexander, *The Secular Squeeze*, 28–33.

No wonder so many kids are in trouble today. Love is scarce and scarcer. It has no place in the scientific mind. So if it happens that at home parents don't love their kids and if in biology the kids are taught that life is an accident, they will have little capacity for love. And therefore little chance of living decent lives. The best many of them will be able to find is someone to have sex with for a time. Which is no substitute. But what alternative do they have if they're taught a worldview in which sex is real and love an illusion? In such a world, promiscuity and divorce will increase. As will child and spouse abuse. And everything bad. In that world oppression makes a lot more sense than selfless love.

The scariest thing in our culture is that our primary alternative to secular evolution is fundamentalism. Which instead of thinking of God as love thinks of God as an all-powerful rule-giver.

No wonder the culture wars are a little short on love.

In biblical times (and in California?), a primary alternative was paganism. In paganism, the gods trick each other, murder their fathers for power, blind each other, and come to earth to seduce beautiful women. Their creation stories normally revolve around violence, deception, and rape. There is no loving creator. That's why the prophets hated pagan religions so much: their violence, injustice, and promiscuity. It's also why we should be nervous about the revival of pagan worship of Gaia.

The Bible gives us quite a different story: "But God, who is rich in mercy, out of the great love with which he loved us even when we were dead through our trespasses, made us alive together with Christ—by grace you have been saved—and raised us up with him and seated us with him in the heavenly places in Christ Jesus, so that in the ages to come he might show the immeasurable riches of his grace in kindness toward us in Christ Jesus" (Eph 2:4–7).

The Bible's story is a story of grace and love. Such a story will enable us to live with one another in peace. As the Holy Spirit applies it to our lives, the fruits of the Spirit will grow exponentially; anger and resentment won't.

THE BIBLE'S STORY OF GOD'S LOVE

The stress on God's love starts in Genesis. I'm inordinately fond of the sentence: "Then the LORD God said, 'It is not good that the man should be alone'" (Gen 2:18). That's when God created Eve. Adam had a beautiful garden, a dog, a picket fence, an American Express Card, and a great relationship with God, but God saw at once that this wasn't enough. God created Adam to need human relationships, too; so he needed another human being to love and be loved by. He needed something like the fellowship of the Trinity. There's something very sensitive and caring about our God.[3]

---

3. I don't know what all to make of this, but Adam already had God. This story clearly implies that that isn't enough. We need human as well as divine love.

SARAH AND ABRAHAM

Then the most important story perhaps in the whole Old Testament is how God cared for Sarah and Abraham (Gen 15–18 and 21.) In their culture almost the worst thing that could happen to you was not to have a child, and Sarah and Abraham were childless. While that's a tragedy for many couples in our culture, it ran far deeper back then.

And not only were Sarah and Abraham childless; they were old. And so the odds of their getting pregnant were negligible. But God took tender care of them, and long after menopause, Sarah got pregnant. Our God is the sort who cares not just about the great events of history (like war and who's king!), but about the "little" things. Like who's pregnant.

Now whenever I say that, someone says, "That's not a little thing; it's the miraculous foundation story of Israel. Every ancient people had some story of how their existence started with a miracle." And that's true. But other miraculous foundation stories are how the founder is himself a god or a half-god and how with his own hands he slaughtered thousands or did some other mighty deed.

But this story—this story is different. It's not about the mighty deeds of Abraham and Sarah; it's about their weakness and impotence. And it's a weakness that was especially disgraceful in their society. Everything turned on fertility. Your fields had to be fertile, your animals had to be fertile, your spouse had to be fertile. Otherwise you were ruined as well as socially disgraced and humiliated. God wasn't blessing you. So Abraham and Sarah were ruined and disgraced because they lacked the potency to get a baby.

In foundation stories it's standard for the founder to face some insurmountable problem. He's given some heroic task to perform to prove that he's worthy. He has to go slay a giant or climb an unclimbable mountain and return with a magic sword. Abraham and Sarah's insurmountable problem is impotence, and the only task they're given is to trust—trust that God will care for them. (In my opinion, this is our whole task, the secret of holiness.)

And Sarah and Abraham don't even do a noticeably good job at trusting God. In fact, at different times, they both laugh at God for promising to get them pregnant (Gen 17:17, 18:12–15). Nonetheless, in their feeble fashion, they believed God, and it's counted to them for righteousness. So Israel's foundation story isn't about Abraham's heroics. Their foundation story is about God and about how God loves Abraham and Sarah. He loves them in a very practical way, a very down to earth way. Abraham and Sarah come into history not as mighty warriors but as failures who believe God and who are loved by God. Which is essentially different from other foundation stories— and so much better.

Perhaps an even more touching story of God's love is about Ishmael, a son Abraham had by a slave while he and Sarah were waiting impatiently and unbelievingly to get pregnant. Not surprisingly, Sarah doesn't like Ishmael or his mother (Hagar), and she has them expelled from the family. They're sent into the desert with only one skin of water:

> When the water in the skin was gone, she cast the child under one of the bushes. Then she went and sat down opposite him a good way off, about the distance of a bowshot; for she said, "Do not let me look on the death of the child." And as she sat opposite him, she lifted up her voice and wept. And God heard the voice of the boy; and the angel of God called to Hagar from heaven, and said to her, "What troubles you, Hagar? Do not be afraid; for God has heard the voice of the boy where he is. Come, lift up the boy and hold him fast with your hand, for I will make a great nation of him." Then God opened her eyes and she saw a well of water. She went, and filled the skin with water, and gave the boy a drink. God was with the boy, and he grew up; he lived in the wilderness, and became an expert with the bow. (21:15–20)

The God of the Old Testament takes gentle care of a small boy and a cast-off sexual partner who were the product of unbelief. That's the kind of loving care God gives from Genesis to Revelation.

JACOB AND HIS CHILDREN

Then Jacob, Abraham's grandson, married Leah *and* Rachel. Unfortunately for Leah, Jacob loved Rachel rather than her. Presumably, this didn't feel very good for Leah. Besides, she wasn't getting pregnant. Sheer misery. In that culture where few cared about barren women, the Bible says, "When the LORD saw that Leah was unloved, he opened her womb" (Gen 29:31). Lovely. Gentle. And loving. Not the image most of us have of the God of the Old Testament.

Then Genesis 37–50 is devoted to the story of Joseph. (It's one of the longest stories in the Old Testament.) Joseph's many brothers are jealous of him, and so when he's seventeen they sell him into slavery in Egypt. There, when his master's wife fails to seduce him, she lies about it, and he gets thrown into prison for years. Not for weeks, but years. What a tragic, miserable life! Hated by his brothers, sold into slavery, imprisoned on a false charge.

But it turns out that God was taking care of Joseph (and his brothers) throughout. To make a long story short, within Egypt Joseph became second only to Pharaoh and thereby saved his family from starving. (Which he wouldn't have been able to do if hadn't been sold into slavery.) The family is reunited, and when their father dies, Joseph's brothers understandably worry that Joseph will get even. However, he tells them, "Even though you intended to do harm to me, God intended it for good . . ." (Gen 50:20).

Even when things seem to be going terribly, God wants us to know that he is loving us and taking care of his people. I bet it didn't feel that way to Joseph about year five of his imprisonment, but no matter what happens, God wants us to know that he's holding us in his arms. So no matter how tough the circumstances, we can thrive.

The Old Testament is filled with such accounts of God's love. That's what God wants us to know more than anything else. That's what we need to know more than anything else. Then we thrive. Which means becoming like the Trinity, which means being loved and loving. Which is the essence of holiness, the fullness of the stature of Christ—the something more of the normal Christian life.

FROM SLAVERY TO A LAND FLOWING WITH MILK AND HONEY

One of the great love stories of the Bible is the story of God delivering the Israelites from slavery and leading them to the Promised Land. Near the start of the book of Exodus, we're told:

> Then the LORD said, "I have observed the misery of my people who are in Egypt; I have heard their cry on account of their taskmasters. Indeed, I know their sufferings, and I have come down to deliver them from the Egyptians, and to bring them up out of that land to a good and broad land, a land flowing with milk and honey." (Exod 3:7–8a)

Our God is compassionate and passionate—a feeler. He feels the pain of his people. After this impassioned introduction, God then proceeds, out of his great love, to deliver Israel from slavery. Which is the foundational event of the rest of the Old Testament. Time after time Israel is pointed back to God's love in freeing them from Egypt. That's what Passover is about: reminding God's people how he loved them so much he delivered them. And as always in the Bible, everything is happening in the context of great promise. They're headed for the promised land, the Garden of Eden all over again.

After their liberation from Egypt, the next major event is the giving of the Ten Commandments. Did you ever notice that they don't start with a command? They start with: "I am the LORD your God, who brought you out of the land of Egypt, out of the house of slavery" (Exod 20:2). Then, and only then, after reminding them of his love, does God give them commands. We need to get hold of that: for ourselves, for our children, for those we teach. Love first. Command later. That's how we thrive in holiness.

I AM doesn't start by giving the Israelites a bunch of rules. I AM starts by loving them. By freeing them from slavery and getting them out of Egypt. Then and only then can the Israelites know that this God deserves to be obeyed. He is on their side and is giving rules so they can live abundantly. (Don't misunderstand me. He does give them rules. That's a crucial way he loves them. But that's not the starting point.)

If all they had experienced was God's power, they might have obeyed him, but it would have been out of fear: "Obey me, or I'll get you." The Old Testament is quite willing to frighten people (the New Testament, too, for that matter), but that's never the essence. Fear is an inadequate basis for life. And an inadequate basis for law. God tells us how to live because he loves us and knows better than we do what will make our lives work. The Old Testament returns to this again and again: "I am the LORD your God, who brought you up out of the land of Egypt. Open your mouth wide and I will fill it" (Ps 81:10).

Because of his great love, God wanted to do more for his people than free them from slavery. (Just as he wants to do more for us than get us saved from Hell.) He wanted to give them everything. He wanted them to open their mouths wide so he could fill them. Therefore, he doesn't just abandon them in the desert, the way the United States did after freeing its slaves. As Lincoln proposed (and Congress unfortunately disposed), God gave each of the children of Israel forty acres and a mule, so to speak. Actually, God did even better than that. First, he gave them the Ten Commandments (what good is forty acres and a mule if you don't know how to live?), and then he gave them a land flowing with milk and honey.

> For the land that you are about to enter to occupy is not like the land of Egypt, from which you have come, where you sow your seed and irrigate by foot like a vegetable garden. But the land that you are crossing over to occupy is a land of hills and valleys, watered by rain from the sky, a land that the LORD your God looks after. The eyes of the LORD your God are always on it, from the beginning of the year to the end of the year. . . . He will give the rain for your land in its season, the early rain and the later rain, and you will gather in your grain, your wine, and your oil; and he will give grass in your fields for your livestock, and you will eat your fill. (Deut 11:10–12, 14–15)

Our loving God is always full of promise. In this case, God loved the children of Israel so much that he gave them the Promised Land. Which is a metaphor for all that's good. That's what God always wants for his people—all that's good. The Garden of Eden, the Promised Land, the kingdom of heaven.

The Old Testament often expresses this notion of all that's good by the word, "shalom." It's usually translated "peace," but shalom is more than lack of war. It means well-being, material and spiritual prosperity, good health, contentment, a sort of completeness in all regards, and, of course, a lack of war and violence. It's like our word "fulfillment"—or rather, it's like what that word is reaching for without the self-absorbed overtones. For "shalom" isn't something for an individual alone, but something for a whole people. Not just military or spiritual peace, not just individual or corporate well-being, not just physical health or economic prosperity, but all of them. A life of complete well-being for an entire people.

To this day, the standard greeting among Jews isn't anything as boring as "Hello." It's "Shalom." And that's also the standard word at parting. Which is how the God of the Old Testament met and parted from his people. With an offer of shalom. He loved them so much that he wanted their total well-being. And that's how much he loves us too.

Here's how Deuteronomy summarizes God's love for the children of Abraham:

> For you are a people holy to the LORD your God; the LORD your God has chosen you out of all the peoples on earth to be his people, his treasured possession. It was not because you were more numerous than any other people that

> the LORD set his heart on you and chose you—for you were the fewest of all
> peoples. It was because the LORD loved you and kept the oath that he swore to
> your ancestors, that the LORD has brought you out with a mighty hand, and
> redeemed you from the house of slavery, from the hand of Pharaoh king of
> Egypt. (Deut 7:6–8)

God's choice of Israel was not based on their impressive size (or, we might add, their great wisdom or unswerving obedience). It was based on God's love for them, nothing else. It was pure love.

Which is why the Judeo-Christian story is so wonderful, so full of promise. It puts love right at the center of the universe. In the heart of God. Not as an afterthought, but as the core of the creator and the created. Letting that soak in is the secret of holiness.

THE SINFUL ISRAELITES

As they made their way from Egypt to Canaan, the Israelites rebelled against God with tedious regularity. In fact, as I've already said, that continues through the whole history of Israel. Their recorded rebellions would take pages to list. If it weren't that we know the same to be true of us, their behavior would seem absurd and unbelievable.

However, their rebellion (and the judgment that follows) isn't the heart of the story. The heart of the story is God's patient, persistent love. Tragically, God's love is largely unrequited. So the prophets often portray Israel as an adulterous lover, but one whom God never abandons. He keeps loving her how ever much she fails to love him back.

That theme is standard throughout the prophets, but Hosea puts it most eloquently. God tells Hosea to marry a prostitute who will be unfaithful to him. He does so, and she does so. When she disappears, he knows she's with another man. According to the law he could have her stoned, and he'd certainly be justified in divorcing her. But instead he wanders through the streets calling for her. Everyone knows where she is except Hosea. Finally, someone tells him. He goes to her and begs her to come back.

Is this God's ultimate word on the nature of love? (And on divorce?) In any case, the point of Hosea's humiliating drama is to live out before the eyes of all Israel how they are relating to God. No, I keep getting that wrong. It's about how God is relating to them. A crucial difference. It's about God's persistent, steadfast love, no matter what Israel does, no matter how badly they do him wrong.

I could go on and on. I could easily write a whole book on the love of God in the Old Testament. I could go through the historical books documenting God's miraculous interventions to defeat heathen armies in the time of Joshua, Gideon, Ahab (even Ahab!), Hezekiah, almost ad infinitum. I could show how when Israel demanded a king in place of the judges that God was giving them, God gave them what they demanded without using it against them. And though they had to live with the consequences of that choice, God used it for their good, turning it to the key positive metaphor of the kingdom of God.

I could point to God's tender loving care of Ruth, Hannah, Esther—and through his care for those women, to his care for all Israel. I could quote a hundred Psalms about God's care for his people, and point to his love for Job in hideous adversity. I could quote the Law, the Prophets, and the Poets to show how tenderly God feels toward the little ones and the oppressed. Understandably, some of us remember the Prophets mainly for their bitter denunciations of Israel or for their eloquent pleas for justice, but I could point out that neither of those is quite the key to the prophets: at bottom, what they're after is finding some way to persuade Israel to grasp God's abundant love for them.

This is the secret of holiness, the key to the Christian life. It's the way that ordinary people can ordinarily become saints. By basking in the love of God.

JESUS

But we haven't even come to the ultimate expression of God's love. God came to live among us and give himself up for us. We're so used to this story that it's easy for us to lose the sense of its power. But think what a mess human beings had made of our lives, of one another. We had invented murder and rape, hatred and greed, closely followed by war and slavery, prostitution and child brutality. If I'd been God, I'd have gone down to Walgreen's and bought a giant bug bomb. However, "God so loved the world that he gave his only Son, so that everyone who believes in him may not perish but may have eternal life" (John 3:16).

Try to get this picture. We're as much lower than God as cockroaches are lower than us. And we're not just lower in terms of intelligence and abilities. God had tried everything imaginable to win us over, and all he got was an occasional person like David and Solomon who almost invariably failed to stay the course and who did invariably fall into serious sin (or should I say invariably *jumped* into serious sin?). The Assyrians had already invented a war machine as vicious as the Nazi blitzkrieg (though they hadn't yet thought of death camps); their war machine had no purpose other than to make themselves rich and powerful. (Unless causing others pain was a purpose.) Meanwhile, they sacrificed their own children to win the favor of their gods.

So what did God do? Set off that bug bomb? No, for reasons that are well beyond me, God sent his son to be a cockroach among us.[4] He lived an under-the-stove sort of life in Nazareth. For thirty or so years. God came not as emperor of the cockroaches, but as a very ordinary one (a carpenter). For twenty years or so, he was in subjection to his parents. For a while he even wet his diapers. Then he sawed on pieces of wood in the heat and cold of Palestine.

I don't know about you, but I tend to think I *deserve* meaningful work—maybe even important work. But here's God, spending a couple decades doing ordinary, semi-skilled labor. On the seventy-third wall he built, did he get bored? Did he start asking

4. Now, it's important to hold this in tension with our being made in God's image, which is also true—importantly true. Otherwise the incarnation would have been a silly thing for God to do.

himself, what am I doing here anyway? He was so ordinary that when he came out from under the stove his neighbors said, we never saw anything impressive about this guy. "Is not this Joseph's son?" (Apparently, Jesus was no one in particular, even among cockroaches.)

And when he did come out of obscurity, it was just in time to be betrayed and murdered. Murdered in one of the most creative and painful ways of torturing people ever invented. Gas chambers are kind by comparison. And in that way, he somehow absorbed our nastiness, evil, and suffering. (I'm not saying I understand this; just that it happened.)

Why would God do this, even for good cockroaches?

Because he loves us. Apparently he loves us desperately and beyond our imagining. Love is what God is about. Also he keeps hoping he can do something startling enough for us to grasp a little of his love. That's it. It's about God's love. Everything that matters is about love. Love is who God is, and he wants us to get hold of it.

"But God proves his love for us in that while we still were sinners Christ died for us" (Rom 5:8). This Greek word translated "proves" is hard to capture. A lot of translations use "demonstrates," and that may well be the best you can do in modern English, but I prefer the King James' slightly archaic, "commends." God commends his love to us. "Demonstrates" and "proves" have a Cartesian, logical ring. "Commends" comes from the heart, from the heart of God. "Here's how I make my love look good to you; here's how I recommend it to you. While you were still sinners, I gave you the life of my own son. So please get hold of my love, and not just in your heads. Get hold of it in your hands, too, in your heart, in your whole being. Then in Romans 8, you have this astonishing conclusion:

> He who did not withhold his own Son, but gave him up for all of us, will he not with him also give us everything else? . . . Who will separate us from the love of Christ? Will hardship, or distress, or persecution, or famine, or nakedness, or peril, or sword . . . ? For I am convinced that neither death, nor life, nor angels, nor rulers, nor things present, nor things to come, nor powers, nor height, nor depth, nor anything else in all creation, will be able to separate us from the love of God in Christ Jesus our Lord. (Rom 8:32, 35, 38–39)

That's it. The whole story. God loves us. Nothing can change that.

But how?

The Bible is full of commands to love. And hope. And trust. Those are the big three, and I can't do any of them. What on earth is going on? I don't even know how to start trying to be loving and trusting and hopeful. I know how to sell my possessions. (I may not do it, but I can't say I don't know how.) I know how to stop lying and stealing. But I have very little idea how to make myself love. Then there's joy, peace, and patience—the second three according to Galatians 5. But how to produce them in my life mystifies me.

If I merely have a duty to make myself do these things, I have no chance. If I live under the bondage of obligation, I have no chance. But if God has already done it for me, then somehow I'm freed to do it. Jesus put it best: "As the Father has loved me, so I have loved you; abide in my love" (John 15:9). Christian ethics consists in basking in God's love. All we have to do is allow ourselves to experience the love that God already has for us and let that love overflow onto other people. Know God's love and do what you want, to edit an old saying of Augustine's.[5] Which of course is another way of talking about the Holy Spirit.

Having begun to understand that, I now see how wonderful it is that the most common sermon text is apparently John 3:16: "For God so loved the world that he gave his only Son, so that everyone who believes in him may not perish but may have eternal life." And the next most common is supposedly Psalm 23: "The LORD is my shepherd, I shall not want. He makes me lie down in green pastures; he leads me beside still waters; he restores my soul. He leads me in right paths for his name's sake." Maybe preaching is in better shape than I thought.

As I begin to grasp God's love, as I begin to grasp that I have been experiencing it for decades, then the confusing parts of Christian ethics begin to take care of themselves. If I know God is taking care of me, I'm freed to love him. And I'm freed to hope when things are going badly because God is going to make everything work out for good. And I'm freed to trust him because he knows so much more than I do. It's the natural outworking.

This isn't an ethical point, and that's crucial to understand. It's a metaphysical point. A point about the nature of reality. If people don't love, we don't need to command them to love as much as we need to help them understand the nature of reality. Once they grasp God's love for them at a deep enough level, they will love.

It's like with my dog. I don't have to command him to love me. I love him, and he loves me back. I'm the same. God loves me, and I respond.

The other day I read a story that explains all this better than I can myself. A boy named Bradley handed his mother a bill for his services. "Mother owes Bradley: For mopping the floor, $3.00. For running errands, $2.00. For baby-sitting little sister, $2.00. Total that Mother owes Bradley: $8.00."[6]

His mother read the note and paid him his $8.00. Then she gave him a piece of paper. (We all know what's on it, right? It's a list of all the things Bradley owes his mother: from childbirth to getting up with him at night to buying his clothes. It will be for thousands of dollars.) The note says: "What Bradley owes Mother. For nursing him through chicken pox, nothing. For making all his meals, nothing. For toys and games, nothing. Total that Bradley owes Mother, nothing."

This story is about love and grace. Not duty. Not difficult things we must do to get to heaven. No, this is a story about love. Bradley's mother does things for him not

5. What Augustine said was, "Love, and do what you want" In *Epist. Joann. Tractatus*, vii, 8.

6. William J. Bennett, "What Bradley Owed" adapted from Hugh T. Kerr, in *The Moral Compass: Stories for a Life's Journey*, 22–23.

because she owes it to him, but because she loves him. That is, she's free. She's free to serve till she drops. And that frees him to serve her till he drops. With joy because they love each other.

And that's how we are to serve God and each other. "Therefore be imitators of God, as beloved children, and live in love, as Christ loved us and gave himself up for us" (Eph 5:1–2a).

My Story

I started reading my Bible seriously when I was in seventh grade. At the time we were going to a church that taught that we were in the dispensation of grace: we were saved not by works, but by our intellectual beliefs. At least, that's the way I understood it. As far as I could tell, that meant that we were asked to do little other than attend church meetings and stop smoking and swearing.

I started reading my Bible at Genesis; so it took all year to get to the book of James, but eventually I got there, and here is what I found: "Faith by itself, if it has no works, is dead" (Jas 2:17). And "Show me your faith apart from your works, and I by my works will show you my faith" (2:18). I really loved the bit about how even the demons believe—and tremble (2:19). So my first sermon, when I was a junior in high school, was on the importance of works. I attacked "easy believism" (a phrase I'd read somewhere in Vernon Grounds).

I was right, of course. At least in some sense. But as I look back on it, I'm suspicious of myself. I suspect that I wasn't so much rejoicing in truth I'd found as I was trying to straighten other people out. Now mind you, people do need to get straightened out: truth is important. Jesus and Amos make that pretty clear. Not to mention Paul. They spent a lot of time straightening people out. But, at least when I do it, there's often something ugly about it.

So anyway, sometime around when I preached my sermon on the importance of works, my dad preached a series of sermons on the cost of discipleship. The point of the Great Commission, he said, wasn't to get people to say a prayer asking Jesus into their hearts and then leave them alone. The point of the Great Commission was to "make disciples of all nations . . . teaching them to obey everything that I have commanded you" (Matt 28:19–20). So among the things we're supposed to be teaching all nations is the Sermon on the Mount. Which is a lot.

For dad that meant that the local church was central. Big evangelistic meetings were worse than useless unless they channeled people into churches that had strong teaching, especially on discipleship. Then by the time I graduated from college, both of us were increasingly emphasizing that discipleship included justice and works of mercy. Dietrich Bonhoeffer's *Cost of Discipleship* made the point clearly, especially his critique of cheap grace. Bonhoeffer had written in the context of the near silence of Lutherans facing Nazi Germany, and to us the silence of American evangelicals facing white racism (this was the sixties) seemed eerily similar.

So we started a magazine called *The Other Side*.[7] The hope was to try to persuade people to live out costly discipleship in the context of a local church. And for the next twenty-five years, even after I left *The Other Side*, I tried to live that out in my life.

And you know what? It didn't work. At least, not the way I was doing it.

BALONEY

Once again, one possibility is that the gospel is baloney. That Jesus and Amos, not to mention James and the Alexanders, were neurotic, controlling people. What we needed was a large dose of liberal tolerance and cultural pluralism (or maybe Lutheran grace) as an antidote to our fundamentalism.

Frankly, I'm drawn to this explanation. If you can get beyond a romantic view, what would you really think of Jesus if he dumped on you the way he did on the Pharisees? Or of Amos if he dumped on you the way he dumped on Israel? Or of Paul if he dumped on you the way he did on the Judaizers?

The flaw is Nazi Germany. And Bull Connors. And the war in Vietnam. And me. What we exemplify isn't cultural diversity, but the cultural monotony of the strong oppressing the weak. Amos and Jesus were right.

But something goes wrong when it drips down to me.

I think it's my failure to grasp the love of God. We're in God's hands, and therefore all will be well. God is taking care of us, and so we can be free in loving others and caring for them. In fact, as we get in touch with the love of God, we are freed to be extravagant in loving God and others.

Which is different from focusing on the cost of discipleship.

Not that discipleship should be watered down to make people comfortable. I hope I've made that clear in the first half of this book. One of the crucial ways churches fail is that they cost too little. But cost is the wrong starting point. In fact, discipleship is the wrong starting point. Or rather, the starting point of discipleship is God's love for us.

All my life I've had a passion that we Christians are wrong about the cost of discipleship, wrong about social justice, wrong about the nature of church. I still think I'm right (roughly) about all that, but I no longer think these things are the heart of anything. The heart is the love and grace of God. All will be well and all will be well and all manner of things will be well because God loves us and is in charge of the universe.

God has done all that matters; we can relax.

The relationship between grace and works is one of the hoariest and hottest debates in theology. It goes back at least to the middle of the first century, or Paul wouldn't have had to write Galatians and Romans. And Paul tells us it goes back to Abraham and Moses. Theologians have argued the details ever since. It seems to be the sort of thing that can't be caught in a sentence, or maybe even in a book. No one's formulation seems to quite satisfy everyone else. No logical analysis seems to quite catch all the

---

7 It was originally called *Freedom Now*.

facets taught in the Bible. Which seems to me to indicate the wonder, immensity, and intricacy of God's truth. God's truth, after all, is always beyond human understanding. When we think we've got it figured, we can be sure we're deeply confused. Still, I think we can be clear on some things about it.

We've fallen off one side of the horse if we say with Luther that the book of James is "a right strawy Epistle."[8] Then we're going to ask too little of works. And our emphasis on God's love will turn into a sentimentalism that can't articulate God's judgment and can't stand up to Nazism. We'll have to ignore half of the prophets and half of Jesus and half of Paul. And we'll create churches that fail to ask for commitment the way Jesus did. So whatever we do, we must never lessen God's law, for it is part of his love. We must never neglect teaching the demands of the Sermon on the Mount, and we must never neglect calling people to repentance. It's just that we call them to repent and obey because God loves them. Not because they have to get it right.

And we've fallen off the other side if we spend as much time talking about God's requirements as about his love. For in the metaphysics of God's creation, love is the heart of everything. We must emphasize God's love more than God's commands.

So we've fallen clear off if we give people the feeling that they really better pull up their socks, that they really have to get it right this time or else. For we can be sure of one thing. We will never get it right. Our socks will always droop, unless we get them too high and tight.

But that's no big deal because Jesus has always had it right.

That then frees us to teach the vision of the Sermon on the Mount without making it a series of legal demands.

Let me put it another way. It's no accident that at the heart of the Sermon on the Mount is the phrase, "Our father." Without that phrase, the Sermon on the Mount would be dealing death. It would be a list of hard things we have to do or God will get us. A list of things we have to be anxious about not doing. And one of the things on the list is not being anxious.

Now a rule against anxiety causes terrible anxiety.

In the Sermon on the Mount, I had long noticed "[D]o not worry about your life, what you will eat or what you will drink, or about your body, what you will wear. Is not life more than food, and the body more than clothing? Look at the birds of the air; they neither sow nor reap nor gather into barns" (Matt 6:25–26a). But I wonder whether I quite noticed the rest: ". . . and yet your heavenly Father feeds them. Are you not of more value than they?" (Matt 6:26b). I suspect I had never quite grasped the centrality of God's love in the Sermon on the Mount. That is the context out of which all other teaching must grow.

For our father is the context of the Sermon on the Mount.

"Don't worry" isn't mostly a command. It's mostly a promise. A promise that God is taking care of us. That's at the heart of everything in the Bible. Not that you must

---

8. Luther, *Martin Luther's Basic Theological Writings*, 112.

gird yourself up to grind through some costly duty but that God loves you so much you're free to stop guarding your rights and to start loving extravagantly. Because God is trustworthy (and only because God is trustworthy), you're free to stop guarding your race (and class and gender and money and sexual orientation). Because God is trustworthy, you're free to live a life of servanthood: for "your heavenly Father knows that you need all these things. But strive first for the kingdom of God and his righteousness, and all these things will be given to you as well" (Matt 6:32–33).

In Luke 12 Jesus gives some of his strongest teachings on possessions. Near the end of them he says, "Do not be afraid, little flock, for it is your Father's good pleasure to give you the kingdom. Sell your possessions." (vss.32–33). Notice the sequence: first, "It is your father's good pleasure to give you the kingdom." Then and only then, the flat, unqualified statement: "Sell your possessions."[9]

Isn't that great?

Those of us with a deep sense of the cost of discipleship better have an equally deep sense of the grace and love of God. Otherwise, we're sowing the wind and will reap the whirlwind. I suspect that that's why house churches and live-in churches often explode. Those who have high requirements for church often have high requirements generally, and if they don't have an equally high view of grace, they will produce explosions wherever they go.

On failing badly

I haven't come to these conclusions because I'm such a good Bible student. I've come to them because I've failed so badly. I've been in many places (sometimes as a primary leader) where people were committed to radical discipleship, and my observation is that in those places we were rarely lovers of God or of each other. That's what failure is—failure to love God and each another.

My conclusion is that confronting people with law, even Jesus' "law," doesn't free them to love. Instead, it sets up a dynamic of condemnation and tension and anger and superiority. An understanding of the law (or better, a misunderstanding of law) sets people up to try to straighten others out. To fix each other, whether anyone wants to be fixed or not. Whenever that happens (which is often), it leads to fiery holocaust. (It's especially common and especially explosive in live-in churches.) All in the name of Jesus.

Trying to fix people makes them frantic. (Except when it makes them furious.) It's a superior talking down to an inferior. No, that's not strong enough. It's me talking down to you so that I can feel better about myself. So I can feel superior to you. That's one of the main functions of law. (If you don't believe it, check with the Pharisees.)

---

9. I'm not making the claim that love must always be taught first chronologically. I suspect, however, that it could be shown from both Scripture and experience that that's the ideal order.

Another primary function of the law is that it gives us something to argue about. We can have endless and unending disputes over details of simple living or nonviolence or baptism or communion.

Oddly enough, none of that frees people to love.

So, every bit as important as our failure to follow the directions on the function of church is our failure to grasp experientially the grace and love of God. (It's actually far more important.) Popular Christian speaker Gene Edwards illustrates this beautifully. Imagine a man buying a horseless carriage when they first came out without grasping where the power came from. Suppose he knew he wasn't to use horses any more, but the person who sold him the car forgot to tell him about the ignition. So some days he sits in the carriage and goes nowhere, and other days he gets out and sweats and strains to pull the carriage himself. This is the Christian life if we don't grasp that we have died and Christ is the power, Christ is the one who lives our life through us. We really can't do it. So we either sit around in our magnificent theology going nowhere, or we strive to be good Christians with tragic failure after tragic failure. We don't quite grasp that our power, the ignition switch, the driving force of our lives, is the love of God in Jesus.

But that doesn't mean we do nothing, that we sit in the horseless carriage without moving. No, it means we zip around on the love of God. We work harder than any legalist ever could.

Perhaps it can't be put precisely. Perhaps it's a tension. That's how Paul leaves it in Philippians: "Work out your own salvation with fear and trembling; for it is God who is at work in you, enabling you both to will and to work for his good pleasure" (2:12b–13).

I love the paradox. Work your salvation out yourself and work hard. For it's God who gives you the power. Full stop. No explanation that would suit rationalists or scholastics. No explanation at all. He just leaves it there. Work your butt off because God's the one doing it.

If folks are trying to pull up their socks, you tell them, "You can't do it. God does that, or no one." And if they're doing nothing, you tell them, "Get to work, because God loves you." Different strokes for different folks—and for different churches and different ages. If you don't find yourself emphasizing both (perhaps at different times), you've got it wrong. But emphasize God's love especially. In the context of the cost of discipleship.

My suspicion is that our failure to play the game God has given us is reflected both in a failure to grasp the abundance of God's grace and in a failure to grasp the cost of discipleship. In either case we're in trouble.

Then again, perhaps only those with a deep sense of God's grace dare to look at the real cost of discipleship. Perhaps we need more stress on God's grace precisely so we can face how much it cost God and will cost us. Perhaps high standards and a high view of grace go hand in hand.[10] If you don't ask much of yourself, you don't know how much grace you need.

INCREASING IN LOVE AND HOPE

These days I'm a pastor in a live-in church, and I'm beginning to get a glimpse of a loving approach. Not that I do it very well or very often, but it's gradually dawning on me that about the only thing I do that helps people much is talking to them about how loving and gracious God is. I ask them to memorize Psalm 23 or Jeremiah 29:11–14. And over the years I see some of us increase in love and hope while decreasing in judgment and fear and anger.

Of course, I also talk to them about the rest of the radical vision of Jesus. (Otherwise, talk about the love of God is sentimentalism.) When to do which is a crucial question. One of the most important there is. And I know no neat answer. Unless it's to do both a lot. So I go over Jesus' rules regularly, but if people don't see it, I feel less need to compel them to agree with me (at least on my good days). It's something about speaking the truth in love and leaving the results in the hands of our loving God. (Which is where the results are anyway, so it's not a bad idea.)

And you know what? A few of them—a few of us—have begun living a life of costly discipleship. And we don't have many explosions anymore.

Except when we forget that we're in the hands of our loving father.

Do you understand? People thrive, live-in churches thrive, all churches thrive when they're basking in the love of God.

Faced with anything else, we shrivel. Especially when faced with judgment and pulling up our socks and getting things right. But anything else too. Anything.

That's basic Christian doctrine. Most of it, anyway. And when people show some sign of beginning to understand God's love, then is the time to start talking about Jesus' rules. The first of which is love. And so is the second.

---

10. I owe this point to Tim Otto, an overseer at Church of the Sojourners.

THIRTEEN
Death to Ego (Servanthood)

The Gospel of John is oddly lacking in detailed ethical requirements. Matthew gets concrete about who can get a divorce and what divorce means; he spells out where not to pray and how not to give alms; he's specific on how to respond if someone hits you or steals your coat; he comes close to listing certain words not to use. But John has nothing parallel.

He deals only with basic principles. Love, serve, wait on God, and (above all) choose Jesus. He seems to assume that if you take care of such things, the rest will take care of themselves.

He's right. Not that the details don't matter (they're often vital) but that they will take care of themselves if the central stuff is taken care of. And if the central stuff isn't taken care of, the details will be meaningless drudgery or destructive self-righteousness.

One of the basics John emphasizes is ego death. He focuses on the greatness of Jesus and brings out how unimportant that makes us. He wants us not to worry about our own significance. To forget ourselves.

So in chapter 3 John the Baptist's disciples are upset because Jesus is baptizing more people than John is. Everyone had been coming out to hear John, but now the whole world is flocking to Jesus.[1] So John's disciples are upset. But John calmly tells his disciples, "He must increase, but I must decrease" (John 3:30). This isn't about John the Baptist, he's telling them; this is about the Messiah. (As is the whole book of John, as is your whole life.)

But most human beings would find that depressing; so that's not where John the Baptist starts. (We "need" to be the center of things.) So he starts by telling his disciples that someone greater than he has come, followed by the killer sentence: "For this reason my joy has been fulfilled" (v. 29)! Only then, only after he has explained that someone greater than he is a source of joy, does he add what I started with, "He must increase, but I must decrease."

In our culture anything that moves us off center stage sounds to us like misery (at least, it does to me), but John the Baptist says joy depends on it. If we're concerned

---

1. The movie *The Keys of the Kingdom*, directed by John Stahl, handles this astonishingly well, especially given that it's a Hollywood production.

about our own importance, we will be forever miserable: no matter how important we become, someone will be more important. Joy is choosing to serve the Messiah instead of yourself, joy is grasping that someone else is ever so much more important than you are. Joy and being off center stage go together. In fact, they're almost the same thing. No one is going to be happy for long who is busy trying to increase personal power or fulfill personal desires. We have to get beyond all that—even to be happy, let alone joyous or holy.

Dying to self is another basic Christian doctrine. (Or is it the same one? The same as the love of God? The same as salvation by faith? And are all the same as the greatness of God?) Another precise prediction: I predict that live-in churches (actually, churches of any sort) will thrive if their members have died to themselves and begun to live to Christ. And they will shrivel if they're mostly living out personal ambitions and desires in the pursuit of fulfilling their potential. I predict that conflict will be directly proportional to how much members are committed to their own potential and inversely proportional to their degree of ego death.[2]

So the passage from John 3 on decreasing the self, ends this way, "Whoever believes in the Son has eternal life; whoever disobeys the Son will not see life, but must endure God's wrath" (3:36). Eternal life isn't just living forever; it's also real life now, a life of quality. True life, fulfilled life, complete life, joy—they aren't the result of getting our silly desires, or even our occasional desire that isn't silly. They're the result of killing ourselves off and letting Jesus live through us.

The things I've said in this book that matter most can be summarized by one of the verses I started with: "It is no longer I who live, but it is Christ who lives in me. And the life I now live in the flesh I live by faith in the Son of God, who loved me and gave himself for me" (Gal 2:20). The foundation of truth is that God loves us so much that he gave his son for us. As a result we can entrust ourselves to him, stop taking care of ourselves, and give ourselves freely to others. Then Jesus takes care of the rest, including living our lives. As we die, we come to life.

Finally.

Mary says it beautifully, "Here am I, the servant of the Lord; let it be with me according to your word" (Luke 1:38). We should all have that written over some mirror we look into every day. It might remind us to ask ourselves at least once a day, "Will I accept the will of God in my life today, or do I have to try to be in control of everything myself?" To the degree that we have control needs, we are dead. To the degree that

2. Several people who read this manuscript in advance were offended by the phrase "ego death." They argue that as used by modern psychologists "ego" is a technical term invented by Freud (or his translator), and it's not equivalent to the "old man" that the New Testament says must die. This may well be correct.

However, my experience is that those who use "ego" as a term for something good can rarely find any strong sense in which the "old man" needs to die. I can appreciate talking about a false self that must die and a true self that needs to be uncovered, but I find no sign of such language in the Bible and I suspect its popularity has something to do with the "me generation." Of course, my "ego death" and "death to self" are themselves quite far from New Testament language. (Paul's language is usually the "old man" being crucified or us dying, and the gospels talk about losing the "psyche" to find it.)

we can leave the control to God, we have faith and are alive. That's what faith in God means—not some intellectual belief that God exists, but complete trust. And having it over our mirror reminds us that dying to ourselves is not once and for all but a process. As Paul says, "I die daily" (1 Cor 15:31, KJV). A long obedience in the same direction. Which is why Luke talks about taking up our cross daily (Luke 9:23).

Jesus talks often and succinctly about dying to ourselves: "I tell you, unless a grain of wheat falls into the earth and dies, it remains just a single grain; but if it dies, it bears much fruit. Those who love their life lose it, and those who hate their life in this world will keep it for eternal life" (John 12:24–25; see also Matt 16:25–26, 10:39; 19:29; Mark 8:35; Luke 9:23–24; 17:33; Acts 20:24; 21:13; Heb 11:35; Rev 12:11; Rom 8:13; Gal 5:24, 6:14; Col 2:12–13, 3:1–5, 9–10). Then, even more succinctly, Jesus prays in Gethsemane, "My Father, if it is possible, let this cup pass from me; yet not what I want but what you want" (Matt 26:39).

Hebrews tells us that "for the sake of the joy that was set before him [Jesus] endured the cross" (Heb 12:2). Not out of asceticism, but for the joy! Real life, real joy, is the result of dying to ourselves. Then the rest takes care of itself. John doesn't worry about the rules because they don't do any good till you're dead—or at least dying.

Perspective

Of course, dying to yourself makes no sense to people of the world with their self-esteem psychology. It can't. They've never encountered our loving and mighty God. So it usually sounds to them like a prescription for negativity and asceticism. Their alternative is to perform well and tell ourselves about it.

Now, of course, some people have been so abused verbally or physically that they can scarcely function. We need to be sensitive to that. But the solution (salvation) is to love them and tell them of God's love, which is quite different from building up their self-esteem.

It's important to be in dialogue with non-Christians to help them see their way through this, but we need to be clear that it's no accident that any Christian psychology will sound like gobbledygook to unbelievers—until they personally encounter the great and loving God (perhaps in us). If a mighty God doesn't exist who loves us all, then they're right: we darn well better take care of ourselves and fight to fulfill our potential.

It's knowing God that gives us perspective on ourselves. That tells us who we are. And what our problems and desires amount to. In the middle of the ocean, it's hard to take yourself seriously. On a night away from city lights when you can see the Milky Way and know that the nearest star is many lifetimes away (even at the speed of light)—on occasions like that it's hard to get all solemn about your importance.

The disconcerting thing is that many Christians are almost as entangled with self-esteem psychology as are those who have the excuse of not knowing God. The secular world is all too successful in squeezing the children of God into its mold. Remember

Baal and the children of Israel. Today, a primary Baal competing with Jesus for lord-ship is self-esteem. It's our messiah in the here and now, the thing we hope will bring us real life on earth. Jesus may save us after death, but today our salvation depends on self-esteem. Or on some other do-it-yourself, pop psychology.

But these do-it-yourself schemes are a hopeless chase. As was Baal. For pagan gods are cruel taskmasters. They require us to perform well. As does self-esteem psychology. In it salvation is by works, by performing well at something, and telling ourselves about it. But the Bible (not to mention life) makes it clear that salvation is by grace or not at all. We're such screw-ups that if we have to do well to be saved, we'd be hopeless.

Salvation is by grace here as well as hereafter. We can be at peace now only by grace. This isn't just theology; it's psychology. Our worth rests in being loved, mostly by God; it doesn't rest in performing well, especially not well enough to have self-esteem.

I have a severely handicapped son. He can do rather few things well. What gives him worth? His psyching himself into thinking he's neat? To the extent that Judy and I love him, he will know that he's worthwhile and will be able to experience the love of God. To the extent that we (and to a lesser extent others) fail to love him, he will fail to know his worth and will have to struggle to know the love of God. To that extent, he will also try to perform well enough to earn our love and boost his self-esteem. But love isn't the sort of thing that can be earned. Nor is self-esteem.

ON NOT BEING JUNK

Now, people will misunderstand what I'm saying here. They will think I'm saying that people are junk. Fallen junk.

That's not it. That's not it at all. My son is not junk.

I learned that we aren't junk from Francis Schaeffer. (Hence his campaign against abortion.) When I first heard him say we aren't junk, I raised my hand and asked, "You mean God made us great, but we make ourselves into junk by our sin?" He got upset and said, "No. The wickedest human beings still aren't junk. They're wicked. And that's different. We human beings can't finally destroy the wonder of God's creation even in ourselves."[3]

Psalm 8 puts it best. It starts by stating the wonder of God: "O LORD, our Sovereign, how majestic is your name in all the earth! You have set your glory above the heavens. Out of the mouths of babes and infants you have founded a bulwark be-cause of your foes, to silence the enemy and the avenger" (vv. 1–2). Then it compares us to God: "When I look at your heavens, the work of your fingers, the moon and the stars that you have established; what are human beings that you are mindful of them, mortals that you care for them?" (vv. 3–4). We're about to be dumped on. We're junk, right?

---

3. This was in 1964, more or less, and I'm sure I don't have his exact words.

Wrong: "Yet you have made them a little lower than God, and crowned them with glory and honor. You have given them dominion over the works of your hands; you have put all things under their feet, all sheep and oxen, and also the beasts of the field, the birds of the air, and the fish of the sea, whatever passes along the paths of the seas. O LORD, our Sovereign, how majestic is your name in all the earth!" (vv. 5–9).

We are created by God, who crowned us with glory and honor. We may well be the greatest thing God has made. Translators are sometimes embarrassed by the strength of the passage and change the Hebrew to say: You have made them "a little lower than the angels" (KJV). But the Hebrew is clear. We are only a little lower than God, than the divine. We are more wonderful than the stars or the ocean or the Rockies. And that is no less true of those who are severely handicapped or who have given themselves over to sin. For our greatness doesn't reside in our ability to perform or our ability to control our lives or to control the universe. Our greatness is that God loves us and gave his son for us so that we can decrease. We can afford to decrease because God gives us so much glory and honor.

The angels were astonished. We should be, too. And we can express this only by being so fascinated by the wonder of God that we gain perspective and forget ourselves in his service. We don't express it by hating ourselves but by realizing that our greatness is in decreasing so that he can increase.

It's like with computers. They're great things (well . . .) if they're plugged in, but by themselves they're nothing, they're incomplete. They become great, they become complete, only when connected to a source of power. Suppose you had a computer that refused to be plugged in. That wanted to increase till it was complete in itself. Or a fish that wanted to get out of the water, a person who wanted to quit breathing, an infant who wanted to get along without her mother.

Or a person who wanted to get along without God. Like Adam and Eve. Like you and me.

How pathetic we are as we try to claim center stage for our self-esteem and our silly little egos. We become fully alive as we leave center stage to God. I'm not junk, but by choice I'm a silly little man. I'm a silly little man precisely to the extent that I trust myself and take myself seriously rather than God. It's God I need to be pushing to the center. Me that I need to be pushing out of the center. It's the only way to avoid complete twititude. The only way to become complete. To get fulfilled.

And find joy.

> If thou couldst empty all thyself of self,
> Like to a shell disinhabited,
> Then might He find thee on the ocean shelf,
> And say, "This is not dead,"
> And fill thee with Himself instead.
> But thou art all replete with very thou,
> And hast such shrewd activity

> That when He comes He says, "This is enow
>
> Unto itself—'twere better let it be,
>
> It is so small and full, there is no room for Me."[4]

Get clear on that, and the details of sin that so fascinate and bind us lose their power. The Gospel of John is right. (Which doesn't make Matthew wrong.)

A SMALL PRACTICALITY

Obviously, I understand this better in theory than in practice. I have a rather limited sense of the love and power of God. And consequently, a rather exaggerated sense of my own importance. Which leaves me with a silly desire to be center stage.

But even a theoretical grasp of the greatness of God helps. It means I can laugh at my folly whenever I start angling to have other people respect me. The pomposity of twits is greatly diminished by friendly laughter, especially their own.

At which point I can remind myself of who God is. Which is a discipline. I have a limited emotional experience of the greatness of God. It would be nice to be charismatic with regular, spontaneous, emotional experiences of who God is. But for me that's not standard. And I suspect that's OK as well as typical. Most of us often have to rely on gritting our teeth and reminding ourselves of the might of our loving God.

And having to remind ourselves is nothing to worry about. That's the long obedience in the same direction. It's reminding ourselves of the truth, as Deuteronomy expects us to need to do:

> "Keep these words that I am commanding you today in your heart. Recite them to your children and talk about them when you are at home and when you are away, when you lie down and when you rise. Bind them as a sign on your hand, fix them as an emblem on your forehead, and write them on the doorposts of your house and on your gates. When the LORD your God has brought you into the land that he swore to your ancestors, to Abraham, to Isaac, and to Jacob, to give you—a land with fine, large cities that you did not build . . . take care that you do not forget the LORD [remembering isn't normally spontaneous], who brought you out of the land of Egypt, out of the house of slavery. The LORD your God you shall fear; him you shall serve." (Deut 6:6–10, 12–13)

Steady slogging more than spontaneous, exciting experience. I've talked a lot about the need to be motivated by love, not driven by obligation. Perhaps I've overstated it. We are at least obligated to keep reminding ourselves of God's great love.

---

4. Thomas Browne, quoted in Madeleine L'Engle, *A Ring of Endless Light*, 20. I quoted this first in *The Secular Squeeze*, 259–60. When I found it, I liked it so much I vowed to quote it in every book I wrote from then on.

A BIG PRACTICALITY

One more piece—a big one. We don't do this well by ourselves. We need a people to keep us honest, a church. (Church is what this book is about, you may recall.) Our selfishness easily becomes invisible when we're alone. Alone, it's easy for us to imagine that we're focused on the love and greatness of God rather than on ourselves. For a reality check on how selfish we are, we need to get married. Or have kids. Or join a live-in church.

Kids were a revelation to me. I was used to going to a movie on the spur of the moment. At 11:00 o'clock at night. Spontaneously. And then sleeping the next morning till 10:00. But suddenly, we had to plan ahead to get a baby-sitter. And the kid woke us up whenever. At 5:00 AM if he felt like it. And he had no respect for my need not to be tugged at while writing a brilliant paper for graduate school.

Then when he had chickenpox even though we were exhausted . . .

He limited my freedom. There were three choices. 1) Kill him (child brutality is no mystery to me), 2) I could wait till he grew up, or 3) I could grow up. Share center stage with him, or shut him in the closet? For me living through this was pain on pain. It was also a step toward growing into the fullness of Christ and dying to self. Maybe that's why God gives human beings the most helpless of infants. For years they're totally dependent, totally selfish, totally demanding. But we love them deeply; so when they thwart our wills, it reveals to us how selfish we are.

Which is why life together rarely works. The average adult isn't as selfish as an infant, but in my experience it's rather rare for another adult to let me have my way all the time. This really makes me mad. Faced with that situation, we either practice child brutality on each other or we begin taking little steps into the fullness of the stature of Christ.[5]

In a way that's what *Shantung Compound* is about.[6] It's a great book, one of the few great books of the twentieth century, in my opinion. But it should be subtitled, *How We Make Life Together Miserable for Ourselves and Each Other*.

Of course, life together in Shantung Compound was intense. It was a prison camp where the Japanese held Allied civilians. As such camps went, this one wasn't bad. The prisoners were treated tolerably and were allowed to elect a board to govern many aspects of their life together. One of the tough things was that at one point 2,000 people were housed in buildings adequate for maybe 300. So you can imagine what happened. The governing board got together and divided the space up equally, and people got along pretty well, though with some complaining. Right? Wrong. All hell broke loose. No one thought they should share their space. Many of the captives were missionaries;

---

5. Alternatively, we can deceive ourselves and pretend we don't mind while inside getting madder and madder. Psychologists call this repression. Jesus calls it lying. In either case, it's a terrible route to take.

6. Gilkey, *Shantung Compound*, 75–89.

so naturally they agreed to share their space, right? Wrong. (The Catholic religious had gone home by then.)

You know, the biggest problem in missions almost always is that the missionaries don't get along with each other. We human beings are incredibly selfish. We want center stage and the best of everything.

Anyway, the governing board of Shantung Compound had no police force. They had to call in Japanese soldiers to get even missionaries to move.

Another time the American Red Cross sent care packages to the compound, enough for each person in the camp to get one and for the Americans to get one and a half. But no, a few Americans objected. They wanted them all for themselves. (It would have meant roughly seven packages for each American.) The governing board, confident they could silence the troublemakers, decided to have the Americans vote on it. Guess what? Almost all of them voted to keep the packages for themselves. This the Japanese refused to do. (Wicked oppressors that they were.)[7]

I don't know this for a fact, but I'll guarantee you that the happiest people in Shantung Compound were those who had outgrown some of their selfishness and were content to be servants of all.

According to Gilkey, one of the hardest things was the lack of meaning. For most, their purposeful lives had been interrupted. They existed to run their company, drink on weekends, make money, impress their neighbors, or evangelize Chinese. Suddenly none of those things was possible anymore. So people existed for the future moment when they were freed. And they could do nothing to further that goal, so they had nothing to do till then.[8]

Nothing to do? Why not serve your neighbor? I realize that this is a heroic standard, but for missionaries camp life could have been only a momentary readjustment. The biggest difference was that instead of serving and evangelizing Chinese people, they could now serve and evangelize people from various European countries. And was that mission field ever needy. Unfortunately, the missionaries were among the worst off.

Those few who managed to keep this perspective must have been the happy ones. They knew what life was about, and that doesn't change if you're in need or have plenty. For they "have learned to be content with whatever I have" (Phil 4:11).

My favorite example is Eric Liddell. He's the hero of *Chariots of Fire*. He was also the hero of Shantung Compound. In the camp, he especially served the boys. He gave one of them his running shoes. And when he died in the camp of a brain tumor, it was the boys who carried his casket to the grave.[9] I suspect that wherever he had been, in whatever state, he would have found someone to serve and love. (What's so hard about

---

7. Ibid., 96–113.

8. Ibid., 193–202.

9. Oral communication with William Shell, then one of the boys in the camp, and known then as William Bonner.

that?) Then wherever he had died, those people would have carried his casket. And wherever he died, he would have died a happy man.

Because happiness depends on dying to ourselves. On becoming saints together. I'll bet half the happiest people in the world belong to the Sisters of Charity. Or at least, that these women are three times as happy as the starlets of soap opera fame. Who have everything.

Anyway, my favorite story about Liddell involves Sunday sports. You may remember from *Chariots of Fire* that his main claim to fame is that he refused to run his event at one Olympics because it was on Sunday. Although I'm a sabbatarian, that smells like legalism to me. That isn't the part of his story I like. The part I like is at the camp. There he was the referee when the boys played soccer. Except on Sunday, naturally. Then he wouldn't do it. Till he learned that when he wasn't there, the boys fought over the game. (Kids are desperately selfish.) So he started being their referee—even on sabbath.

He understood that life is about serving God and people, not about keeping your principles.

A SMALL MISUNDERSTANDING

I realize that my argument sounds a little odd. What we need to do is start crowded prison camps and call them churches to deal with our selfishness? First Church of Shantung Compound. People probably would not join by the thousands, but those who did would mean business. Or alternatively, we could require all Christians to move to Los Angeles and learn patience by driving the freeway every afternoon during rush hour. (Actually, just having to live in Los Angeles would do it for most of us.)

Hardly the point.

In fact, most of the people in Shantung Compound didn't grow into the fullness of the stature of Christ. They were at least as selfish when they left as when they arrived. As are most people even after years with live-in groups—if they've joined because it's a rule.

My claim, or at least my hope, is quite different. We're called to share with our church the gifts that the Spirit has given us. Within limits, we can do that on Sunday morning. But if we limit our contacts with people to that extent, we will have proportionately fewer conflicts. Of course, we will also have proportionately fewer opportunities to share the gifts. This is all because of our bone-deep selfishness. Because of our desire to be center stage, not plugged into the power source.

So we have to decide. Of course, we have to have enough space to breathe and be nurtured. Studies of rats prove that much. But within some nurturing limits, are we going to die to ourselves so that we can be connected to one another and share our gifts, or are we going to hide in a corner with two friends from our favorite affinity group?

It's not a question of law, but of vision. Don't move into a live-in church or join a small group because it's a law. A required form. Do it if you have a vision to share the gifts of the Spirit. Do it if you have a passion to grow with others into the full stature of Christ. Otherwise, don't. You'll just be bothering others with your legalism.

SPOONS AND THINGS

I like things organized. Clean isn't too important to me, but I hate to go to the silverware tray and find soupspoons mixed with teaspoons mixed with serving spoons. Don't people know that spoons come in three sizes? Why do you think silverware trays usually have five slots: one for forks, one for knives, and *three for different sizes of spoons*? But no, not if you live in community. One of the profounder insights I've come to in community is that at least half the people in the world seem unable to tell the difference between teaspoons, soupspoons, and serving spoons.

Besides, although our kitchen has only matching silverware, when they set my place, do you know what they do? They give me a knife from our set and then go borrow a spoon and fork from some neighbor—solely to irritate me. And we have three full sets of glasses. But do they set the table with one set? No-o-o-o. They search the kitchen for the maximum number of unmatching glasses and spread them randomly around my dinner table.

And tape measures. I have lost enough tape measures in community to give one to each person I've ever lived with. What do people do with tape measures? I may have been a socialist when I was young, but I no longer have any intention of loaning my private property to people who don't know what things cost. And the next time I open my toolbox to find no seven-inch crescent wrench, I'm going to suspend my commitment to nonviolence.

No, I'll just move out.

People aren't worth it. If you live together, you have to deal with disorder and noise and dogs scratching their collars at 6:00 AM (It's not well known, but Newton's fourth law of thermodynamics is that the more tags a dog has the longer he will scratch early in the morning. If such laws were better understood, live-in churches would be even rarer.)

But seriously, have you ever noticed what annoying habits others have? People are worse than dogs. And the truth is, life together is a series of those annoyances.

Why bother?

Because teaching the three sizes of spoons isn't central to following Jesus. And my learning that is important. It helps me deal with my selfishness and focus on what discipleship is about.

And allows me to receive the gifts the Spirit has given others for me. And the other way round.

'Till I learn a little about not being upset about spoons, I'm a prisoner of my own obsessions, and I have to isolate myself from most meaningful human contact. Not to mention contact with God. (I get so busy sorting spoons I have no time for our wondrous God.)

ON BEING A GOOD BROTHER OR SISTER

Let me try to say it less ironically. In church, our task is simple and clear. We're to serve. We're to be good brothers[10] or sisters. We're to clean the toilets. Like the sisters in Shantung Compound. Like the janitor when you were in third grade.

That's about all we have to do. Is that really so hard? This is not a requirement that we leap over buildings in a single bound. But take care of this minimum, contentedly, and the rest will take care of itself. (As long as it's not a compulsive way to keep busy, and as long as you're aware of resentments you have about it. Those are huge provisos that deserve a lot of attention, but I'm not going to deal with them here.)

Which is why Jesus washed his disciples' feet. Contentedly. Or do you think he was annoyed to have to do that just before he was murdered? It was almost the last thing he did with them. He wanted them to learn that much.

The great danger of talk about gifts is that we all use our gifts as weapons, to enhance our power or importance. (Selfishness can ruin almost anything.) In churches people moan endlessly, especially new people, about their gifts not being used enough. Often they're right. Churches have to keep reminding themselves to identify the full range of gifts the Holy Spirit has given us.

Nonetheless, the main gift the Spirit has given each person is the ability to clean the toilet. (A contemporary equivalent of washing feet.) We are clear on that for others but often not for ourselves. So in the body of Christ, it has to be an incantation: for each of us, our task is to clean the toilet, wash the dishes—in short, be a good brother or sister. That's our mission. Clean up after the party, and when the baby down the hall starts crying at night, go get her. Or take the disabled person to the movies, hang out with your sisters in the evening, study the Bible to the extent of your abilities, and pray for your housemates.

Wash their feet. And don't worry much about using your other gifts. Is that so hard?

A live-in church is a quick way to learn to die to ourselves. By reminding ourselves of how much greater God is than we are . . . and by washing feet. Contentedly. Then our gifts become usable.

"Here am I, the servant of the Lord; let it be with me according to your word."

JUST SAY YES

I've talked a lot about ego death. But be clear. That's not the goal here. The goal is to increase God. Decreasing me is secondary. The idea isn't to say no. The idea is to say yes. Yes to God. Yes to a mighty and loving God.

The source of all hope and joy. The source of extravagant abundance.

10. I learned this phrase from the Bruderhof.

1 Corinthians 1–4

Several years ago, our church studied 1 Corinthians together. We did it because we knew it had a lot on serving one another, a lot on gifts, and a lot on church conflict. (An interesting combination.) That study became formative in our life together.

But we didn't know what we were getting into. I didn't anyway. I didn't realize that the book is really a handbook on church unity in a church already claiming the gifts of the Spirit. It's precisely about how to deal with the church conflicts I've been talking about. And it's annoyingly simple. You deal with them by taking Jesus more seriously, yourself less seriously, and by serving the body. That's the basis of unity. Not getting people to understand the various sizes of spoons. Not getting them to live the way I want them to so I can have my way and be at peace. Not by getting them to recognize the importance of my gifts. And not by getting their ideas straight.

I don't mean to say that ideas are unimportant. They're part of the way to unity, but not the main way. Jesus comes first, then the cross, then servanthood, then unity of Spirit, and then last of all, agreement on ideas.

But let me back up. The church in Corinth had been taught about gifts by Paul himself. They were big on them. They spoke in tongues, they prophesied, they worked hard at developing godly wisdom. Paul praised them for it (1 Cor 1:5–7). But despite their extensive use of the gifts of the Spirit, they were in deep doodoo. They were having conflicts over everything under the sun and were about to go up in a fiery explosion. Paul doesn't tell them to quit speaking in tongues or to speak in tongues more. He tells them to put Christ center stage, get off it themselves, and serve one another. He tells them repeatedly. In a series of ways. He obsesses on it.

The first four chapters talk about their conflict generally and tell the Corinthians that they need to get their leaders off center stage and Christ on center stage. The gifts are about God and his greatness, not about themselves. I said Paul focuses on Christ, but actually he focuses on Christ crucified. Not Christ the great speaker or Christ the healer or even Christ resurrected, but Christ crucified. The ultimate in servanthood.[11] When he talks about preaching Christ crucified, he's not worried about abstract theology;[12] he's worried about practical theology. He's worried that the Corinthians aren't serving each other the way Christ served them.

Paul didn't come as a great speaker with clever words or clever philosophy. That would put him on center stage and distract from the cross of Christ. Paul came as a servant. And he warns the Corinthians not to take themselves too seriously. They seem to think they're pretty smart, but he reminds them that among them not many are wise

---

11. To another group, one who understood something of servanthood and were feeling defeated, he might well focus on Christ resurrected. Even in 1 Corinthians, he spends a whole chapter on the resurrection and God's final victory.

12. By practical theology, I don't mean what is taught by that name in seminary. I mean roughly the topics taught in seminary as abstract theology handled with an eye on how they nurture life.

or mighty or noble. They're twits whom God has chosen for their weakness "so that no one might boast in the presence of God" (1:29).

It's about God. We're servants. In fact, we're lower than servants. We're fools. For Christ (4:10). Who is what life is about. He's our honor and glory. This whole chapter of mine on ego death is little more than a paraphrase of 1 Corinthians 1–4.

Then Paul gets concrete.

1 Corinthians 5–7: Lawsuits, sex

Chapter 6 is a killer. The Corinthians may speak in tongues, but they're cheating each other in business and fighting it out in court. If someone in your church wrongs you, don't take him to court. You're to deal with the conflict yourselves. And the way you're to deal with it! "Why not rather be wronged? Why not rather be defrauded?" (v. 7b). Be a servant. Let yourself be crucified instead. That's how to be unified.

It's pretty easy. Or at least it's straightforward. Not hard to understand at all.

In the rest of that section (chapters 5–7), Paul talks about sex and marriage and the divisions they cause. He's not only practical, but so intimate it's almost embarrassing. If your spouse wants sex, give it to him or her. Sexual pleasure isn't about you but about your spouse. So "the wife does not have authority over her own body, but the husband does; likewise the husband does not have authority over his own body, but the wife does. Do not deprive one another" (7:4–5a). Serve your spouse even in bed. (Those who believe in male headship need to find a way to work this in. And they need to ask whether Paul is talking only about sex.)

These days, if a couple in conflict go to a marriage counselor, the counselor will try to find a way that both can get more of what they want. Usually, it will be a compromise of some sort. The couple may sign a contract where each gives up certain things for the sake of getting other things. That's today's notion of conflict resolution, and it's not silly. But as always, the Bible goes deeper and asks more. Paul asks each spouse to give the other everything. That's how you get unity, whether in marriage or church. By self-sacrifice and by serving one another.[13] Totally.

Like Jesus on the cross.

Not only is the lack of self-esteem and of assertiveness unintelligible for modern people, but the logic is also troubling to our either/or minds. You either have to let the other person have her way, or you get your way, or you reach a compromise. But Paul is setting the standard for how to deal with conflict: both of you give all the other wants. To heck with the logic. Only in the spirit of both giving all, where your rights don't matter, can you come to the spirit of unity. (Of course, when we think we're giving all, we're doing well if we're meeting the other nearly halfway!)

---

13. Notice the lack of sexism in this passage. It's not just the wife who doesn't have authority over her own body. That would be deeply troubling. It's also the husband. At least in bed, the wife has authority over her husband. And vice versa.

Obviously, unity requires some cognitive agreement (see Galatians) and behavior that isn't wicked. So how you serve others is limited by principle (though I suspect that we should have far fewer principles than most of us do). Paul's argument against using prostitutes turns on the same point as the rest of the book. Not on some abstract notion of ethics, but because "You are not your own. For you were bought with a price" (6:19b–20a). Like a slave, you've been bought and paid for and can't just do what you feel like. We're to be servants, Jesus' servants, even in sex.

1 Corinthians 8–10: Eating meat

Next Paul deals with meat offered to idols. Whether idols are backed by real spirits seems like an important theological question. Yet for Paul it apparently isn't important enough to argue about. (Perhaps because it doesn't go to the heart of the gospel?)

And the very people he agrees with, he's not in unity with. He goes after them for acting superior and not caring about those he and they disagree with: "So by your knowledge those weak believers for whom Christ died are destroyed. When you thus sin against members of your family, and wound their conscience when it is weak, you sin against Christ" (8:12). This is a family matter; so don't be lording it over your brothers and sisters, but do what they need, especially for the weaker and less important ones.[14]

Then in one of those stunning embodiments of the gospel found in the Bible, he says, "Therefore, if food is a cause of their falling, I will never eat meat, so that I may not cause one of them to fall" (8:13). Now, I hate to admit it, but second only to glazed donuts, my favorite food is New York steak. If some of my vegetarian brothers and sisters were offended by that, could I say I'd quit eating meat?

For that is much of the practical meaning of the gospel. Serve your brothers and sisters. That's how you avoid the sort of conflict that tears people apart as soon as they get close.

In chapter 9, Paul explores the question of rights. They didn't have that exact concept yet (there's no word for it in Greek), but he asks whether he doesn't have the "authority" to eat what he pleases, the "liberty" to do what he feels like. His answer is "Yes, but." Yes, but "I have made myself a slave to all, so that I might win more of them" (9:19b). He doesn't care what he has the right to do; he cares about finding ways to win others to Christ, and he'll do almost anything and give up almost anything if it might help.

He goes on: "To the Jews I became as a Jew, in order to win Jews. . . . To those outside the law I became as one outside the law . . . so that I might win those outside

---

14. Who to consider weaker is a tough question. It's fairly standard to suppose that the weaker brother in our churches is an elder who is opposed to using alcohol. Younger people are to avoid offending him. This seems odd. Isn't it more likely that the weaker conscience would be younger, less mature Christians? But Paul's main point doesn't turn on how you apply this to such situations. His main point is to serve the person you disagree with.

the law. To the weak I became weak, so that I might win the weak. I have become all things to all people, that I might by all means save some" (9:20–22). There are things Paul cares about more than his rights—namely every single human being he meets.

That's what servanthood is. Paul will be learned if he needs to; he'll be simple if he needs to. He'll eat raw monkey eyes if it will help, or he'll clean toilets. Because he has died to himself and become the servant of all for the sake of Christ and his people. In chapter 10, he offers another classic summary: "'All things are lawful,' but not all things build up. Do not seek your own advantage, but that of the other" (10:23b–24).

Peace isn't hard to come by. If a few people take Paul's servant attitude in your church, there will be few conflicts. Somehow, disputes over spoon size seem pretty silly. As do disputes over baptism and maybe even the details of predestination. (Of course, disputes over whether I have to do others' share of the dishes remain pretty important to me.)

1 CORINTHIANS: SUMMARY AND EMBODIMENT

Through the rest of 1 Corinthians, Paul repeats himself about unity coming through servanthood. I'll leave the details for you to find for yourself, except for a quick summary. How should we handle the Eucharist? In a way that serves all, and no one is left out. What about the spectacular gifts of the Spirit? They're the gift of God. But remember that they're for building up the body. How should we do worship? Organs, guitars, nineteenth-century hymns? Paul is the supreme pragmatist. However builds up the body. He says this not once, but seven times.

Seven.

Joe Peterson was the last community leader of Shiloh Youth Ministry. I once heard someone ask him whether Shiloh had a covenant or statement of faith that all members had to sign. He said, "Yes, only we call it the dish-washing list." I don't want to be quite that casual about doctrine (the whole point of this section, if not the whole book.) But we need to be clear that the doctrine means little apart from embodying it, in this case apart from washing the dishes.

PART FIVE

Love and Reconciliation
(Reclaiming Church, Revisioning Church)

FOURTEEN

The Mark of Church (Love and Unity)

The mark of church is love. In different times and in different places, churches may take various forms. But the enduring, unvarying, non-negotiable characteristic of the church is love. If we are to reclaim churches from their frequent waywardness and irrelevance, the first step is to put love at their center.

How we baptize, whether we use an organ or guitars, whether we meet in homes or in buildings with steeples, whether we emphasize predestination or free will, whether we have a common purse or not, whether we use high liturgy or low—on such things, our visions can and do differ. And at least within reasonable limits, differing on such things doesn't call faithfulness into question and shouldn't call our fellowship with each other into question.

But we cannot disagree on the centrality of love. We may not be able to agree on the wording of our theology of love, but we must love: "I give you a new commandment, that you love one another. Just as I have loved you, you also should love one another. By this everyone will know that you are my disciples, if you have love for one another" (John 13:34–35).

Here's how outsiders will know that we're for real: By our having a beautiful liturgy? By our getting our theology right? By our apologetics being compelling? By our having the right sort of buildings? By our giving away all our money?

Hardly. By love. Love is at the center. The rest overflows from that. Everything good grows out of love. And out of nothing else. Good doesn't grow out of getting the five points of Calvinism right or out of speaking in tongues or getting church structures the way they had them in AD 50. Love is the foundation of church; it's the mark of church. That must be our vision.

Now, that doesn't mean that churches always love well. It means that love is the game we're playing. We may drop lots of fly balls. No, we *will* drop lots of fly balls. We will fail to love, and sometimes that failure will be spectacular. But outsiders watching us will understand that love is what we're about. Even at their frequent worst, the Cubs are undeniably playing baseball. Heck, even in the worst of Little League games, I've never heard anyone ask, "What game are they playing? Are they playing basketball or tiddlywinks? Or are they perhaps eating lunch?"

That's what it means for love to be at the center. That's what Jesus means when he says: everyone will know that you are my disciples if you keep trying to love however much you fail. Then outsiders will begin to get it.

But don't misunderstand me. This emphasis on love doesn't mean that theology is unimportant or that it doesn't matter what forms our churches take. It means rather that we evaluate our theology and our forms by how well they encourage love. It means we shape theology and liturgy by what tends to support love. So, a form for church that tends toward anonymity is a form we'll move away from, and a form for church that tends to encourage relationships (loving, committed relationships) is a form we'll move toward. Similarly, we'll avoid theology that tends toward endless hairsplitting, and we'll be drawn to theology that articulates practices of love that get beyond sentimentality and rhetoric.

By the same token, if love is central in our vision for church, we'll see everything else as relatively minor. My guess is that we won't spend much time arguing about forms of baptism, and we'll find ways to avoid the worship wars. When tongues become an issue, we'll follow Paul and point toward the "still more excellent way" of love (1 Cor 12:31). When simple living or liturgical forms become an obsession, we'll try to refocus things by quoting Paul, "If I give away all my possessions, and if I [invent the most beautiful liturgies], but do not have love, I gain nothing" (1 Cor 13:3). And if people need to persuade us to be vegetarians, we'll find ways to accommodate them while trying to help them see that food isn't what it's about; it's about love, not about what we eat. And on and on.

This makes it all the more important to get clear that church isn't a building or a preaching service that happens just before or after Sunday school. Church is a society that's about love: about God's love for us, about our love for God, about love as our motive and practice, about our loving one another and our enemies and everyone else.

Love is our function and ministry. So we'll minimize other stuff while going for forms and worship styles and theologies and life styles that support love. That's the vision for church. The vision we must reclaim. Or else we're playing some other game.

God

Now people can misunderstand what I've said lots of ways. One of the most serious is to suppose that love is a work instead of a gift of God. So be clear that I'm not taking back any of the things I've said about God or grace or any of that stuff. It's crucial for us to be clear that churches, the people of God, are constituted by God and not by our work, even our works of love.

So when God first makes a covenant promising a people, he tells Abraham, "I will make you a great nation, and I will bless you" (Gen 12:2). He doesn't tell him, "Go make yourself into a great nation—all by yourself—and I'll lend a hand when things get tough." No, God assured Abraham of his love and told him that he was going to make his descendants a great people. God does this, not us. The Bible makes it clear that the way God does this is to love us and thereby enable us to love one another. The people of God are constituted unilaterally by God, especially by God's love. Therefore, we are constituted as a people of love. Getting hold of this frees us to love. For love is a function of God's grace.

If we're to be a loving people, we'll need to get burned into our souls and brains that God is doing this, not us. This isn't easy to get hold of deeply. Remember Abraham and Sarah. After God had promised them a huge and blessed family, they got nervous and decided they needed to help God out. So after they had laughed a little at how silly God was, they got to work making a baby: not the traditional way, but by making Hagar a breeding mare. And their descendants have been paying for it ever since.

God didn't need Abraham's help. And he doesn't need ours. Our job is to relax and wait on God. Wrestle with God all night, and then leave it to him. In that gracious atmosphere (and only in that gracious atmosphere), love will start bubbling up from all sorts of places, and God's work will be done among us. By God.

If he has to, God will nail the point down with us the way he did with Abraham. You remember how God told Abraham to sacrifice Isaac—Isaac, the only possible source for the people of God. Apparently, Abraham had started to think he'd succeeded; he'd finally created the people of God. So God taught him, "No, I am creating my people, not you. I can do it with you or without you."

Similarly, God will take our favorite examples of being the people of God, our favorite church, and kill it off so that we can be clear who makes God's people.

It's not us.

You see, if we're doing it, we have to control things. Control people. Have tantrums when others do it wrong. Which is reasonably close to the opposite of love. But if God is bringing together his people, I don't have to be so controlling. I can leave the controlling to God. (It's called faith.) Which frees me to love people whom I think are screwing up. (I don't have to fix them.)

And God won't need us to sacrifice Isaac. As Genesis says and Paul takes as central, Abraham "believed the LORD [about Isaac]; and the LORD reckoned it to him as righteousness" (Gen 15:6). A trusting people doesn't have to worry about its own righteousness or that of others. Which frees us to love.

So our vision of church is a vision of love. A love that grows from how gracious God almighty is to us.

Tough Love

Another way of misunderstanding this topic is to suppose that love is sentimental and romantic. If anything is clear in the Bible it's that love is tough. This is clear in: "I give you a new commandment, that you love one another. Just as I have loved you . . ." (John 13:34).

Just as I have loved you. Now, I'm sure that Jesus had lots of warm feelings in his heart for his disciples. And I suspect that he gave them lots of warm fuzzies. He must have because he loved them passionately. But the text isn't especially clear about his handing out warm fuzzies to them.

What's ever so clear is that he died for them. (Just after he told them to love as he did.) He served them. He was patient beyond patience even when they were complete twits. He kept gently telling them the truth. (Without denouncing them, by the way. He was much gentler with them than with the Pharisees.) And then telling them the truth, again. Then washing their feet. Then dying. And eventually, with a little help from the Holy Spirit, the disciples got the idea that Jesus was trustworthy. That no matter what happened, he was going to be there for them. That they could entrust him with their lives and dreams and spouses because he loved them.

So tough love is washing the dishes. Encouraging people. Cleaning their toilets. Telling hard truths without getting mad. Getting up at night with someone else's baby. Reminding each other that Jesus has already done it. Laughing a lot. Dusting the blinds. Forgiving seventy times seven. Making a nice dinner for everyone. Skipping the movie you want to see to talk to a lonely person not in your affinity group. Throwing a party.

That's what love is. Hard work. One of the endless paradoxes of the gospel. Since God is doing it and we don't have to, we work far harder than if it were our job.

THE CENTRALITY OF GOD'S LOVE

The mark of church is love, but let me be more specific. The primary mark of church isn't our love. It's that we are a people who know that God loves us.

The centrality of God's love in the Bible is obvious; so I'm not going to argue it in too much detail. But I want to argue it enough to make it clear that God's love for us is a theological point, a biblical point, a point that isn't negotiable. It's not just my opinion or an optional form that Christians can disagree on. Knowing God's love is the first thing that marks us as the people of God.

The Bible says so.

We need to be clear that this teaching on the centrality of God's love goes clear back to the founding of Israel. It can be seen throughout Genesis with God's loving care of the patriarchs, wretches that they were. He causes Abraham, Isaac, and Jacob to prosper, he provides them with wives who aren't pagan, and (most important, from their point of view) he gives them children.

One of the most wonderful and surprising stories in all literature is the ancient story of how Yahweh cared for his people in a famine. (We call it the Joseph story, but that's a misunderstanding.) It starts with a standard biblical account of hate and murderousness, showing the depravity of the human heart. The sons of Jacob sell their little brother, Joseph, into slavery. (The origins of Nazism and slavery are no mystery to people of the Book.)

If you're like me, at this point you're thinking this is just another depressing if realistic story (like *Oedipus Rex* or *Agamemnon*). However, it then seems to turn into the sort of hero story common in all literature, including religious literature. Joseph overcomes incredible obstacles and performs incredible feats. But then comes the great turn in the story—the turn that marks it not just as great literature or national myth but as the very Word of God. Years after selling him into slavery, his hateful brothers are about to starve, and what does Joseph do? Serve them their children in a stew? Sit back and gloat? No, he feeds them. And then he lays out the basis for the great turn that marks stories as God's stories, "Even though you intended to do harm to me, God intended it for good" (Gen 50:20). That is, at the dawn of recorded history, Joseph already knows that God is a God of unimaginable love and power who cares for his people. God's love for us is the mark of God's word from Genesis to Jesus to Revelation.

From this ancient story comes a paradigm for forgiveness and the reason for it. Yahweh is so great and loving that even when terrible things happen to you, you can trust God to take care of you and forgive those who imagine they did it. Note well, forgiveness isn't a work of magic or heroism available to atheists or pagans. It's a gift (the gift?) from the God who rules and loves. We have no need to hate our enemies because even when they are doing us harm, God may use them to give us more than we can ask or think. Forgiveness in any other worldview is ever so much harder.

But I'm ahead of myself, again. After 13 chapters of this story about God's love (one fourth of the book of Genesis), the next story is the story of the Exodus. It spends twenty more chapters on God's love for his people. (Or is it a thousand more chapters?) The Exodus is the central event of the Old Testament, the paradigm for how God loves Israel. The children of Abraham were in slavery in Egypt, and "the LORD said, 'I have observed the misery of my people who are in Egypt; I have heard their cry on account of their taskmasters. Indeed, I know their sufferings, and I have come down to deliver them from the Egyptians, and to bring them up out of that land to a good and broad land, a land flowing with milk and honey'" (Exod 3:7–8a). This Yahweh tenderheartedly proceeds to do.

From here on, the Hebrew Scriptures refer back again and again to God's loving care in the Exodus: "I am the LORD your God, who brought you out of the land of Egypt, out of the house of slavery" (Exod 20:2). I've never done a verse count, but some form of this statement must appear a couple hundred times by the end of the Hebrew Bible. There's hardly a book in the Old Testament that doesn't go on and on about it.

I could give dozens of other stories about Yahweh's love, but I'll offer only an inadequate summary. The Hebrew Scriptures often say not only that God delivered Israel from Egypt, but also that he gave them "a land flowing with milk and honey." Other writers emphasize the goodness of God in giving the Jews his law, in giving them peace and prosperity under David and Solomon, or in bringing them back from Babylon. So Judaism is built around the love and goodness of almighty God. This is a theological, biblical point, not speculation or a statement of personal preference. You could say that the function of the Jewish Scriptures is to record the love of their good God and God's might in serving them.

For the people of God are founded on the love of God. First and foremost.

Then in the New Testament, we have a new Exodus. God frees his people from the slavery of sin through the life, death, and resurrection of his son. This was much more costly for God than the exodus from Egypt. This time it wasn't the sons of the Egyptians who died; it was the son of Yahweh himself. God took the suffering on himself. (Can you picture letting one of your children be tortured to death for the sake of others—others who aren't nice?) If we can grasp this even cognitively, we will be deeply moved. We'll be done with a sentimental view of love, and (far more important) we'll begin to trust this God and love him back. Which will overflow onto others in forgiveness and grace.

I could cite many New Testament references to the centrality of God's love in the death of his son, but let me remind you only of three:

> For God so loved the world that he gave his only Son, so that everyone who believes in him may not perish but may have eternal life. (John 3:16)

> He who did not withhold his own Son, but gave him up for all of us, will he not with him also give us everything else? . . . No, in all these things we are more than conquerors through him who loved us. For I am convinced that neither death, nor life, nor angels, nor rulers, nor things present, nor things to come, nor powers, nor height, nor depth, nor anything else in all creation, will be able to separate us from the love of God in Christ Jesus our Lord. (Rom 8:32, 37–39)

> In this is love, not that we loved God but that he loved us and sent his Son to be the atoning sacrifice for our sins. Beloved, since God loved us so much, we also ought to love one another. (1 John 4:10–11)

Those of us inclined to read the Bible as a handbook of behavioral obligations must notice that God's love for us isn't another duty that we or God must carry out. And though it's the foundation of our ethic, it isn't a command. It's a metaphysical fact, which neither we nor anything else can change. God's love is a reality in which we can revel and luxuriate.

So God's love is the first mark of church, the core of our vision. The people of God are above all a people who know that God loves them.

Our love for God

If the first mark of the people of God is God's love for us, the second mark is our love for God. The ancient origins of this in the Hebrew Scriptures are clear. Here's the Shema, the daily prayer of Judaism (kind of like the Lord's Prayer of Judaism): "Hear, O Israel: The LORD is our God, the LORD alone. You shall love the LORD your God with all your heart, and with all your soul, and with all your might" (Deut 6:4–5).

Jesus emphasizes the centrality of this for both Judaism and Christianity by his answer to the scribe's question, Which commandment is first?

> Jesus answered, "The first is, 'Hear, O Israel: the Lord our God, the Lord is one;
> you shall love the Lord your God with all your heart, and with all your soul, and

with all your mind, and with all your strength.'" (Mark 12:29–30; see also Matt 22:34–38, Luke 10:25–28)

So the people of God have always been up to loving God wholly. What's more, this wasn't an abstract moral principle that anyone of any faith or lack thereof could understand and practice. No, Jews saw their love as a response to the very being of Yahweh: Yahweh is our God, Yahweh alone, He is one, the almighty God, our God, the one who delivered us from Egypt; we who have these specific facts love him utterly.

So they (and we) aren't called to love any old god in abstraction. We're called to love a particular God, not because he's more powerful than us, but because he's Yahweh who has shown himself trustworthy, loving, and lovable. This is not the Unmoved Mover of Western theism, but Yahweh who does things like sending his son to die for us.

Loving God isn't mostly an obligation, but lest my rhetoric against obligation overtake me, let's be clear: We human beings are astoundingly self-absorbed. We readily forget about God's love for us, and when we do love stops overflowing on others. That's why we have obligations, duties. So it's especially important for us to remind ourselves of how much God loves us, how much pain he has taken on for us and at what cost. So right after the Shema, Deuteronomy goes on:

> Keep these words that I am commanding you today in your heart. Recite them to your children and talk about them when you are at home and when you are away, when you lie down and when you rise. Bind them as a sign on your hand, fix them as an emblem on your forehead, and write them on the doorposts of your house and on your gates. . . . Take care that you do not forget the LORD, who brought you out of the land of Egypt, out of the house of slavery. (6:6–9, 12)

OUR LOVE FOR ONE ANOTHER

The third mark of the people of God is our love for each other. Jesus calls loving one another a new commandment, but it's also "an old commandment that [we] have had from the beginning" (1 John 2:7). So in giving the next most important commandment, Jesus again refers back to the Hebrew Scriptures, "You shall love your neighbor as yourself: I am the LORD" (Lev 19:18, quoted by Jesus in Matt 22:39, Mark 12:33, Luke 10:27).

Paul and James give perhaps even more emphasis to loving one another. Paul says that all the commandments "are summed up in this word, 'Love your neighbor as yourself.' Love does no wrong to a neighbor; therefore, love is the fulfilling of the law" (Rom 13:9–10). And, "For the whole law is summed up in a single commandment, 'You shall love your neighbor as yourself'" (Gal 5:14). And James says, "You do well if you really fulfill the royal law according to the scripture, 'You shall love your neighbor as yourself'" (Jas 2:8).

But let me make my standard point one more time: our love for one another isn't our work. It's a response to God's love. "In this is love, not that we loved God but that he loved us. . . . We love because he first loved us" (1 John 4:10, 19). "As the Father has loved me, so I have loved you; abide [rest, revel, luxuriate] in my love. . . . I have said these things to you so that my joy [not your joy] may be in you, and that your joy [not your obligation] may be complete. This is my commandment, that you love one another as I have loved you" (John 15:9, 11–12; see also 2 Cor 5:14, 1 Thess 4:9).

This is the vision of church that we must reclaim.

LOVING ONE ANOTHER AND OUR MISSION

I deliberately organized the chapter as I have to make it clear that our love for each other is third. God's love for us is primary; everything good grows out of that. Then our love for God is secondary: we keep from getting enmeshed in the joyless duty of being good by being motivated by love for God. And then when God's love for us and our love for God are embedded in our deepest being, the third mark appears: then we are we freed to love one another by letting God's love overflow on others.

But to say that loving one another is third doesn't make it unimportant. It's the new commandment, the royal law, the summary and fulfillment of the law and the New Testament. John, Paul, and James say those things because of the inevitability of loving one another as we grasp God's love for us and begin to love him back.

It's easy to blather on about love, but it can quickly become meaningless talk. Apparently that had happened in the church 1 John was written to. So John says: "Those who say, 'I love God,' and hate their brothers or sisters, are liars" (1 John 4:20a; see also 1:6–7, 3:17–19, 4:7–8, not to mention most of the rest of the book). So the reality of God's love for us and our love for God (or the lack of them) are revealed in our love for each other (or the lack of it). That's how we tell love-blather from love. Which means that loving one another is central in our vision of church.

That is to say, though love for one another is third, it is the primary *visible mark* of church. God's love for us and our love for God are invisible except in their fruit—in our love for each other. That's why I practically started this book with, "By this everyone will know that you are my disciples, if you have love for one another" (John 13:35). Loving one another is the reality test for the first two.

And since loving one another is the primary visible mark of church, it's not going to be surprising if loving one another is important in evangelism: "By this everyone will know . . ." Loving one another goes to the heart of our mission. It's the key to calling others into the kingdom of God's beloved son. The key isn't apologetics, isn't verbal witness, isn't evangelistic rallies or street preaching or social action, isn't even loving our enemies; in fact, it's not even loving the person we're trying to evangelize.

It's loving each other.

Churches embodying love for one another is the key to carrying out our commission to make disciples of all nations.

Now, to keep loving one another from being just religious talk, we have an obligation to discipline ourselves into habits of practical love for our brothers and sisters. If we don't feel like doing it that day, we act anyway. If God's love isn't overflowing on us well that day (!), we fight ourselves and out of sheer duty practice specific acts of kindness toward our sisters and brothers. Till those practices become ingrained habits. Till we become people with a culture of love.

UNITY AND RECONCILIATION: JOHN 13–17

One of the annoying things about the Bible is its lack of sentimentality. Another is its failure to be airy fairy. As usual, so in this case: the Bible is annoyingly clear that love has less to do with warm fuzzies than it does with cleaning the toilet for a brother or sister. Or feeding them when they're hungry. Or dying for them.

But most Christians know that much, at least in theory. What we're less likely to know is even more annoying and even less airy fairy. It's that love shows itself in peace and reconciliation between people. People who love each other are at peace with each other; they're reconciled; they're in unity. They've let God deal with their resentments and coldness toward each other.

At least, that's what the Bible says. So Jesus started his long discourse in John by saying that people will know that we're his disciples by our love for each other, and he ends with what I take to be almost the same thought: "I ask . . . that [my followers] may all be one. As you, Father, are in me and I am in you, may they also be in us, so that the world may believe that you have sent me" (John 17:20–21). Here's how the world will know that Jesus is from God: when we're as at one with each other as the Trinity is.

We have here a clear indicator of the essence of love: unity. Unity isn't just not fighting. If our unity is to be like the Trinity's, it will also be warmth toward each other with no shadow of distance or resentment or irritation. And out of this will grow lack of conflict, or at least the conflict will be transformed.

We also have here a large hint why so much of the world hasn't believed our Messiah: we're too divided. We're too hostile toward fellow Christians. (And if you don't believe it, listen to the world, and notice how quickly they get to the folly of our divisions and dislike for each other.)

But to understate the matter a tad, all this is asking a lot. How can we possibly be as united as the Trinity? Yet as if to emphasize that he means it, Jesus repeats it a few verses later. He goes on to pray "that they may be one, as we are one, I in them and you in me, that they may become completely one, so that the world may know that you have sent me and have loved them even as you have loved me" (John 17:22b–23).

Completely one? I don't know about you, but personally, I could do without the adverb. Which brings us back to the central problem of this book, the central problem of life. How do we live with each other *completely* at peace? Does this text mean that Jesus thinks we shouldn't fight all the time with those we're close to? That we don't have to keep everyone at arm's length? That we shouldn't resent each other?

Yes. I suggest that reconciliation is the nature and purpose of church. Our function and form and vision and ministry and life. Our role is to be a demonstration plot where the world can observe unity and reconciliation. By our living together as a family at peace, the world will come to believe in the Messiah. And so far as the Bible tells us, there's no other way they'll come to believe.

The centrality of peace is already clear in the Hebrew Scriptures. Arguably, their organizing spiritual principle is shalom. Peace. Not just with the Philistines, and not just private peace of mind, but also (and maybe mostly) peace with each other. That's what it's all about. That's God's ultimate promise.

The centrality of peace and reconciliation to evangelism may seem strange, but if you think about it, what is the heart of the world's predicament? Isn't it our inability to get along with each other? Isn't unreconciliation at the heart of racism, divorce, war, and fights with neighbors, friends, and fellow workers? So the world needs us to be reconciled. It needs to see us living together—in peace.

That's our mission, our great commission, our vision. Love one another. Be at peace with one another. That's what church is. That's how we have to revision ourselves.

UNITY AND RECONCILIATION: EPHESIANS

Paul makes the same point in Ephesians. Only he's even more annoying. Not satisfied with Jesus' general prayer for unity, he makes it specific. He prays for (and promises) racial unity. This must have been at least as astonishing to first-century people, especially Jews, as it was in Montgomery, Alabama in 1963.

The heart of Ephesians is that God is calling together a people to live in unity and peace, a people to love him and each other. To Jews, that wasn't new news. As I've argued, Jews already knew that; it has always been God's plan for his people. Yet in Ephesians Paul talks about the mystery not made known in other ages (3:3–9). The news is that this loving people is to include Gentiles.[1] "Now in Christ Jesus you [Gentiles] who once were far off have been brought near by the blood of Christ. For he is our peace; in his flesh he has made both groups into one and has broken down the dividing wall, that is, the hostility between us" (Eph 2:13–14). Paul's vision is of a local church composed of Jews, Romans, African Americans, Latinos, Russians, Palestinians. All living in unity. With the dividing wall of hostility broken down. Not just mutual toleration, but out and out tenderheartedness with racial resentments and feelings of superiority laid aside. Laying our lives down for one another in mutual service.

Elsewhere, Paul makes it all too clear that this unity between formerly hostile groups isn't just between races. It also crosses gender lines, economic classes, the distinction between slave and free, communists and capitalists, liberals and conservatives. "There is no longer Jew or Greek, there is no longer slave or free, there is no longer

---

1. Of course, Isaiah already says it (see, for example, Isaiah 19) as do other parts of the Hebrew Bible. But few people got it.

male and female; for all of you are one in Christ Jesus" (Gal 3:28; see also Col 3:11; 1 Cor 12:13).

This is already close to the vision of love and unity in John 13 and 17, but Paul gets even closer to that vision when he gives the evangelistic significance of unity. By living in unity, this newly constituted family will "make everyone see what is the plan of the mystery hidden for ages in God who created all things; so that through the church the wisdom of God in its rich variety might now be made known to the rulers and authorities in the heavenly places" (Eph 3:9–10). They will know us by our unity.

Notice Paul goes even further than Jesus. It's not just that all people will know God's plan by racial unity; even angels will know it that way.

But how?

The theory is great. But the practice is a little tricky. How on earth are we supposed to do this? Especially since historically churches haven't been brilliant at unity. And while contemporary churches may be better at it than often in the past, we still come up far short. The thought of having to pull off love and reconciliation is overwhelming. Not to mention discouraging. So I've tried to structure this chapter (in fact, the whole book) so that the how question is already answered.

How do we pull it off?

We don't. God does. Or rather he already has. "I have made you a great nation." We couldn't do it if we wanted to. So fortunately it has been done once and for all in Jesus. Notice how clear this is in the key passage from Ephesians: "Now *in Christ Jesus* you [Gentiles] who once were far off have been brought near *by the blood of Christ.* For *he is our peace*; in *his* flesh *he* has made both groups into one" (Eph 2:13–14). He has already done it. One of the most amazing things about human beings is that we can read this passage as if it were giving us another thing we need to do. We read it as if it says: "Now you Gentiles who once were far off must bring yourselves near by your own efforts. For you must make your own peace; in your flesh you must make both groups into one . . ." (Eph 2:13–14, Radical Discipleship Human Effort Version, hereafter RDHEV, an extremely popular translation among all Christians, Protestant, Catholic, Orthodox, liberal, evangelical, charismatic, and fundamentalist).

No, this is something that's already done. In the past. "He *has* made both groups into one and *has* broken down the dividing wall." So we can relax and revel in our unity, which is already accomplished.

When and where were you saved? Not at an evangelistic rally when you were twelve, but one Easter weekend nearly two thousand years ago. On Calvary.

Without this understanding, we have no hope. With this understanding, we can have a ball. God has already worked decisively and unilaterally among us; so we can be confident that he will continue freely giving us everything else. Even the feeling of reconciliation.

The next step is to bask in God's love for us till it begins to overflow into our love for God. Then the next step is to let it overflow on all the people and groups that we really don't like and on the people we're close to (who all have such peculiar failings). And encourage them to know that God loves them and has already created a united people for them to be part of.

We can pray with Paul:

> I bow my knees before the Father, from whom every family in heaven and on earth takes its name. I pray that, according to the riches of his glory, he may grant that you may be strengthened in your inner being with power through his Spirit, and that Christ may dwell in your hearts through faith, as you are being rooted and grounded in love. I pray that you may have the power to comprehend, with all the saints, what is the breadth and length and height and depth, and to know the love of Christ that surpasses knowledge, so that you may be filled with all the fullness of God. Now to him who by the power at work within us is able to accomplish abundantly far more than all we can ask or imagine, to him be glory in the church and in Christ Jesus to all generations, forever and ever. Amen. (Eph 3: 14–21)

Did you hear that? Paul is talking about God's riches in glory, not our meager inner reserves. About the power of the Holy Spirit, not our pathetic fumbling. About our being rooted and grounded in love, not about our being rooted in depressing and depressed duty.

What a vision to reclaim! Rejoice, for the kingdom has come and is coming.

So we are free to work our tails off joyfully in unity and for unity.

The essence of our work for unity (as in contrast to God's already completed work), I spelled out in the chapter on death to self. Unity is no problem at all if I have died and Jesus is living in me. If I don't have to run the show but am content to wash the dishes, then unity happens. If someone else is opposed to eating meat and I'm willing to give meat up for the sake of their soul, then unity has already come. It's no accident that it's hard to tell whether 1 Corinthians is on church unity or on servanthood or on being crucified; that's because they're all the same topic.[2]

You see, unity isn't acquired by pounding out common statements of vision or by coming to cognitive agreement on things we disagree over. No, unity is a spirit, a spirit of joyfully serving the other, of wanting the best for them, of laying down competition and resentment. Then it's possible to begin discussing the issues—and occasionally coming to agreement on them. If our spirit has changed first. Or should I say Spirit? (1 Cor 12:13).

---

2. In the next chapter I will get more concrete by giving a specific example of racial reconciliation.

FIFTEEN

Straight Talk (Love and Unity Again)

Another mark of the people of God is straight talk. Where God is at work, people speak to each other frankly and kindly. Paul treats this as central to spiritual growth: "But speaking the truth in love, we must grow up in every way into him who is the head . . ." (Eph 4:15).

Jesus covers some of the same territory in Matthew 18. There he gives unusually detailed instructions on what to do when we know fellow Christians are sinning. The idea is that you go to them alone once, and then if they don't listen, you go to them with someone else; if they still don't listen, you involve the whole church. This not only helps the sinner grow spiritually but deals with the cancer of gossip (one of the opposites of unity).

In Eberhard Arnold's classic statement:

> Love means having joy in others. Then what does being annoyed with them mean?
>
> Words of love convey the joy we have in the presence of brothers and sisters. By the same token it is out of the question to speak about a brotherhood member in a spirit of irritation or vexation. There must never be talk, either in open remarks or by insinuations, against a brother or sister, against their individual characteristics—under no circumstances behind the person's back. Talking in one's own family is no exception.
>
> Without the rule of silence there can be no loyalty, no community. Direct address is the only way possible; it is the spontaneous brotherly service we owe anyone whose weaknesses cause a negative reaction in us. An open word spoken directly to the other person deepens friendship and is not resented. Only when two people do not come to agreement quickly in this direct manner is it necessary to talk it over with a third person who can be trusted to help solve the difficulty and bring about a uniting on the highest and deepest levels. (Matt 18:15–16)
>
> Each one in the household should hang this reminder up where he works and can see it all the time.[1]

Straight, loving talk is crucial to living together in peace. One of the reasons our churches don't live together in unity is that we don't practice this clear teaching of Jesus

---

1. Arnold, *God's Revolution*, 113–14.

and Paul. We don't follow the instructions, and so we wind up eating lunch on the infield instead of growing into the full stature of Christ.

Paul and saying the good stuff

I've heard many sermons on speaking the truth in love. For some reason, most all of them assume that speaking the truth in love means saying hard things. And while that's surely included, isn't saying good, encouraging things also the truth?

Much of straight talk is saying the good stuff.

We may imagine that it's easy to say the good things, that the hard part is confronting people. Perhaps, but that's not my experience. My experience is that an awful lot of people, especially men, have a terrible time saying the good things.

I heard an analysis of why Bill Clinton was elected and Bob Dole wasn't. It went something like this: If you're a male from Arkansas and like someone, you tell them so—clearly and extravagantly. But if you're a male from Kansas and you like someone, then you say, "That pickup you just bought is [four letter word] ugly; it's almost as ugly as your face." So Bob Dole lost the election.

You may think that's funny. And in politics it may be. But in church, it's not.

Now, as a male born and raised in Kansas, I feel a need to say that this is partly a problem of communication. It's not the fault of males from Kansas that people from Southern California don't grasp that insults are a way of declaring affection. But even giving due weight to that (which won't take long), more of us are from Kansas (or is it Mars?) than we like to admit. I'll bet that even most women from Arkansas could learn a lot about encouraging others. Which is a large part of telling the truth in love. (And by the way, don't bother to tell people about their sins if you aren't also telling them the good stuff, like the love God has for them.)

John Gottman has researched why marriages succeed.[2] He says that pop psychology notwithstanding, people can do all sorts of odd and obnoxious things to each other without undermining their marriages—with one proviso: they have to affirm each other five times as often as they criticize each other. Couples can yell and scream and caricature each other providing that soon thereafter they're having fun together and telling each other why they like each other. They can be as obnoxious as they like providing they're supportive five times as often.

Gottman maintains that a 5:1 ratio of good things to bad things is relatively precise. So couples who rarely praise each other will do OK providing they criticize even more rarely. And perhaps surprisingly, people who praise each other endlessly and criticize each other rarely are in trouble; they don't make it either, in Gottman's opinion, because they're skirting the problems all couples have with each other.

2. Gottman, *Why Marriages Succeed or Fail.*

Interesting. I'd bet this is a good indicator of healthy churches as well as of healthy marriages. Praise each other a lot. And don't forget to talk to people about their sins. But only one-fifth as often as you show them that you enjoy them.

That's essential in reclaiming church.

BUT IT BOTHERS ME

It's a dogma of most live-in groups and many small groups that you need to tell people if they do something that bothers you. In that discussion Matthew 18 is often cited. So communitarians and small groupies spend much of their time sitting around talking about how they make each other feel bad. We then try to work out compromises so that I can do the things I like while causing you minimum distress and vice versa. We wind up with mutual contracts where you agree to put soupspoons in the right place if I agree to put the toilet seat down.

This is fine, and in our church we certainly do a fair amount of it, but it's not the flow chart Judy worked out from 1 Corinthians. I don't think Paul was saying that if you disagree about eating meat offered to idols, then work out some way that you can all get what you want. No, he was asking us to lay down our lives for each other, to let ourselves be crucified.

Nor is it what Jesus said in Matthew 18. He just didn't say, "If someone bothers you, go and tell him when the two of you are alone." He says, "If someone sins," go tell the person.[3] And the last time I checked, bothering me isn't necessarily a sin. Christians need to get clear on this.

I suspect that the idea that telling people our feelings is important has more to do with romanticism and Freud's theory of repression than it does with Jesus. The notion that we need to express ourselves, that it's unhealthy not to act on our feelings, is not one of the major themes of Jesus or of any other part of the Bible. So why should it be a major part of doing church together?

Now, I suppose it's possible that a couple hundred years ago romantics and psychologists discovered something that had escaped all previous wise people. So Rousseau and Shelley and Freud (whose personal lives have to be ranked among the less stellar in world history) discovered the importance of expressing your feelings. But unfortunately, it's a point that was missed by the Bible.

Jesus is trying to get us to do something quite different. He's not asking us to express our feelings (unless perhaps they're good feelings), and he's not offering a technique to maximize people getting their preferences. Instead he's asking us to focus on the spiritual state of other Christians to help them grow. If we see them sinning, he wants us to find a way to talk to them about it so they won't get even more messed up. But he doesn't spend a lot of time on how other people make us feel. The question for

---

3. Some texts have sin "against you," but that's omitted in many of the best manuscripts. So it's omitted in the NASB.

Jesus isn't what bothers you about someone, but what does that person need in order to grow spiritually?

That's different. So before you go to tell folks something hard, ask whether you're concerned mostly about their spiritual state. Are you dealing with sin, or do they just annoy you? If it's annoyance, stay home. If you believe they're sinning and you love them enough that you're concerned for *them*, go talk to them. It will add to unity. Otherwise, stay home.

The purpose isn't to lessen your annoyance but to rescue your sister or brother.

RESCUING LOST SHEEP

That brings us to the context of Jesus' teaching in Matthew 18. Without the context, we're liable to read Jesus as giving us the legal procedure for excommunication: Talk to the person about sin. Then, if that step fails, get another person to go with you so you have a witness against her for the final step, which is to bring it to the whole church, at which point she will be excommunicated. But that's not the context.

That sort of reading at least counts as reading the directions. So perhaps I should cheer, but my observation is that literalistic, quasi-legal readings of the Bible are death dealing. And reading Jesus that way is (for some reason) especially death dealing—at least as death dealing as overlooking what he says. In fact, my experience is that reading this passage quasi-legally is a primary cause of the death of many serious churches.

The context makes it clear why. In the passage just before the one we're working on, Jesus tells about the shepherd who has a hundred sheep and loses one (18:12–14). The shepherd is so concerned about the one lost sheep that he leaves the ninety-nine and goes out to look for the one. And when he finds it, he rejoices over that one more than over all the others.

Only then does Jesus tell us how to approach someone in sin. So part of his instructions are to talk to people who are sinning out of deep compassion. In hope of rescuing lost sheep. Isn't that what he's saying? Isn't he telling us, "Don't go in annoyance, frustration, or anger. Go like a shepherd concerned for his sheep." That's the spirit of Matthew 18. Otherwise, you'll add to disunity.

Notice how different this is from going to straighten someone out. And notice how far removed it is from a courtroom procedure. We're not trying to prove we're right, as in court. We're trying to rescue the person from disaster. That's a different spirit. The Spirit that leads to unity.

FORGIVENESS

Then Jesus gives us the outlines of the famous procedure for talking to individuals about their sin. Immediately, bright young Peter misses the point again. He asks how often we should forgive each other: "Lord, if another member of the church sins against me, how often should I forgive? As many as seven times?" (Matt 18:21).

Or is Peter missing the point? I doubt it. Peter has understood that Jesus' instructions are mostly about forgiveness. When you talk to someone about their sin, it usually doesn't go well. So, Peter asks, Should we talk to them seven times before we excommunicate them? (Peter is oh, so generous.)

But Jesus is not impressed. He suggests that seventy times seven would be more appropriate. (A number that is quickly reached if you live with someone more than a month.) That's how many steps there are in struggling with a sister's sin: 490, where 490 isn't a limit to forgiveness but an indicator that our generosity in forgiveness needs to be excessive.

To put it more cautiously, instructions on talking to people who have sinned is put next to a passage about forgiving them 490 times. It tells us the spirit we need to have when talking to people about their sin. A Spirit of forgiveness, grace, patience. Matthew 18 tells us how patient we need to be with people who don't get it.

Very.

We talk to brothers assuming we'll have to forgive them for their sin. Then we'll have to forgive them again. And again. And again. And that will be OK.

Lest we miss the point, Jesus pounds it home by telling a parable, the one about the unjust steward (18:23–35). This is the guy who owes the king a million dollars, and the king forgives him the debt. The steward then goes out and refuses to forgive another guy who owes him a few bucks.

That's who we're not supposed to be. We have been forgiven much; we should forgive much. As the bumper sticker says, "I'm not perfect; I'm forgiven." So we are freed to forgive. It should be easy for us to have this spirit since we've had to be forgiven so many times ourselves.

The church is a culture of having been forgiven. Therefore we can also be a culture of grace and forgiveness toward others. For grace and forgiveness are just another way of talking about love. Which is just another way of talking about unity. This is the vision we need to reclaim.

Humility

One more piece of context. Matthew 18 begins with the disciples asking Jesus who is greatest in the kingdom. Jesus answers by taking a child and saying, "Unless you change and become like children, you will never enter the kingdom of heaven. Whoever becomes humble like this child is the greatest in the kingdom of heaven" (Matt 18:3–4).

Now I've spent too much of my life around children to have a romantic view of them. While I usually like children, it has never been obvious to me that their qualities are to be indiscriminately admired and strenuously copied. Average children are at least as selfish as average adults, and what's more they haven't learned to hide it yet.

Furthermore, they're given to whining and moaning and fighting for imaginary rights. Not especially Christian virtues.

So Jesus can't be praising the general behavior of children. He is being specific, and the one quality of children that he specifies is humility. ("Whoever becomes humble like this child.") But if Jesus is teaching that children have mastered moral humility, I'm still puzzled. (I've known more than a few children who were arrogant.) So Jesus is almost surely not talking about a moral virtue of children but about the role of children in Mideastern society. Which was pretty low: that is, pretty humble. Much lower than in our culture. They were to be seen and not heard. They had no power. No legal rights. They were the property of their father (in ways that are appalling). It was the elderly who were respected and who had status and power. Kids were nothing.

So Jesus is telling his disciples: Here's how to get someplace in the kingdom—take the lowest place with the least status and power. In other words, become an outcast; take the role of a slave and wash everyone's feet. That's the route to reconciliation. (Perhaps Paul read Matthew 18 just before writing 1 Corinthians!)

So that's the context of going to talk to those who have sinned against you. Jesus mustn't be read as giving us a legal procedure whereby for your own sake you righteously drag your brother to court to straighten him out or to punish him for his failures. Jesus is calling instead for a servant who first washes the person's dishes and then (after a little bowing and scraping the way servants do) says something like: "I wonder if you've ever wondered whether the sort of thing you did the other day might be sin?" And when the person pays no attention, the servant is no more surprised than a little Mideastern boy in AD 30 when his father doesn't give him what he asks for.

Oh, by the way, this model works better than the quasi-legal approach.

Doing it

Only when we have emphasized humility, compassion, and forgiveness as Jesus did, only when we have emphasized encouragement, can we go on to talk to people about their sin. However, in the midst of all these qualifications, don't miss the point of Matthew 18:15: Jesus does say to tell people when they sin. We should do it in a spirit of humility and love, no matter how often they've sinned, but we should do it. It's important, important like rescuing lost sheep.

And forgiveness and humility and love don't imply pretending that people don't sin—against me or against others. I'm not loving a person if I let my brother sin repeatedly without telling him. In fact, love mandates telling people when they sin. You wouldn't be loving your kids if you saw them playing on the freeway during rush hour and let them continue. And sin is often as serious as playing on the freeway.

Jesus is saying, "Talk to people when they sin. God is not concerned about whether they can distinguish between teaspoons, soupspoons, and tablespoons. So you shouldn't be either. But you should be concerned when they sin. And then you should go talk to them alone in love, humility, and forgiveness."

Now, as you may have guessed by the way I'm writing about this, I'm not someone who enjoys telling individuals things they don't want to hear. I don't mind doing it if I can hide behind a pulpit or a book, but I'm a ten on conflict avoidance when I'm talking to someone alone. But Jesus thinks it's important.

A HARD SAYING THAT'S EASY

Having acknowledged the difficulty, I want to say that this hard saying turns out like most of the hard things Jesus says. They seem impossible but turn out to be freedoms.

> "Come to me, all you that are weary and are carrying heavy burdens, and I will give you rest. Take my yoke upon you, and learn from me; for I am gentle and humble in heart, and you will find rest for your souls. For my yoke is easy, and my burden is light." (Matt 11:28–30)

The unity Jesus assumes isn't so hard after all.

Since I'm a major conflict-avoider, Jesus' words sound like words of doom to me. But they turn out to be great. Instead of having to be angry at people for their sin, I'm freed to just go talk to them about it. Instead of having to feel superior to sinners and fight for my image to be better than theirs, I'm freed to take my place alongside them as a brother—not at all superior. Instead of having to fight not to gossip about people's weaknesses, I can just talk directly to them. It's a release.

Part of the reason is that it turns out not to be all that hard. In a culture of grace and forgiveness, it turns out that you talk quite openly and easily about each other's sins. Well, "easily" may be too strong, but it's doable. In such a culture, talking straight isn't something we do out of a terrible obedience to Jesus; it's something that grows naturally among a group who together are experiencing the love and forgiveness of God.

After all, close to the heart of our story is the notion that we all sin badly and often and that God loves us anyway. And having experienced his love for sinners, we're to model ourselves on that experience. So we have no need to hide that we're sinners—for two reasons. First, because everyone knows it anyway. Second (and even more important) because we've learned that our being loved doesn't depend on a fake image of goodness. People's admiration for me may depend on my projecting an impressive image, but my being loved is destroyed by my projecting images of myself. So when someone talks to me about my sin, we may disagree on the details, but we both know going into it that my sins are probably far worse than the other person has any idea of. This frees both of us to talk openly and kindly. Without embarrassment or tension. Almost without much interest. We're all in the same boat.

So the starting point for a culture of straight talk is clear, regular teaching on the love of God, the continuing sinfulness of his people, and how the two connect. Then you get people to talk about their own sins in public, to let each other in on that. And you have small groups (very small groups, maybe of three or four) where you talk freely about each others' sins. The Church of the Sojourners had a breakthrough in developing this sort of culture when Judy assigned each of us to figure out our core sin, talk about it, and explain how particular sins grew from it. From then on, without my quite noticing it, I gave the people who knew my core sins permission to talk to me about that sin. (Well, at least it wasn't quite as big a struggle to give the permission from then on.)

And I no longer needed to avoid talking to those folks about their sin. We both knew; so it wasn't conflict.

TEFLON AND ALL THAT

But I didn't figure this out by studying theology. My first clue was noticing that some people are Teflon coated. That is, they can confront people about sin without getting blamed for it, without stuff sticking to them. And other people can hardly say anything. I'm not certain what all is involved in this, but parts seem clear.

One thing I noticed is that a Teflon-coated person isn't annoyed when she talks to people about their sin. She talks as matter-of-factly as if she were discussing the weather. She communicates little or no negative emotional load, and when the folks respond to her, they're freed not to dump an emotional load back. That is, people often speak back as they're spoken to. Which isn't surprising, especially in this case. After all, people usually have a pretty good idea of their sin; so if you mention it like it's something everyone already knows (which it usually is), they hardly notice you've said anything, and you can talk about it the way an optometrist talks to a client.

Recently, I had an appointment with my optometrist. He looked in my eyes and flashed lights at me for a while, and then proceeded to say quite calmly that I had the beginnings of cataracts. I wasn't unduly pleased, but neither did I feel any need to yell at him.

How do you suppose I would have responded if he had gotten angry at me for having cataracts? If he had yelled at me?

Now, I have confidence in this observation of mine: not being annoyed gives you some Teflon. That's obvious. But I have more confidence because I think it's said in Matthew 18. Go in compassion and forgiveness, not in anger and annoyance: we're all sinners.

The approach works. And it makes Jesus' yoke easy. To put it succinctly, if you make people feel loved, you can tell them most anything.[4]

A second thing that seems to give people Teflon is humility. If you come in as superior, knowing it all, then telling someone the truth about their sin will often cause

4. Although telling people all you feel isn't commanded in the Bible, if we develop a culture of speaking straight and kindly, then telling people that something bothers us will often be natural and appropriate. But we should be careful if we find ourselves spending hours sitting around talking to each other about how we feel and how we can all get our way; then we're doing something other than working on living out the reconciliation Christ has provided for us.

bitter division. But if you talk like we're all in this together, like you're as big a screw-up as she is, like you know you don't have all the pieces, like this time around you may well be wrong both in the details and in general and that you certainly could be wrong about the motives—if that's your spirit, then the person is freed to own quite a lot.

Much of it is being able to be wrong. We're all wrong a lot, of course, but being able to own it soon and openly is a great gift to others. (It's an even greater gift to yourself, but never mind). The question is how you react if you tell a brother how he's sinned and he gives you a reasonable explanation that gets him off the hook. Are you then pleased that this sin you thought you had observed doesn't exist? Or are you upset that you're wrong, that he got off the hook? Our stance must be hope that we're wrong and the other person right. That's the spirit that brings unity. And it allows people to chat about their sin as matter-of-factly as about the weather. This of course is merely an embodiment of Jesus' comments about the child and of his story about the unforgiving servant.

Another way of saying it is that a person is Teflon coated if she goes in treating the other person as Teflon coated, treating the other person as someone whose sin won't stick to him. Then the person is freed to grow through the sin.

PRESSURE COOKER

Some groups develop a culture where they can talk straight to each other, where in fact sin doesn't stick to anyone. Other groups develop a culture of judgment and anger; such groups become pressure cookers—places where any sin, difference, or disagreement causes tension, pressure, and explosion. This is especially common in live-in churches that are taking Jesus oh so seriously. They're not like standard churches who never read the instructions.[5] They're more likely to explode. How ironic. We exist to live in unity like a body and wind up splattering each other all over the walls.

Unfortunately, much of this is sociologically inevitable. To live as a body means rejecting one of the deepest underpinnings of Western culture—individualism. Who is going to undertake this? Not to put too fine a point on it, those who consciously reject their own culture are almost certain to be rank individualists. What chance do individualists have of living as a body?

To say the same thing in different words, who will leave buildings with steeples to start living as a body? Especially at first, won't it be mostly those who are independent, critical, dissatisfied malcontents? These are precisely the people who are constitutionally incapable of forming into a functioning institution, let alone a functioning body.

So those who lead such bodies will have to spend the first ten years teaching and trying to practice love, grace, interdependence, contentment, and unity. A church dies

---

5. In the Anabaptist tradition, telling people their sin is often called the rule of Christ. I find that frightening, the sort of thing that poisons a church. Matthew 18 as a whole might be the rule of Christ, but not those few verses. And anyway, if we're to call something the rule of Christ, it should be to love God and our neighbor. Or to love one another the way Jesus loved us.

when a spirit of criticism and judgment rules. It dies when I know how to do it and no one else does. That church becomes a pressure cooker. To flourish, its members will have to unlearn deep habits of carping and become people of grace, contentment, and gentleness. They're a people who will learn to affirm five times more than they criticize.

Teflon, not pressure.

In other words, we're not about fixing each other. Obviously, we hope to help each other grow, but that's different from fixing broken equipment. If you're fixing a broken machine and can't get a nut off, you take a hammer and chisel to it. That's not growth. In life together, if a brother doesn't get it and continues a sin, the temptation is to use a hammer and chisel on him. And if that doesn't work, you get a bigger hammer. Which isn't what Jesus was telling us to do. He was talking about compassion and forgiveness and humility. (Those who call for a bigger hammer are normally lacking in both humility and grace.) Jesus calls for something more like watering a plant, fertilizing it, putting it in the sun, and leaving it to grow. From time to time, you have to pull weeds, but a plant will die if that's all you do. Better to have it growing so fast it outgrows the weeds.

One characteristic of a pressure cooker is haste. They cook faster than a regular pan. Likewise in life together. We're usually in a hurry. If there's a conflict, we want to get through it fast. That's understandable, often praiseworthy, but I gave up on that some years ago. That was when the leadership of a community I was close to knocked on a couple's door at 11:00 PM and told them they wanted to get things settled before any of them went to sleep. Around 2:00 AM, the couple decided to leave the community. No amount of mediation helped. My reading was that if they'd all gone to sleep at 10:00, by morning the conflict would have been half over. But by 2:00 AM, it was too late.

I'm conflict avoidant, of course, and you can't let things go forever, as Judy often has to tell me. But wounds take time to heal, and in my experience the Spirit of God often works slowly. Give people the time and space to grow.

Notice how little Jesus hassled his disciples. And it wasn't because they were so good. He watered them instead. And shone on them.

INTENSITY

Maybe the key thing I've been learning personally over the last few years at Church of the Sojourners is that I often kill things by getting intense. If people are being wrong-headed about something important, I tell them so directly and with intensity. I'm told I don't sound much like I'm discussing the weather. I'm not mostly angry when I get intense; I mostly just really, really want people to agree with me. Suddenly it seems obvious to me that everyone should be able to see that we're, let's say, too crowded to take in anyone else for emergency housing.

I express no doubts. I leave no room for disagreement. I want everyone to agree with me right away. My voice gets louder (or quieter). I shut everything else out and focus entirely on whoever I'm "talking" to. I'm unwilling to be wrong (or wronged). All discussion seems like a waste of time to me. Not only am I right, but the issue is also clear and of the utmost importance.

Normally other people retire before the force of my, uh, personality. Either that or we have a fight. Unity is not reached.

Often my intensity is silly, and I see pretty soon that the issue isn't important. But at least occasionally the issue is genuinely important, and I'm right that it will have a lasting effect on the health of our little church. Am I supposed to discuss it as if it didn't matter? Should newscasters announce the start of World War III in the same measured tones they announce the weather? I doubt it.

But the rest of the church is clear that when I get intense, the meeting is over. Or I have to repent. Or leave. (They're capable of sending me out, I'm glad to say.) And my experience is that when I get like that, we can't reach meaningful consensus on anything.

To date, I'm not sure I understand this well. But I think it's mostly a matter of my trying to control things. I'm forcing my way, not listening to others, not serving in humility, not trusting the Holy Spirit to rule. After a meeting where I do that, I go to bed exhausted and feeling misunderstood.

This is precisely the opposite of Matthew 18. If you talk to folks about their sin with the sort of intensity I've described, even if you're right, they won't listen. And your church will not be growing in the grace of God. Even if you're right, it's grace that brings growth, not straightening people out.

Grace.

WHEN THE RUBBER HITS THE ROAD

Let me give a different sort of illustration. One about how racial reconciliation is experienced between people. One of the great burdens and greater joys of Judy's and my life was counseling Spencer Perkins and Chris Rice about their relationship.[6] Their primary visible role in the church at large was modeling racial reconciliation. Spencer (who died suddenly of a heart attack in January, 1998) was African American, and Chris is European American. They wrote a book together on racial reconciliation, put out a magazine on racial reconciliation, traveled around the country speaking on racial reconciliation, and were part of Antioch, the only interracial, Protestant community in the United States.

Trouble was, they didn't get along. Naturally, this was embarrassing. What's more, their conflicts had a lot to do with race. Which made it very embarrassing. Like marriage counselors filing for divorce. Or child psychologists with wretched kids.

---

6. Editor's Note: Chris Rice has written about his relationship with Spencer Perkins and the lessons they learned from John and Judy Alexander in *Grace Matters: A True Story of Race, Friendship, and Faith in the Heart of the South.*

So they felt unworthy. We evangelicals are good at that. We feel unworthy. Spencer and Chris were right, of course. They were unworthy. In fact, they were a mess. They called Judy and me in, hoping we could fix them. Well, if I may say so myself, we failed. When we were done, they were still a mess. As we all are.

However, Chris and Spencer also approached greatness. Not because they got fixed, but because before it was over they accepted God's grace. They finally got it. Finally they figured out the gospel. They figured out that being a mess is just part of the story. It's very freeing, grasping that being a mess is OK. I don't know about you, but I can't do much about being a mess. And neither could Spencer and Chris. They really wanted to fix each other so they could tell others how to fix race relations, but the harder they tried, the more they failed.

Then they decided to accept each other instead. Accept each other before they were fixed. "While we were yet sinners, Christ died for us" (Rom 5:8, KJV). Just as I am, without one plea. That's how Jesus accepts us; that's how we need to accept each other. That's how Spencer and Chris did accept each other.

To return to the topic at the end of the last chapter, that's the only way racial reconciliation happens in practice. Or any other kind of reconciliation for that matter. That's how people in churches become one. Accepting each other before they're fixed.

You see, Chris and Spencer were sinners. They were also forgiven. And that's almost the only thing that matters. The rest is details. That we white people often, uh, annoyed Spencer isn't important. That African Americans often annoy Chris isn't important. Almost the only thing that matters is that Spencer and Chris were sinners whom God loved. Whom God had forgiven. And here's the only other thing about them that matters: they knew it. In the end they understood that they were sinners whom God loved and had forgiven. Then they were freed to accept each other in grace.

It's odd to say that they knew this grace only toward the end, because they'd known it for decades. Grace, after all, is the central doctrine of us evangelicals. Yet somehow we often convey judgment and condemnation. We say grace is central, but we aren't known for our deep sense of being loved by a God of grace, nor are we especially known for that love overflowing from us onto those around us. We're more likely to overflow disapproval and our need to fix others.

As that changes we will become a reconciled people—accepting each other, not fixing each other. Not making the other person acceptable first, and then accepting them. Not confronting them till they get it, not waiting for the other person to repent before accepting them.

That's what Spencer and Chris did. While they were both still a mess, they were reconciled. And they started telling people that that's the heart of racial reconciliation. African Americans have to accept European Americans while we're still racists. And European Americans have to accept African Americans just as they are, rather than moving into the city to fix them. That's at the heart of Ephesians' teaching on the reconciled church.

P<small>ANIC</small>

Of course, people get panicky at the mere suggestion of not fixing each other. Won't you lose control of people if you do that? (Well, it feels that way, doesn't it? But when was the last time you controlled anyone anyhow?) Won't they take advantage of you? (Sometimes. Pretty often in fact.) You mean you're just going to let people sin? (As if you can do anything else.)

White evangelicals just can't stand the idea of not fixing African Americans. I thought this was just white racism, part of the disease of us white people, that we have a deep need to fix everybody and everything. And then without thinking, I made the parallel point to some African Americans: They shouldn't expect to change us white people; they need to accept us as we are.

You think white people need to fix black people? Let me tell you, apparently the feeling is mutual. After I said that, I thought for a minute I was going to get lynched. But the folks I said it to were nice, and so they just writhed on the floor.

Writhing is, I think, the universal human response to grace. "What shall we say then? Shall we continue in sin, that grace may abound?" (Rom 6:1). Paul anticipated that response when he gave his classic explanation of grace. People would panic at the notion of grace (to others) and think it would make sin expand and expand.

But Paul's answer is the right one: "God forbid" (Rom 6:2). We all have deep needs to control people, to fix them, and we have the imaginary idea that we can do it by holding out on them emotionally till they've become good people. And if anyone suggests anything else, we writhe. But the fact is that insofar as we can fix people at all, help them sin less, we do it by giving them grace and leaving them to our loving father. But that's almost entirely foreign to human nature.

A few months before Spencer's death, he and Chris got fed up with each other. They called us to say they were close to quitting. Chris wasn't getting fixed, and neither was Spencer. (Well, that's not quite what they said; they're more sophisticated than that.) Could we come help? This time, however, they'd wised up. They'd figured out we weren't going to fix them. But would we come hold their hands while they broke up? (That's not what they said either; they were good Christians, but that's how it felt.)

So we flew down to Jackson, Mississippi (their home) with all the joy of people going to get seven teeth pulled. Spencer and his wife, Nancy, met us at the plane, and on the way to the house we told them they had to give Chris permission to leave. Spencer had to give up the dream of his life. He had to give up modeling racial reconciliation. He had to give up on the only genuinely interracial Protestant community in the United States. What he had to do was extend grace to Chris.

He told us that if he did that, Chris would leave. We told him that Chris was going to leave anyway and that he might as well let him go graciously, that there was no point holding their relationship together by emotional intimidation. If he let Chris go, if he released him, he wouldn't have to spend the next twenty years hating him.

And it might free Chris to stay.

Well, over the next few days, we had meetings and we had meetings. Chris and Spencer were both jerks. All kinds of garbage came out. They were hopeless. Like all of us. The bottom was a meeting in Chris's office—just them and us. Chris was such a jerk I thought Spencer was going to punch him. Chris was probably just as angry, but that didn't worry me. White men can't jump, let alone fight. But in high school, Spencer was an all-Mississippi power forward, and over the years he hadn't gotten any smaller.

Afterwards, Spencer freed Chris to leave. Which freed Chris to stay. Which he did. That's how the Gospel works. People respond when they are loved and accepted.

Like flowers. They grow when they're watered and given sunshine. Not when they're hacked at and beaten.

Like children. They thrive when they're respected and adored. Not when they're yelled at and abhorred.

ACCEPTANCE

Now I've talked a lot about acceptance, which is a tricky word. A favorite of secular psychologists, for whom there is no sin. I'm OK, you're OK. Positive reinforcement, no spanking. Talk yourself into thinking that everything is fine.

That's not grace. That's idiocy. And it's certainly not what I'm talking about. Grace assumes evil. Deep and horrible evil. Racial hatred. Battered children. Couples once in love turning to hate. So when we asked Chris and Spencer to accept each other, we didn't mean they were OK and just didn't see it. We meant that neither of them was OK, and Jesus had taken care of it. Jesus has already died for them. For each of them. Their job was to forgive each other and take care of each other while trusting God instead of themselves or each other.

You don't do that by persuading yourself the other person is good. You do it by understanding that you're as big a mess as the person you're struggling to fix. You're in the same boat together. That way you don't have to feel superior to them anymore; you're freed to bring them coffee.

That's one of the few how-tos in the New Testament. It's the parable about a man forgiven a huge debt who refused to forgive another person a small debt. Persuade yourself that you're as bad as the other person, not that he or she is as good as you. Think about what a pain you are to live with. That sounds depressing to secular psychologists, of course. Because it is if we aren't in the hands of a loving God who has taken care of our sin.

RACE RELATIONS

So does this mean that justice doesn't matter? Should blacks just let us whites off the hook and not tell us how we've sinned? Well, no.

Chris thought he worked harder than Spencer. It wasn't fair. Their conferences would never come together if Chris worked 9:00 to 5:00. Spencer had no drive. It wasn't fair.

At Spencer's funeral, a white activist told of coming to see Spencer and finding him watching the Chicago Bulls with his family. He reported his pleasure that Spencer took time out of his busy schedule to watch the Bulls with his family. Well, maybe the activist had it backwards. Maybe Spencer took time away from watching the Bulls (and fishing with his son) to work on his sweeping vision of reconciliation. Which was great for his family, but tough on Chris.

Supposing that that interpretation is true (and I don't finally know), should Chris have just accepted it? Well, no.

White people are racists. It comes out of the hide of African Americans. Should black people just accept it? Well, no.

People of grace speak the truth. We talk straight. We call sinners to repentance as concisely as Jesus did. We talk about justice as bluntly as Malcolm X did.

But with grace and love. With forgiveness before it's asked, before the person has repented, before the person even knows he or she is a sinner. We talk about justice, not as a superior helping a hopeless idiot, but from the boat we're all in.

And the time comes, "if the offender refuses to listen even to the church" that we treat "such a one . . . as a Gentile and a tax collector."[7] But not nearly as soon as Peter or most of us would like.

So we all need to be learning to speak gently, knowing that we're as bad as the people we're calling to repentance. However, we also need to be learning to speak all the more clearly because people of grace know how bad sin is. We aren't denying sin's existence or trying to ignore it. We're forgiving it and matter-of-factly pointing it out.

As I have come to understand grace a little, I have become more honest. Less apologetic as I speak hard truth. And as Antioch came to understand grace a little, they became blunter with each other. They talked about things that they didn't dare mention before.

It may seem odd, but in a context of grace truth seems less offensive and more important. If you love someone, you can't bear not to tell them how they're messing up their lives. (Which is a different dynamic from telling someone to straighten up because they aren't living up to your high standards.) If you all know you're sinners, it's no big deal to tell each other how you're sinning; at most you're quibbling over trivial details. (Which is a different dynamic from talking to people who need to defend themselves against attacks on their self-esteem/self-righteousness.) If you know you're a sinner like everyone else, other sinners will feel less put down when you mention who they really are. (It's a different dynamic from a superior fixing an inferior.) If you've given up the need to control, others will feel less need to fight you. (It's a different dynamic from nagging, which escalates to threats, which escalates to breaking off the relationship.) If

7. See also 1 Corinthians 5–6.

you talk about people's failures as matter-of-factly as about the weather, they'll have an easier time not reacting with frenzy. If you talk about their successes five times as much as their failures. If you let them talk about your failures.

Once again, it's like with children. They need to be loved, part of which is telling them the truth about how to live, telling them clearly when they screw up. Without rejecting them. A child who is given no limits isn't being loved or given grace. Neither is an adult.

Let's learn to speak the truth in love and grace.

Not that grace is guaranteed to work. The human race provides ample evidence of that. I don't recall a lot of Pharisees repenting after Jesus forgave them from the cross. Few white people have ever repented of their racism.

But it beats the alternatives. One big alternative is shaming. Another is control. If I hold onto my anger and flash my disapproval enough, I'll be able to control people, I'll be able to fix them.

You will? When was the last time it worked for you?

In racial reconciliation meetings activists are likely to try to persuade whites that they're bad, that they're rotten people who can only be accepted when they're good enough to almost be African Americans. This is a pleasant change from hearing whites talk as if African Americans will only be accepted when they're almost good enough to be white. But where is the Gospel in all this? This isn't grace; it's shaming.

Perhaps we evangelicals understand the gospel and grace when it comes to personal salvation. But we rarely practice grace when it comes to race or day-to-day human relationships. When Christians are addressing race or politics or psychology, we aren't being Christian unless we're constantly mentioning Jesus and grace and the cross and accepting suffering.

But we understand the gospel so little that in relation to race we can't imagine a good alternative to treating whites as inferior for their racism. If we can't just tell them off, the only thing left is explaining to them that African Americans aren't as bad as whites think they are, that the stereotypes are untrue. We're all nice people. (We hear a lot of this in race relations conferences, too.) Now there's a lot of truth in this, but it's not the gospel. It's not grace. I can't remember Jesus trying to persuade the Pharisees to accept tax collectors and sinners on the grounds that they weren't so bad, that they were as good as the Pharisees.

In this mess together

The way of the cross is knowing that white people are a mess and black people are a mess. We're all in this mess together. Whites sure aren't superior, but neither are blacks. In this we're equal. We need to persuade whites not that blacks aren't so bad but that whites are as bad as blacks and blacks are as bad as whites. We aren't going to fix each other; God is going to have to do that. Jesus wants to save us, and he can only do that when we've all come to the end of ourselves. The only way out is to forgive each other, love each other, hold each other, speak the truth to each other—while trusting God to grow us up together into the fullness of the stature of Christ.

Let me put it this way. Several decades ago, I was at a race relations conference with an African American friend. One afternoon he came running up to me (we were much younger then) and said, "The black caucus is meeting. Let's go." Now, I was deeply honored that for a brief moment he forgot what color I was. I liked being an honorary black man.

But I am not black.

And I'm not just talking about my skin color. I am a white male to the core of my being. Some of this is fine, but some of it needs to be repented of. I fit the white male stereotype: for example, I am driven. And people who aren't irritate me. Even when I'm trying to relax, I work hard. My favorite form of relaxation is running till I'm exhausted. And I watch the 49ers with the intensity of someone who believes his eternal salvation depends on their making a touchdown on every play.

With the love and support of my wife, I'm trying to repent of this. She figured out a long time ago that it would take me a couple hundred years, that she'd have to accept the pain of that or file for divorce. I will be a white man to the day I die. That's a cross that others have to bear for me. It comes out of their hide.

And Spencer was a black man to the day he died, and Chris will be a white man.

As much as I liked being an honorary black man for a moment, that's not what I need. I'm not going to earn that very often or for very long, and I don't have to. I'd like to, mind you. I'd like to earn my own salvation. Be a perfect model. But I keep screwing up. So what I need is to be forgiven, a forgiven white man.

That's the best I can do. It's the best Chris can do. That's what Spencer offered in the end. He forgave us.

Only something like that can lead to a reconciled church, racially reconciled or reconciled any other way. It's all about grace and love: talking straight and lovingly.

SIXTEEN

Rebellion, Submission, and Cooperation (Love and Unity Yet Again)

The goal of God's universe is unity and love. Which means that the essence of the human predicament is our failure to be united and loving. Which means that the role of church is to live out unity and love with one another. This is the essential vision that we need to reclaim for church.

So this book is about helping us become who we're meant to be—a people of unity and love. One step toward this is to name correctly the source of our disunity. This the Bible does in several ways. One name the Bible gives this source is rebellion. We cannot be united, we cannot love one another, because we have rebellious spirits. Our spirits are rebellious with God and with each other. And those with rebellious spirits can't work well with one another.

To modern people, this concern with rebellion sounds extremely odd (supposing they hear it at all). Our nation grew out of rebellion, and much of Western culture is based on rebellion. We believe that the horror of Nazi Germany and the Vietnam War could have been prevented if people had been more rebellious. So "Question authority" is a popular bumper sticker; "Question questioning authority" is not. Which means that if they understand it, many people in our culture find the Bible's analysis of the core human problem somewhere between offensive and foolishly archaic.

But I suggest that the story of Adam and Eve, virtually the first story in the Bible, goes deeper than any other in explaining the human predicament. Our culture's failure to appreciate this story merely shows how far we've fallen from wisdom, how enamored we are with disunity. To witness to Christ in our fallen, rebellious culture, we need to lead lives that are the opposite of rebellion. Only that will produce love and unity.

A cognitive critique of rebellion has little chance of getting past our cultural defenses. So let's look at rebellion in story form, the story of Adam and Eve:

> Now the serpent was more crafty than any other wild animal that the LORD God had made. He said to the woman, "Did God say, 'You shall not eat from any tree in the garden'?" The woman said to the serpent, "We may eat of the fruit of the trees in the garden; but God said, 'You shall not eat of the fruit of the tree that is in the middle of the garden, nor shall you touch it, or you shall die.'" But

the serpent said to the woman, "You will not die; for God knows that when you eat of it your eyes will be opened, and you will be like God, knowing good and evil." So when the woman saw that the tree was good for food, and that it was a delight to the eyes, and that the tree was to be desired to make one wise, she took of its fruit and ate; and she also gave some to her husband, who was with her, and he ate. (Gen 3:1–6)

Those few verses say it all, beautifully and succinctly. In fact, they tell my own story. And much of the story of humanity. Eve knew perfectly well what God had said. She also knew perfectly well that God had given her all the other fruit in the garden. That is, she knew perfectly well that God loved her and was taking good care of her. So she had every reason to believe that God's telling her not to eat this one fruit grew out of his love for her. But no, she wanted more. Not the good things that God had already given her in abundance, but something that looked good that God had kindly forbidden. It would make her like God. So she rebelled from God's clear and loving instructions. In favor of her own preferences. In favor of her desire to have it all. In favor of her desire to be God. She knew best. That is the human predicament. The will to power. Covetousness. Unbelief. The desire to be above others. Lack of contentment no matter how good things are.

I love to study and write and teach, and I do them well. I'd love to sit in coffee houses most waking hours, studying and writing. Books are easier to deal with than people; so except for my family (and not always them), I prefer the sort of minimal human contact you have with the people you know in coffee houses. You see, I'm not comfortable talking to people one-on-one. I stuttered when I was a kid and was a nerd. One-on-one, people scare me.

Meanwhile, Church of the Sojourners has asked me to spend much of my time pastoring, mentoring, and talking to people—many of whom are even more troubled than I am.

I'd rather collect garbage.

Now, no doubt, being a pastor flatters my ego. But it's also hard work, especially for someone who's afraid of people, for someone who's conflict avoidant, for someone who's afraid he might start stuttering again (though I haven't for forty-five years), for someone who's afraid that if he opens his mouth people will realize that he's not a wise leader but a nerd who's faking it.

So I don't want this job. (At least, on bad days I don't.) It disturbs me that I have to spend so much time with people. So little time studying. And I get resentful. I want something other than what I have. Like Eve.

Many years ago in another church, I was on the leadership team. I resigned and immediately became deeply resentful of the new team. If God gave me an orange, I suspect I would want an apple. Maybe it's a general rule: whatever God gives us, we want something else. We covet. We can't be satisfied.

I'm fascinated by theology, and I'd really like to become a competent theologian. Or a biblical scholar. And my academic training is in philosophy of science, epistemology, and ethics, with a fair amount of psychology. I love all that. That's what I want to do, not be a pastor. And besides, I'd like to run more than my allotted fifteen miles a week.

Really, I'd like to do almost everything (that isn't one-on-one). I find twenty-four hour days limiting. And annoying. Being finite is something I don't prefer. My discontent and resentment mean I don't sleep well. I have colitis. And eczema. And a deep sense of dissatisfaction.

I'm not a workaholic: I love vacations. They're my best chance to study. (In fact, I'm writing this while vacationing in Biloxi, Mississippi!)

So I have no trouble understanding Eve. She wasn't especially vicious or malicious. Nor am I. (Sometimes I am, but not usually.)

It's not exactly that I want to be God. I just want what I want when I want it. I don't want to be limited. Nor do I want to be crossed. "Don't tread on me," as the rattlesnake said on the first American flag. So I get intense when people don't see things the way I do. I tend to mow them down. To dominate them—or try to. For some reason, crises seem to follow me around. Shalom is rare. At least, where I am. As is unity. (At least, that's who I am when I let myself go.)

This is the story of the human predicament. My story. Adam's story. Eve's story. You live some variation on it. The particulars will be different, but the heart is the same. Your heart is my heart is Eve's heart. The will to power. Dissatisfaction and covetousness. Resentment and rebellion that things aren't the way I want them, that I have limitations, that my son has limitations. So I attempt to force the few things in my power to be how I want them: I'll seize what I want, even if it means dominating and oppressing you.

But this story Jesus brought to an end. He gave us a different story to live. A new game—love and unity. It's OK to drop some flyballs, but this is the game we're playing.

Blame shifting, or the woman whom you gave me

The story of Adam and Eve goes on.

> They heard the sound of the LORD God walking in the garden at the time of the evening breeze, and the man and his wife hid themselves from the presence of the LORD God among the trees of the garden. But the LORD God called to the man, and said to him, "Where are you?" He said, "I heard the sound of you in the garden, and I was afraid, because I was naked; and I hid myself." [The LORD God] said, "Who told you that you were naked? Have you eaten from the tree of which I commanded you not to eat?" The man said, "The woman whom you gave to be with me, she gave me fruit from the tree, and I ate." Then the LORD God said to the woman, "What is this that you have done?" The woman said, "The serpent tricked me, and I ate." (Gen 3:8–13)

I love it: "the woman *you* gave me." One of the most profound lines in all literature. And it's thousands and thousands of years old. Sophocles never matched it.

Shakespeare never matched it. All that blame and resentment stuffed into one line. "It's not my fault; it was her. In fact, it's you. The woman, she did it, and *you* gave her to me. So it's really your fault, God. Why did you screw me up like this? I really resent you." No mention of his own covetousness or disobedience.

It's hilarious when other people do it. Invisible when I do it. Invisible to me, that is. And it makes unity impossible. Along with love. It's hard for me to love people while blaming and resenting them. Especially for what I did myself. And hard for them to love me.

Rebellion, defended by deception and self-deception, compounded by blame and resentment, leading to my seizing what I want, which then fails to produce satisfaction, which leads to my using increasingly extreme attempts to dominate and control, in the belief that the next thing will be different and produce satisfaction. Unless I despair and give up to resentment. That's the human predicament. It's depressing and would be hopeless if it were the end of the story, but it's not. It's the beginning. For Jesus has given us another story. A story of hope that his people have the joy of living out together.

But we have to stop rebelling, blaming, resenting, dominating, and trying to get more. Only as we turn away from those things will we have love and unity.

ON NOT BLAMING

We often have a hard time telling whose fault things are. Adam wasn't just lying when he said, it was "the woman you gave me." He was right, as far as he went. But he fails to mention that he hadn't spent a long time arguing with her. He fails to mention that he could have told her, "No, I'm not going to eat the fruit. God told us not to, and I'm going to obey."

And Eve wasn't just lying when she said, "The serpent tricked me." (At least she doesn't say, "The serpent whom you created.") But she, too, fails to mention that she didn't have to eat the fruit. She could have told the serpent, "No, I won't rebel. God loves me."

Close to the heart of the human predicament is our failure to take responsibility for our lives. We rebel and then we shift the blame, which makes growth almost impossible. It also makes those being blamed angry. And they rebel, too. Especially when the blame is justified. The cycle begins.

Jesus' solution is simple. Take the blame. Whether it's yours or not. That's the cross. The pain of crucifixion must have been terrible, but I'll bet being blamed and misunderstood at the trial was tough, too. And being hidden from God, like Adam and Eve. But in Jesus' story and only in Jesus' story, peace and unity become possible. Among a people where blaming has stopped and responsibility is accepted. Not as a great burden, for one thing is clear in Jesus' story. No, two things. One, we're all rebelliously selfish like Eve. And two, Jesus has taken care of it. We're vile and wretched creatures. Even when we're not vicious and malicious, we're ludicrously dissatisfied (another word for rebellious). But God loves us anyway. While we were yet sinners, God gave his only son. The blame is gone.

God has forgiven us, and so we can forgive ourselves and each other. And get on with living in peace by reminding each other how uninteresting it is that we sin. After all, God loves us. Then with support from our brothers and sisters and with the love of God, we can face our self-deception and get on with growing into the fullness of the stature of Christ. Into our Head. Into love.

THE LIBERAL LIE

Our culture has a different story. Naturally. Everything is someone else's fault. So I need to rebel. That tax on tea was a terrible thing. It was George III's fault. So it was OK to kill thousands. For a few cups of tea. Not our fault. Don't step on us.

Or take something like slavery. Slavery is terrible beyond words (unlike a tax on tea). Perhaps nothing in history has been worse. (It included unending sexual abuse if the wrong person took a fancy to you. Or a dislike.) We must never forget that. Yet the time comes when former slaves and their descendants need to get on with their lives. I'm a fierce supporter (intense even) of affirmative action, but my observation is that people are not alive who spend their time blaming society (even rightly). People are not alive if their life is rebellion against society (even an abusive society).

The same is true for white males blaming affirmative action for their problems. Our problem isn't undocumented immigrants or affirmative action or women or people on welfare. It's us. We need to stop mumbling about stuttering, and get on with what God has given us. Whether you've been wronged (which in the case of white males, I usually doubt) or not.

I was present recently when an older woman told the story of a long marriage to a miserable, promiscuous, mean man. It was clear that she had carried on with her own life before God and done rather well at it. Afterwards another woman said to her, "You must have been terribly angry." She replied simply, "No, it wasn't worth it."

That's what I'm trying to say. Bad things happen to us. Many of them imaginary, but enough of them real. We rebel and ruin the rest of our lives. We do that our-selves. What we need to do is forgive and be content with the life God has given us. Resentment and blaming are poison. Poison for us. They aren't worth it.

DEPRESSION AND BEING A VICTIM

We've got to get beyond this cycle of resentment, rebellion, and blame, or we will die. Die in disunity and depression. Like Cain. (I'm not sure Cain was wrong about his offering, either. Maybe that's part of the point of his story.)

Like Israel. All forty years they were in the wilderness, they complained. I don't especially blame them. My favorite cereal is Total. My wife figured that out and kindly began buying box after box of the stuff. In a month, I was bitching and moaning. If she bought me manna for forty days, let alone forty years, I wouldn't be a happy camper. Especially if we ran out of water from time to time. Within a week, I'd be saying:

> "If only we had meat to eat! We remember the fish we used to eat in Egypt for nothing [dissatisfaction and rebellion], the cucumbers, the melons, the leeks, the onions, and the garlic; but now our strength is dried up, and there is nothing at all but this manna to look at." (Num 11:4–6)

Egypt had been the place of Israel's worst misery, but suddenly they remembered it as one big Jewish deli. Now, don't misunderstand me. The food may have been better in Egypt. Knowing myself, I doubt that, but let's specify that it was. Nonetheless, the Israelites were in slavery in Egypt. But they forget that right off. Their children were murdered in Egypt, but as soon as they get bored with desert food, they forget all about that. God lovingly delivered them from Egypt, but life still wasn't good enough for them. Like for Eve and me. Life was so great before affirmative action. Or before the rape. Instead of rejoicing in what we do have, now we're victims. God's victims. We must be. The food is boring. Or maybe it really is something serious, like rape. But what's the point of being embittered for years and decades?

"There is nothing at all but this manna to look at." Oh? Nothing else to look at? Well, I don't know what the Sinai desert is like, but there must have been a cactus or a bush or two to look at. And what about the sunset? And in those days before pollution, the stars must have been unutterably beautiful. But when you're dissatisfied with your lot, everything else disappears and all you can see is the dark hole of your misery and depression. There must be someone you can blame and resent. How about Moses and God? Or God and your spouse.

When I'm depressed, I can go to a brightly lit room where everything is wonderful and go over to the wall and find a dark spot. I'll put one eye up to the dark spot, close the other, and start swearing that the whole room is full of darkness and misery. For darkness is all I can see—all I have chosen to see. It takes work, but with sufficient scrunching and squinting, I can fix things so that all I see is my misery. My wife never gives me the food I want; my housemate always leaves his towel on the bathroom floor.

That's how Israel chose to see the world. There's nothing to see but this manna. Nothing.

The story continues, switching to Moses' side of the story, which is the same. The text says, "Moses was displeased" (Num 11:10b). You can't blame him. Leading these miserable people must have been hideous. Besides, he had one eye right up to a dark spot, and the other eye was closed. Life wasn't perfect, so it was terrible. And Moses believed, quite plausibly, that he had a right to a life that wasn't terrible. It would be silly for him to claim he had a right to a perfect life. So he had to rephrase it. And he couldn't just say he didn't like the limits God had put on him.

The text puts it wonderfully, hilariously. (Whoever wrote the first four books of the Bible was a comedian.)

Moses was displeased. So Moses said to the LORD, "Why have you treated your servant so badly? [Ah, the joys of blaming.] Why have I not found favor in your sight, that you lay the burden of all this people on me? Did I conceive all this people? Did I give birth to them, that you should say to me, 'Carry them in your bosom, as a nurse carries a sucking child,' to the land that you promised on oath to their ancestors? [His moaning has real quality.] Where am I to get meat to give to all this people? For they come weeping to me and say, 'Give us meat to eat!' I am not able to carry all this people alone, for they are too heavy for me. If this is the way you are going to treat me, put me to death at once—if I have found favor in your sight—and do not let me see my misery." [I love it; it reveals me to myself.]

So the LORD said to Moses, ". . . say to the people: Consecrate yourselves for tomorrow, and you shall eat meat; for you have wailed in the hearing of the LORD, saying, 'If only we had meat to eat! Surely it was better for us in Egypt.' Therefore the LORD will give you meat, and you shall eat. You shall eat not only one day, or two days, or five days, or ten days, or twenty days, but for a whole month—until it comes out of your nostrils and becomes loathsome to you— because you have rejected [rebelled against] the LORD who is among you, and have wailed before him, saying, 'Why did we ever leave Egypt?'"

But Moses said, "The people I am with number six hundred thousand on foot; and you say, 'I will give them meat, that they may eat for a whole month'! Are there enough flocks and herds to slaughter for them? Are there enough fish in the sea to catch for them?"

The LORD said to Moses, "Is the Lord's power limited?" (Num 11:10b–16a, 18–23a)

There you have it: the source of our disunity and endless fighting. I require things to be perfect. Otherwise, I'll reinterpret reality and claim that things are terrible. Then I'm justified in rebelling, complaining, and resenting. I'm unwilling to be limited in what I have, limited to Total for breakfast. So I will blame others.

Oh, and the Lord can't possibly take care of things.

We need to give up complaining and blaming (even when we're right). And rejoice in the limits God has given us. "Here am I, the servant of the Lord; let it be with me according to your word" (Luke 1:38b).

Rejoice. Stopping complaining is too cautious, not drastic enough; it won't work. Instead we need to choose the opposite, choose to rejoice in the good things (limited though we imagine them to be). We need to open our other eye and not stand so close to the dark spot. Then we will find unity. On the other side of blame and rebellion. But if we keep complaining about others and finding fault, we will fight with each other till Hell freezes over with us in its gullet.

THE OPPOSITE PICTURE: SUBMISSION AND REJOICING VS. REBELLION AND

ANGER

The solution to rebellion is joy. One of the best places to find this picture is Ephesians. Chapter 5 projects it especially well (in yet another monster sentence):

> Do not get drunk with wine, for that is debauchery; but be filled with the Spirit, as you sing psalms and hymns and spiritual songs among yourselves, singing and making melody to the Lord in your hearts, giving thanks to God the Father at all times and for everything in the name of our Lord Jesus Christ [, being] subject to one another out of reverence for Christ. (Eph 5:18–21 NRSV, author's translation at brackets to show how Paul's grammar is one single sentence.)

Here's the opposite of disunity and rebellion: Don't look for satisfaction in drugs but in being filled with the Holy Spirit, which will produce rejoicing and song; out of the overflow of this joy, will flow mutual submission—the opposite of rebellion. This is how we must revision church if we're to be a loving and united people who can call the world to become part of us.

I'll bet it's no accident that Paul combines rejoicing with being subject to each other. To put it differently, I suggest that the emotional opposite of rebellion isn't submission but rejoicing. And when we begin to rejoice, mutual submission is natural. Therefore, submission is especially hard for angry, complaining people. To put it differently, people in rebellion are always angry—unless they're depressed, which is a sort of anger.

But what is submission?

We live in a time when submission is a bad word. In the coffeehouse where I often write, someone has written on the bathroom wall, "Don't submit, or you're like everyone else." I understand that. After Hitler and the Gulag Archipelago and Pol Pot, blind obedience is repulsive.

That should be apparent to those of us with a history in live-in churches. One of the plagues of live-in churches has been leaders who require blind obedience. Jim Jones got his people to drink Kool-Aid laced with cyanide and hundreds died. This sort of submission is especially serious since such leaders inevitably get distracted by something trivial, like by the details of eschatology or by some sexual addiction. Even though such leaders don't normally do anything dramatic like Jim Jones, they lead people to nowhere.

So what is submission? Unfortunately, Greek and New Testament studies aren't a lot of help, but in my experience, submission is more like rejoicing that you have other people to listen to. It's more like listening in an attitude of openheartedness, supported by a spirit of servanthood.

So submission doesn't mean blind obedience; it doesn't mean believing your church if they tell you a red sofa is blue or that Jews or capitalists or women cause your problems. But it does mean knowing you don't know everything. It means knowing that the people of God gathered know more than you do by yourself. It means being willing to listen with an open heart when the body has the audacity to differ with your views. It means being willing pretty often to try out others' views for awhile to see if maybe you're the one that's confused.

Isn't it odd how after years of proving ourselves wrong we still instinctively believe ourselves—even when the whole body tells us something else? Maybe submission is occasionally betting that other people know a little something, too. Not turning off your brain, but living out what they suggest until and unless you see it doing harm. Then you stop obeying, preferably calmly and kindly; but in any case, you stop.

Of course, you can't listen that way to everyone you pass on the street. But you better be able to find a church somewhere that you suspect might be wiser than you by yourself. If you can't, check your arrogance level and go find someone you can listen to. That's all submission means. Not blindly following Hitler.

Respect and DWEMs (dead, white, European males)

When I was twentyish, B. A. Farrell (my tutor in philosophy) had me write a paper on Ludwig Wittgenstein's view of private language. I obliterated Wittgenstein. Farrell suggested that perhaps I had misunderstood Wittgenstein, and he proposed an alternate interpretation. I explained why that couldn't possibly be what Wittgenstein meant. Farrell made a couple more attempts to defend Wittgenstein, and I made a couple more brilliant replies. He became agitated and began rocking back and forth. Then he said something like, "You almost persuade me that I don't understand Wittgenstein, but I feel confident that if you came to understand him, you'd be a much wiser young man than you are."

That silenced me. I knew I'd been told something like no tutor had told me before (or since). But I tried to tell myself that Farrell had turned off his brain and was hero-worshiping the icon of English philosophers. But the next week I wrote and spoke with more respect. I'd heard a spirit that seemed deeper than the one I knew and lived. This is a large part of the vision of church that we must reclaim—for the sake of the gospel, for the sake of ourselves, and for the sake of a world that is lost and confused because it has rejected that vision.

And that's all submission is. Rejoicing that someone is wiser than us, that there are others whom we can respect. That frees us to rejoice that we don't have to know everything ourselves—betting that others know something, too. It's a spirit, an attitude. Out of which grow unity and wisdom.

One of the tragedies of postmodernity is that no one is left to respect. There used to be a cultural canon, an agreed-on group of people whom folks apprenticed themselves to. Not just as an exercise to sharpen their wits, but in the belief that these people were wiser than the average bear or wrote more beautifully than the rest of us. Young people were taught that the thought of these people needed to be mastered by anyone who hoped to stop being a fool. Teachers weren't especially interested in the thinking of their students, except whether it showed they were apprenticing themselves to the masters.

The masters. A notion long dead. Along with the classics. In seminary I took a Luther seminar from an eccentric professor. Whenever anyone said "I think," he'd interrupt cheerfully: "I don't care what you think. I want to know what Luther thinks and whether you know what Luther thinks. This is a seminar on the thought of Luther, not on the thought of John Alexander. When your thinking is worth knowing, I'll schedule a seminar on you. But it may be awhile. Meanwhile figure out what Luther thought."

The loss of the masters is tragic. As tragic as it is understandable. By now, it's obviously odd that virtually all those masters were dead, white, European males. Very odd. And some of them turned out to be fools. Can anyone still take Leibniz's monads seriously? And how can anyone defend the Revolutionary War? Or most of the Presidents of the last few decades, not to mention the rock stars and other celebrities who have replaced the classics? Everything is debunked.

To some people this feels neat. They think it's fun to be on their own. To be deciding all by themselves. To have no idols.

I doubt that it's fun. Independence does not bring life, not for long. It's just another name for rebellion. If the wise white men of the past all turn out to be fools, won't everyone else, too? Then what hope is there for any of us? Soon it will seem equally clear that women and blacks and Asians are fools, too. Everyone.

Including the postmodernists who are teaching this to our young people.

Here's one of the great things about the body of Christ. We have an agreed-on hero to whom we can apprentice ourselves. A huge book we can study for hundreds of years without completion. Then there are the millions of others who have tried to follow our master and understand our book. We can study them for many lifetimes. And we have a local body that can encourage us and against whom we can sharpen ourselves and who will tell us when we're being fools.

COOPERATION AND REBELLION

Be clear: blind following of leaders is a terrible thing. But so is blind rejection of leaders. Passive acceptance of the way things are destroys, and so does aggressive destruction of everything established. It's a question of spirit. A spirit of passivity destroys as does a spirit of rejection. Maybe the only thing as deadly as conventional thinking is the need to debunk.

In my experience, more people have a need to debunk and complain than have a need to follow blindly. I know lots of complaining rebels, few blind followers. In my experience, a lot of people in our culture know how to question authority. Not so many know how to cooperate on a deep level. Not many know how to watch and listen till they know what's going on before they start rejecting and fighting.

We all know people who have a counterproposal for every proposal, whether it's about which restaurant to go to or which God to serve. And we all know people for whom most things are wrong most of the time. (Me, for instance.) People whose complaints are as extensive as the children of Israel's. People who are always testing authority, trying to prove that their wisdom is great, greater than God's. Life among those people becomes wearing and wearying.

In any case, blind following and blind rejecting isn't the full range of options. And I don't mean some moderating position between the two. On another continuum altogether is active, hopeful listening, where you aren't blaming and debunking but cheerfully cooperating while still asking friendly, pointed questions.

Remember the graffiti in the bathroom? "Don't submit, or you're like everyone else"? Someone wrote below it, "Are you kidding? We need people who know how to cooperate." Cooperation. I suspect that's a fair modern translation for submission.

Did you ever spend time around an uncooperative child? That's a spirit of destruction. (Maybe it was a first-grade teacher who wrote that second graffiti.) Occasionally I meet a child (and once in a while even an adult) who throws herself into what's suggested with enthusiasm, who seems to have no need to test you or herself. That's what submission means—enthusiastic, cheerful cooperativeness. (By the way, I doubt that anyone would describe Hitler's followers as cheerfully enthusiastic or as cooperative. So insofar as leaders engender genuine cooperativeness, we don't need to worry too much about them becoming little Hitlers.)

Instead of being passive followers or angry rebels, we can become people who are filled with the Spirit, singing psalms and hymns and spiritual songs among ourselves, making melody to the Lord in our hearts, while being enthusiastically cooperative with one another out of reverence for Christ.

SEVENTEEN

Leaders (Final Thoughts on Love and Unity)

Which brings us to leadership. In the years I spent in what we called intentional Christian community, I advocated minimizing leaders and maximizing whole group processes. We talked mostly about facilitators, enablers,[1] consensus, empowerment, and the need to maximize each person's gifts and potential. This was supposed to help us listen to the Holy Spirit instead of to leaders' egos; it was supposed to help us grow, and to do so without hierarchies that put so many people on the bottom.

However, that wasn't what happened. What happened was that we had endless meetings trying to agree on vision. We'd seem to agree on a vision, and three months later the cycle would start over. Meanwhile, people wandered aimlessly. Without much vision or with conflicting visions. And lots of people didn't get the pastoral care they needed because we didn't give anyone the authority to pastor us.

The trouble was that we'd watched so many intentional Christian communities go down the tubes because their leaders became petty dictators. They took themselves too seriously, and soon they began to preach submission two nights a week and became subtly abusive to those not adept at the leadership's line.

But as the futility of trying to talk our way to consensus on vision became more and more obvious, I began to say that maybe the only thing worse than strong leadership is weak leadership. Maybe communities are healthy only in that brief period between when we acknowledge the need for authority and when the leaders we acknowledge go bad.

COOPERATION

But gradually I found my way to another paradigm. To what I call a cooperative spirit. On some level, most of us can probably agree that to have any kind of life together, we need to be cooperative. We may know it reluctantly and more in theory than in practice, but most of us know that a cooperative spirit is important if we're to live in peace. So we can accept cooperating as we sit in a circle with no one in charge.

---

1. This was before the days when enabling meant helping someone continue dysfunctional behavior. Then an enabler was someone who empowered others to do things instead of doing everything herself.

But what if we're at a rectangular table with someone sitting at the head? Leaders are tricky, especially for egalitarian Westerners. Maybe we shouldn't cooperate with the leaders. What if they turn into little Hitlers or minor Jim Joneses? I suggest that churches need to model for the world a new vision for leadership. Or rather we need to reclaim an old vision—the vision of leadership in the teaching and life of Jesus.

Unfortunately for egalitarians, both the Bible and experience suggest that leadership is crucial. To help us Westerners understand this, let's forget the word "leadership" for the moment and try to get at the function at issue. Instead of talking about leaders, let's talk about "mothers." To fulfill our purpose of growing into the full stature of Christ, I suggest that churches need mothers. Mothers who inspire cooperation rather than rebellion.

Mothers won't seem necessary if we think of church as a large institution to be maintained or as a group gifted at beating on each other. Why would you need mothers for that? But if church is mostly a family that needs nurturing and loving, then mothers are important.

That's why Luke includes this famous story in his account of the Last Supper:

> A dispute also arose among [the disciples] as to which one of them was to be regarded as the greatest. But [Jesus] said to them, "The kings of the Gentiles lord it over them; and those in authority over them are called benefactors. But not so with you; rather the greatest among you must become like the youngest, and the leader like one who serves. For who is greater, the one who is at the table or the one who serves? Is it not the one at the table? But I am among you as one who serves." (Luke 22:24–27)

In our culture, we no longer have servants. So who serves us? Who bounces up and down at dinner and has little chance to sit at the table? Not the young. Not working men. Not starlets. Mothers.

Let me suggest a modern paraphrase: "The greatest among you must become like a woman, and the leader like a mother who serves. For who is greater, the one who is at the table or the one who serves? Is it not the one at the table? But I am among you as a mother."

Now if you don't like my translation, don't worry about it. But please get my point. What's needed to make a family thrive is clear—the same things needed to make any intimate group of committed people thrive. That has been the topic of much of this book. Thriving has little to do with saluting when given an order; it has everything to do with grace, love, serving. It has everything to do with caring for one another, nurturing one another—the way mothers try to do.

Any group of people whose lives are deeply interconnected needs a person or three who have experienced so much grace that they exude it onto others. We need people who accept sinners and screw-ups with a minimum of annoyance and judgment. That doesn't mean they put up with sinful behavior; it means they tell the person about it directly and kindly, without making the person feel rejected. The more people we have who are full of grace and gentle truth the better, but we must have one or two, or we will burn.

That is, we need a few mothers. Or something reasonably close to our cultural ideal for mothers, anyway. Mothers who take joy in their children and freely correct them without making them feel rejected and abandoned. That's what Jesus is doing in the gentle straightforwardness of his reply about the desire for greatness. The disciples have been with Jesus for three years, and now they're at the Last Supper. Jesus is preparing to die and the disciples are at the end of their training. And what do the disciples talk about? They talk about which of them is most important.

Surely, this is the time for Jesus to body-slam them. But he doesn't. Mothers rarely body-slam. Not if their children survive. Mothers offer firm correction again and yet again. Followed by dinner and other forms of encouragement and serving.

That's what a leader is in the New Testament. A nurturer. Someone who brings milk and cookies after a rebuke.

To put it differently, we human beings are so self-centered and rebellious that we can only stay together if we have pastors to help us through our struggles with one another. Whether it's a live-in church or the music committee of a church-with-a-steeple, people fight when they're together much. We aren't so different from five-year olds in play group. We all want the same toy at the same moment, and we still will when we're ninety. If we're not going to kill each other, Mom needs to step in and call a time out. She needs to tell us we're being selfish little piggies.

That's what leadership is in church. It's how we learn to cooperate, to stop the rebellion we learned in the Garden.

But it's complicated by our imagining that a seminary degree equips us to lead churches (a degree in nannying might equip us better). And besides, in the case of church, everyone is a five-year-old, including the mom who stops the fights. (Well, it helps if she's six.)

Criteria

Which gives us some crucial criteria for choosing leaders. We need people who don't get as entangled in fights. I don't say someone who doesn't get entangled in fights. That's impossible; we're all five or at most six. But we need someone who gets less entangled, who can eventually step back and say, "We all need a time out." And who can say it with grace. It's called speaking the truth in love. Moms do that better than average.

We need moms who will cheerfully shake us awake when we become self-absorbed, when we forget everything except our wants. If in our quest to be God we become intolerably demanding about having our own way, we need a mom to quietly point out what we're doing.

In other words, we need pastors, shepherds. By "pastors," I don't mostly mean people who know a solution whenever someone brings a personal problem.[2] Nor do I mean people gifted at premarital counseling or at conflict resolution (while carefully not taking sides). Rather, I mean people with pastoral hearts, mothers' hearts. I mean people who, when others bring their convoluted problems, may have no idea what the answer is but still find some way to point back to what matters: love, trusting Jesus, forgiving, stopping being piglets. Pointing back not just in words, but also by what they exude. Like ideal mothers.

When Paul talked about speaking the truth in love, I doubt that he mostly meant giving good advice or being able to explain the implications of being the oldest child. I think he mostly meant talking about Jesus, who is the way, the truth, and the life. So I suspect that good pastors will often say things like, "I don't know whether you should change your job, but I do know that if you expect to find your satisfaction in your work, you'll be disappointed. Only Jesus can fulfill your dreams." Like mothers who say, "I can't think of a perfect solution to this, Christopher, but it doesn't matter if Verah has your toy; the one on the floor is just as good."

I'm wandering from my mother metaphor, but the same kind of thing needs to be said about the importance of leaders trusting God and his grace. A leader may be as big a screw-up as Jacob. Not having such leaders isn't the point. The point is having leaders who exude confidence in God, exude a sense of serenity about their own failures because their hope is in God rather than in themselves. So church leaders should often say things like, "I don't know the solution, but I do know that God loves us and is taking care of us at this very moment. God will just have to intervene, or we're lost."

GREATNESS

Now, I know I'm not exactly exegeting Jesus' reply to who would be the most important. In his reply, Jesus wasn't focusing on leaders as people who speak the truth in grace and love, or who keep pointing back to him. He was focusing on the importance of being the one who gets up from the table to get more butter.

Which wasn't who the disciples wanted to be. They wanted the opposite. They wanted to be the ones for whom others got up to get the butter. They wanted to be admired—or maybe to have status and power. When Jesus took his proper place on the throne of Israel, they each wanted to be his chief of staff. Or maybe his secretary of defense. With lots of people at their beck and call. No popping up for butter for them.

Which seems pretty silly to us. After all Jesus had said and done, how could they be so embarrassingly stupid? Yet the answer is close at hand—as close as our hearts.

---

2. Nor do I mean a preacher or teacher. Good teachers of the word are as important as pastors, and they may be the same person, though the roles are different. Actually, the roles go together so often in my experience that I suspect there's some connection between the gifts. I've never met a good teacher of the word who wasn't also at least a fair pastor, though I have met good pastors who aren't good teachers. In any case, you can't teach the word well without at least a pastor's heart.

We all want importance and admiration; at least, I do. And those who don't want those things want other things equally stupid.

It's not the disciples who are idiots. It's all of us; it's the human heart. It's our desire to be God. For whatever else being God includes, it includes being important and admired. So I want to be important and admired. Now. Or someone's significant other. Now.

Which is tragic. Perhaps the only thing we need other than physical necessities is to be loved. Being loved is the only thing that can fill us. But naturally that's not what we want. We keep trying to get filled with other stuff. With counterfeits. Like importance and power. Or maybe money and sex. I suppose the preferred counterfeit varies from person to person, but being important and admired are pretty high on most lists.

Here's one way of writing an anatomy of the fallen human heart: list the things we'd rather have than love. Almost everything has been on my list at one time or another. Yet love is the only thing I need.

Perhaps it's because we human beings rarely appreciate the things we already have. We've got God's love; so who wants it? It's like manna on the fourth morning.

But Jesus puts it less abrasively. He tells us that wanting to be great is fine. Then he redefines greatness! It's being the biggest servant. The word he uses becomes one of the main New Testament words for leadership. It's the word from which we get "deacon." One of the main offices of church is being a deacon. Do you know what it means literally? A person who waits on tables.

Like a mother.

That's the sort of thing that's so exciting about Jesus and the New Testament. Can you imagine Aristotle or Plato advocating that their disciples become good waiters? Or can you imagine Norman Mailer or Jacques Derrida advocating that? Ours is the best story around.

So we pick leaders who are servants in the deepest fiber of their being. And we avoid leaders who aren't servants. If their leadership isn't a disaster at first, it eventually will be. You can count on it. It would be better to be led by a person who had been addicted to children for sex and was broken by it (a sort of Jacob type) than by someone who thought himself too important to wash the dishes.

I tend to read this passage as a way to know who not to make a leader, as a criterion of exclusion that will save us from ordaining Jim Joneses. And I suppose that's right as far as it goes. But Jesus means more than that. He means that serving is about all leadership is. There's only one job in church. It's being a servant. So naturally those who do it best, we make our leaders.

Whatever a church's official leadership may be, its real leaders are the people who stay to wash the dishes and straighten up after meetings.[3] That's what Jesus told the disciples. (Which is interesting for the standard dispute over whether women should

---

3. Some people clean for show or obsessively or out of guilt, which is a different matter, of course. My statement is partly metaphorical, a way of saying that the real leaders are the people who do the tough work without concern for who gets the credit and without much concern for whether they're tired.

be leaders in church. So far as I can tell, almost all the leaders in church are in fact women.)

What kind of leaders does a group need if they're to live together in peace? What's the function needed here? It's someone to clean up the poop. After the baby has diarrhea all over the living room or after the congregation has a fight over the sort of music to have in the worship service. You can always find someone to play the piano or do the accounting. What's hard to find is someone to hold your head while you vomit on them. Church leaders are like Mother Teresa, not like Julius Caesar or Maria Calas.

Such people rarely become Hitler or Jim Jones. More important, sometimes even we rebels learn to cooperate with them.

Informal decision-making and leaders

So, if we understand the heart of Jesus, we will soon have servants sitting at the head of our rectangular table. They're the only sort of people whose judgment we can trust.

Of course, it's easy for us to imagine that we don't need people at the head of the table, to imagine that all our tables should be round. The "servant of all" can do her job perfectly well without being appointed elder or overseer or deacon or bishop. What's this need for titles and offices and authority? Let's have Jesus as our head and no one else. Isn't that the sort of thing Jesus meant when he said, "Call no one your father on earth, for you have one Father—the one in heaven" (Matt 23:9). We need to be following the servants among us, but it won't help to formalize their authority. That just confuses them and messes with us.

This is a sensible argument. At least, I used it for years. In those days, I loved to point out that when the Gospels use the word "elder," they're usually referring to wicked rulers of Israel. We don't need rulers, I'd say. (And on that I was probably right.)

I was intrigued by the notion that in the early church spontaneous groups of Christians made their decisions informally. As the decades passed, however, churches got larger and needed formal procedures for making decisions. Only then did they institute more traditional forms of leadership. So it's not till 1 and 2 Timothy and Titus, which were written quite late, that you get teaching on church offices. Institutional churches may need elders to run their bureaucracies and do fundraising, but God never intended for churches to be that big or require that kind of money. If we get back to churches small enough to meet in homes, maybe we won't need elders anymore and maybe we'll practice the priesthood of all believers. Then maybe we'll be able to hear the Holy Spirit more like they did then.

And maybe not. The first crack in my armor came from practicalities. Do you have any idea how long it takes people sitting in a circle to decide what color to paint the living room? At Jubilee Fellowship of Germantown, we used to spend half our lives trying to decide things that didn't matter. So we appointed a sort of administrative committee to deal with trivial matters and to run business meetings. Members rotated off after a year and almost anyone could be on the committee.

But being trained in epistemology, I began to wonder how those people decided what was a trivial matter. Didn't you have to have a vision to decide what mattered? Didn't it depend on what that vision was? And what if your committee was composed of people with bad vision? About then Ron Sider pointed out the obvious to me. He said that by Acts 15 (which was early), churches had elders and that together with the apostles, they at least focused the decisions. (See also Acts 11:28–30; 14:19–23; 20:17, 28–32.) And I wondered if maybe these were the people with vision. With a sense of what was trivial and what affected the gospel.

OVERSEERS AND UNDERROWERS

Two biblical terms began to intrigue me. One was overseer.[4] I struggled with the word because its primary meaning in our culture is those who ran slave crews. Nonetheless, I was beginning to think that even quite small communities (or house churches or small groups) need people with an overview, a spiritual overview. Someone needs to have a sense of the whole ball of wax (both of the gospel story and of where the congregation is); someone needs to have the pulse of the group as a whole and be sensitive to the spiritual state of each member. A lot of us run on automatic or develop tunnel vision and wind up in the corner doing something irrelevant or uncoordinated with the needs of the body. Those people (all of us?) need help keeping on track. That's where vision comes in and where people come in who have a sense of whether people are living that vision out. A vision, at least a good one, also inspires and encourages people. It points them in the right direction when they have energy and sustains them when they're tired.[5]

The second biblical term that intrigued me was "servants of the word" (Luke 1:2). Luke says stories about Jesus were handed on by eyewitnesses and servants of the word. Not just by those who saw what Jesus did, but by those who saw and were servants of the word. You see, being an eyewitness doesn't tell you how to interpret what you saw. (A point postmodernists were well behind Luke in figuring out.) You have to have a word, an interpretive framework, or you don't know what you've seen. And local bodies need people who are servants of the word to help them understand what they're experiencing.

I was encouraged that Luke saw these people as servants, just what Jesus had told his disciples to be. They aren't people who are following their own egos. No, they're serving something larger than themselves—God's revelation of himself.

Later, I was intrigued to learn that the word Luke uses for servants here literally means "under-rowers, subordinate rowers." They're people who row to the beat of

---

4. *Episcopos* in Greek. "Overseer" is a reasonably literal translation of the Greek word.

5. This role is especially important in a group that is adding new people or that deliberately takes in people who are less healthy emotionally than average. Otherwise, you have to require people to be mature and trustworthy before they can become members. Jesus didn't require this even of his disciples; he didn't need to because they had a clear leadership structure.

someone else's drum. A different drum.[6] (I don't mean to use this as an argument. This is only an illustration. My argument is the regularity with which the whole Bible talks about godly leaders—like Moses, David, and Paul—as God's slaves.)

Underrower. It's almost the opposite of overseer. Those who oversee the body of Jesus better be subordinate (submissive) to something larger than themselves. How about to Jesus, the word made flesh?

Overseers must be more submissive than the rest of the congregation. More submissive to the congregation, and above all, more submissive to the Word. For He is the source of our vision. The alternative to our rebellion and blaming.

The vision that overseers themselves bring will be nothing but trouble. But the vision that underrowers have of the Word can bring life to the churches they lead. If they got their vision from the Word (from the Bible, from Jesus and his life, from the Holy Spirit) and keep getting it there, then they will bring peace and unity.

I have nothing more important to say in this book than this: overseers must be people who are dying to themselves in such a way that they can often hear the Holy Spirit. They must be people who are losing interest in their own visions so that they can be seized by God's vision. They must be people (and there are months and years of pain in this sentence) who can generally surrender the fight for what they want in favor of what God and his people need.

When people ask me what to look for in overseers, I have always talked about servanthood, about not being rebellious, about being the most submissive person in the congregation, about people who are followers of the word and not of themselves. Increasingly, however, I put all this in terms of whether they need to fight for things to go the way they want.

Let me explain it this way. I'm an overseer at Church of the Sojourners, and not fighting for my way is a struggle for me. Fortunately, I usually don't care much about details; so I often do OK when I'm overruled on trivia. But I have a hard time giving way on things I think are important. I'm an overseer, aren't I? Why won't they do what I say? If I draft a policy statement for the congregation, I get crazy when they won't accept what I've written. I tend to persuade myself that every third thing is a matter of principle that I need to take a stand on.

But it has become clear to me over the last few years that the things I fight for often don't finally matter. The other night in a discernment meeting, we were discussing whether to buy another house, and if so, which one. It seemed clear to me that we should buy a house, and it also seemed clear which one. To my unhappiness, none of this was at all clear to the church. They had the audacity to keep asking questions and raising objections. They weren't being at all submissive. What was worse, their spirit

---

6. The term is derived from Thoreau: "If a man does not keep pace with his companions, perhaps it is because he hears a different drummer. Let him step to the music which he hears, however measured or far away." (*Walden* reprinted in *The Portable Thoreau*, 564–65.) However, Thoreau's different drummer is the self. There is perhaps no sharper picture of the difference between the biblical vision and the modern vision than to compare Thoreau's drummer to Luke's underrower.

was so good, I couldn't complain. But for once I was able to keep my mouth shut and not be a bimbo. (And by now, I can tell they were right.)

In those situations, I'm learning to ask myself two questions. First, do I have a word from the Lord on this? And second, does our faithfulness to the gospel stand or fall on this decision? Or (and this is the same question) will the name of Jesus be dishonored if we make a poor decision? Sometimes the answer to those questions is Yes. But not nearly as often as I like to think.

Whether we buy a house surely isn't trivial; it's important. But it's crucial for me not to let that mystify me. Whether we buy a house now is a pragmatic calculation, a time/money question. The gospel won't be undermined if we go broke. Only our pride. Which might be good.

And in this case God hadn't given me any clear sense of spiritual issues. For an underrower of the Word, the main questions aren't time/money calculations. They're things like: Are people being extravagant in their demands for space without regard for the kingdom? Or are they being ascetic in calling us to tough it out for Jesus when that doesn't do anything? If the answer to questions like that is yes, then as an overseer I need to say so. And maybe fight it out. But otherwise I hardly need to enter the struggle over which house to buy. (I've often proven that being an overseer doesn't make one good at business.)

What's important in the vision of the world and what's important in the vision of the Word aren't the same. For an underrower of the Word, it's crucial not to confuse the two, not to fight for my preferences or even my economic analysis, but only for the Word of the Lord. And that's not easy. At least for me, it's a much harder form of service than washing the dishes.

One of the hardest times for me to be a servant is when the church is editing policy statements that they asked me to write. As someone who spends a lot of time writing and who for many years made my living editing, I tend to believe it's a sacrilege for anyone to change a single word from my pen. However, I don't have all wisdom. And, besides, people need to own a policy that may guide their lives for years. I just need to grow up and listen to people. Forget graceful language and incisive thought (which I'm the ultimate judge of?); forget keeping meetings brief. That's what I'm called to; that's my story.[7]

However, it's not the whole story. The time comes to ask whether wording is being softened so the idea won't be clear. The time comes to ask whether people are editing because they need to leave their own ego tracks. The time comes to ask whether people are tinkering with trivia long after it's worth doing so or altering meaning in ways that will undermine the integrity of the gospel. Those are overseers' questions that sometimes need to be addressed. (Preferably by an overseer other than me. I can't always tell whether I'm protecting my ego tracks and neither can others. But if I think I have a word from the Lord, I better say it, especially if no one else does.)

7. In *The Chronicles of Narnia*, the children keep asking questions about other people, and Aslan keeps telling them that that's not their story. This is a crucial notion in life together.

QUALIFICATION FOR LEADING: GIFTS AND DEATH TO SELF

People have different gifts. This enriches the church; it's the source of our growth, according to Ephesians 4. Some of us are hands, some feet, and some adrenal glands. We need not to be cut out by the same cookie cutter, or we're depriving ourselves of the gifts of our Lord. We're depriving ourselves of each other.

But these gifts aren't necessarily natural. It's a serious mistake to assume that natural leaders can lead church. The pushiness and immense egos that qualify people to lead in the world have little connection to serving in church. At Church of the Sojourners, we've been surprised at who God made into leaders. (Often not until they were really needed.)

So it's no surprise that when Paul gives the qualifications for elders and overseers, he doesn't even mention gifts (1 Timothy 3 and Titus 1). He talks only about the spiritual state of potential leaders. What keeps people from being overseers is rarely lack of ability to lead or even lack of ability to see the whole picture. The thing that keeps us from having an overview is self-centeredness. As people repent, surprising gifts emerge. I'm sure cognitive and emotional intelligence help, but the main thing is learning to tell the difference between God's will and one's own. And that takes years of discipline and has more to do with spiritual state than giftedness.

So it's no surprise that the Bible often calls overseers "elders." It takes time to learn to distinguish between your own will and God's. Maybe you have to get old and be bored with yourself before you have much hope of telling the difference. It's alarming, but at fifty-seven I'm only just beginning to ask myself some of the questions necessary for sorting out whether I have a word from the Lord or am projecting my own ego calculations.

Put differently, natural gifts aren't always accompanied by maturity in Christ. I often find myself thinking, "This man knows music so well, it's too bad he can't get along with people well enough to lead the music team." Or, "This woman has such a good vision for church, it's too bad she's so self-absorbed she can't tell what anyone else is feeling." I often then get annoyed at the person. When a part isn't working the way it's supposed to, the cost is immense.

But we need patience. Growth takes time. Years. Maybe decades. And that's OK. God will give us the leaders we need when we need them. Maybe not before.

Another important characteristic of elders is a sort of learned focusedness. A clarity of intention where other things get stripped away—the need for approval, for getting rich, for having my own way. Ideally everything gets stripped away—everything except the Word of the Lord and the growth of his people. We need a biblical overview combined with biblical tunnel vision that excludes everything else.

My daughter and I have a basset hound named George. When George is on a scent, everything else disappears. He's no longer concerned about my approval or Jenny's. My guess is that he doesn't even hear us if we call him. They tell me that if bassets are tracking with other hounds, the other hounds will follow the pack if it leaves the scent. But not bassets. When they're on the hunt, they simply don't care where the rest of the pack thinks the trail is or whether anyone else admires what they're doing. Normally, George lives to eat. But if he's on a scent, I doubt he'd know if dinner time came and went.

Within the confines of mutual submission, we all need to be like that, especially elders. We need to stay on the scent of the Word. And that is no natural gift. It's a lifetime of questing and discipline. And grace. And you never get there, not even close. Or rather, the closer you get, the further away you realize you are.

LEADERS AND REBELLION

Now I'm going to be offensive. Our desire to become like God isn't an endearing foible as I once heard a psychologist describe it. It's the source of all our misery and the misery of everyone else in the world. We can begin to challenge it as we learn to rejoice together, as we learn to cooperate with and listen to the rest of the body.

This process will be greatly helped if we have a few elders to mentor us in grace and love and faith. To help the world make sense of their experience, we need elders who don't give us reason to rebel the way DWEMs, politicians, police, and rock stars often do.

Perhaps only with a few such elders can we deal with the rebellion that the Bible treats as the root of the human predicament. If our rebellion is the source of the domination and blaming and resentment of human history, then we need some workshop where we can be learning to curb our rebellion.[8] Church is the place that God means us to be doing that. That is one important way to revision the function of church. Our task is to stop rebelling and complaining so that we can love one another and live in unity, reflecting the light of our Savior out to the world.

Of course, the idea that leaders are crucial in this process is offensive to many modern people and for reasons that aren't hard to understand. I once took a graduate course on Ephesians. The professor suggested that the submission of Ephesians 5 and 6 is an aberration. It grew out of the benighted culture of the time and shouldn't be treated as the Word of God. As attractive as this argument is to people appalled by slavery, Hitler, Jim Jones, and the continuing oppression of women, Ephesians 5–6 isn't an aberration in the Bible.

In the Bible submission and related notions are surprisingly central. You can't reject them and keep the rest of the story intact; they're part of the deep logic. So the Israelites weren't just freed from being the slaves of Pharaoh; they became the slaves of God. Moses, David, and Paul were some of the best leaders in the Bible; they were also deeply submitted to God. So the Bible refers to them regularly as slaves (often mis-

---

8. I'm using "rebellion" to name the human predicament because I think it covers the cluster of unbelief, disobedience, resentment, blaming, and covetousness. But if you prefer one or two of those other words, the point still holds.

translated as servants) of God. The Prophets often see the core of Israel's sin as being rebellion and lack of obedience (especially Jeremiah). Or try these verses from Isaiah:

> Hear, O heavens, and listen, O earth; for the LORD has spoken: I reared children and brought them up, but they have rebelled against me. The ox knows its owner, and the donkey its master's crib; but Israel does not know, my people do not understand. Ah, sinful nation, people laden with iniquity, offspring who do evil, children who deal corruptly, who have forsaken the LORD, who have despised the Holy One of Israel, who are utterly estranged! Why do you seek further beatings? Why do you continue to rebel? The whole head is sick, and the whole heart faint. (1:2–5)

> Oh, rebellious children, says the LORD, who carry out a plan, but not mine; who make an alliance, but against my will, adding sin to sin. (30:1)

So it should come as no great surprise that the New Testament continues to see a submissive spirit as important and to sometimes apply this to listening to people in authority. Hebrews 13:17 isn't odd: "Obey your leaders and submit to them, for they are keeping watch over your souls and will give an account. Let them do this with joy and not with sighing—for that would be harmful to you." Neither are it and Ephesians 5–6 alone. The list is long. (See, for example, Acts 20:28; Rom 13:1–7; 1 Cor 16:16; Phil 2:12; Col 3:18—4:1; 1 Thess 5:12–13; 2 Thess 3:14; 1 Tim 6:1–2; Titus 2:9–10; Heb 13:17; 1 Pet 2:13—3:1, 5:5.)

Of course, leaders aren't perfect and leadership is open to terrible abuse. That's why it's important that we choose leaders who are servants of all. And perhaps that's part of why the New Testament consistently seems to envision leadership as plural. If a leader becomes abusive or monarchical, we better not be silently obedient.

We have to keep in mind that church leaders may be elders, but they aren't very old. If the rest of us are five, these folks are only six. They haven't completed the process of growing up by a long shot; what they've done is begin it in a way that others can see some fruit. For their growth to continue or their leadership to be meaningful, they will need the love and cooperation of the whole church.

Let's get on with it.

EIGHTEEN

Sabbath (the Sovereignty of God)

One of the quainter doctrines in the Bible is Sabbath rest. It was already omitted from seminary by the time I got there. The basic Christian doctrine that I learned in seminary was salvation by faith. Which makes omitting Sabbath odd, because it comes to the same thing. Or rather, Sabbath rest is little more than an embodiment of salvation by faith. At least, that's the way it seems to me.

Salvation by faith is the essence of Augustine, of Luther, and of the entire Protestant tradition. Especially of evangelical and fundamentalist Protestants. Faith is the whole ball of wax in that tradition, my tradition. So most of us know that salvation is by faith.

But few of us live it. Or understand it deeply. You can tell that by our neglect of Sabbath. For what is Sabbath if it doesn't include quitting our laboring in the confidence that we can trust God with our lives and needs? We don't have to spend every minute shoring up our defenses and trying to get others straightened out. Once a week, we can trust God to do it!

Now for one of my "scientific" predictions: I predict that individuals and churches who don't practice Sabbath rest will be marked by anxiety, crisis, conflict, and urgency about trivia. And live-in churches who don't rest in God will explode, unless they implode first. And those who have learned to rest in Almighty God will be at peace—whether as churches or as individuals, whether with others or with themselves.

SABBATH REST

Of course, in modern culture the whole notion of Sabbath rest is almost unintelligible. We're so spiritually impoverished that we tend to understand it either as legalism or laziness.

Tilden Edwards tells about a teacher who began classes with a time of meditation. The parents complained—not because they wanted religion out of the classroom but because meditation isn't productive.[1] You don't make any money meditating. Or in Sabbath rest. They're not efficient. (Stress, frustration, anger, high blood-pressure, and cardiac arrest are efficient?)

1. Edwards, *Spiritual Friend*, 69.

Others reject Sabbath rest on the grounds that it's legalistic. That's understandable because we human beings have an amazing ability to forget the meaning of things and turn them into silly rules. So we decide how many paces we can walk on the Sabbath or that we can take naps but not swim. My personal favorite is that downhill skiing is OK but not cross-country. (The one is entertainment, the other exercise!)

But that tells us nothing about Sabbath. It just tells us how silly we are. It tells us that in ethics the second law of moral thermodynamics is legalism: left alone, any good thing tends toward the entropy of trivial rules. (And in spirituality any good thing tends toward religion: learn the right formula, put in the right nickel, and the gods will magically give you any silly thing you want.) So the question becomes: What is Sabbath meant to be about?

Sabbath is about God being in control of the whole universe and lovingly holding his people in the palm of his hand. And this God (not some angry or lecherous god) loves us enough that he wants us to rest in him. He wants even the oxen to rest (Exod 20:10). He wants us to stop our labor every seventh day—or if you count all holy days (holidays) and jubilee years, he want us to stop our labor every third day. Not to see if we can jump that high, but because he knows that laboring all the time will poop us out and ruin us. God made human beings so that we thrive on cycles of rest and work, and we shrivel if we work all the time or rest all the time. (It's as inefficient to work all the time as to play all the time.)

Not that efficiency is the end goal. The end goal is to rest in God. Work is just a temporary interference—as Jesus tried to explain to Martha.

The book of Hebrews ties all this in with salvation by grace. At Kadesh-Barnea, the Israelites refused to enter Canaan. The people there would defeat them, they feared. They were afraid to trust God, and so they rejected God's salvation. Hebrews puts it this way: "They were unable to enter [God's rest] because of unbelief" (3:19). In other words, God's rest is tied to faith and salvation. In not entering Canaan, they were refusing to believe the "good news" (4:2). Only "we who have believed enter that rest. . . . So then, a Sabbath rest still remains for the people of God," who can "cease from their labors as God did from his" (4:3, 9, 10). By trusting God.

I often get overwhelmed by problems in the church I help pastor or by the needs of the world. On bad days I then feel like staying in bed, and on good days I bounce up and start trying to save the church or solve the world's problems. In either case I get badly stressed and my colon becomes an ulcer farm.

But then once in awhile I remember that I have the privilege to "cease from my labors as God did from his." I can't make church happen. I can't solve the world's problems—any of them. Nor are those things my responsibility. They are God's responsibility. My task is to do the job God has given me as well as I can with the limited time and gifts God has given me. Then I can leave the consequences to God. Which isn't a bad idea since God controls consequences anyway.

And as a symbol of that I take one day every week when I rest, when I don't try to save anyone or solve any problems. And once in a while, I take a week or two in

Yosemite. Or a year to pray and write. And all the rest of the time I work as hard as I can to rest in God's grace and goodness. (That's another of the Bible's lovely oxymorons that it doesn't bother to explain: "Let us therefore make every effort to enter that rest" [Heb 4:11].)

I love it.

TRUSTING GOD

Let me explain it this way. I can get through most days without artificial emotional respiration. Yet some days I get hit by a freight train. Even when so far as I can tell there's no train track anywhere around. With all my degrees, with all my compassion, with all my brilliance, all my likeableness, I'm always getting shocked by life. And that's a good thing—a very good thing. It teaches me that I can't trust myself.

And that maybe I should try trusting God.

You see, I can't cure my handicapped son. I can't make a depressed person trust God. I can't keep it from raining when I'm at Yosemite. I can't add a cubit to my height.

It gets worse. Neither can I stop wanting bad and silly things. Nor can I count on figuring out anything useful to say to my wife when she's sad or my daughter when she's lonely or to a church member who's frightened. And I can't keep from saying the wrong thing to the wrong person at the wrong time for the wrong reason—without even noticing it. As a result, people get mad and freight train me. With some regularity. Out of the blue so far as I can tell. And I can understand that; it's not the least unusual for them to be justified.

After all, I'm a wounded person. Wounded mostly by my own sin and perversity and finitude, but also by the sin and perversity and finitude of those around me. So I'm not very good relationally (even though that's the heart of life, at least Christian life).

Till I was about thirteen, I stuttered. Getting stuck on a sound was the most horrifying thing that happened to me. So I learned not to look at people. (If you look people in the eye, they're liable to say something that requires a response.) I learned to answer almost anything with an inflected grunt. (You have no idea how many inflections can be put on a grunt.) In short, I learned not to speak.

This is not a strength in a pastor.

It's also a great strength. It gives me lots of time to figure out that I don't know what to say and that God is going to have to bail me out. Perhaps that's what God means by "My grace is sufficient for you, for power is made perfect in weakness" (2 Cor 12:9). Stuttering left me with lots of time to listen and notice and think.

The point is, I can't provide myself with Sabbath rest. (And, by the way, neither can the NFL or medical doctors or military might or the money for a vacation home in Maui, though that is what they all promise.) It is God who provides Sabbath, and only God. Grasping that, and acting on it, is salvation. It is faith. It is grace. It is love. It is hope. It is theology proper. It is most any doctrine they teach in seminary.

Churches that understand this experientially, who know they don't know enough to come in out of the rain—those churches will thrive. The rest will shrivel and die, no matter how large they may grow numerically or in buildings.

THE FEAR OF GOD

The Bible calls this the fear of God. It's the beginning of wisdom.

In the years I didn't talk, one of the things I had time to notice was that people couldn't do much to me, that few things were worth pursuing, that not many crises deserved the name. For me, this was mixed with arrogance and Stoicism and cynicism, but it still gave me a way of understanding what Jesus meant by, "Do not fear those who kill the body but cannot kill the soul" (Matt 10:28). In other words, focus on God and don't worry about the other stuff, which doesn't matter anyway. You have nothing else to fear.

This made it easier to stop stuttering. For me at least, stuttering was very little other than fear. Fear of other people's opinions, but also primal fear. And I noticed that this fear wasn't of anything real.

Don't think I appropriated these things deeply, but I did begin reaching toward ignoring all but God. And in the long run, that's the opposite of cynicism and arrogance. In fact, it's hope and humility.

As we begin to understand that we are in God's hands, we have every reason for hope and no reason for cynicism. And as we begin to understand the greatness of God, we tend to take ourselves less and less seriously.

When I was eighteen, I crossed the Atlantic on the Queen Elizabeth. Since I'm from Kansas, I had no trouble noticing the ocean was larger even than your average wheat field. The ocean is immense. Once New York City disappeared (which was soon), we saw no land for five days. And the ship, which was huge (the largest passenger liner of the day), got tossed around like a gum wrapper in the wind. Where did something as huge and powerful as the ocean come from? What sort of power must its creator have? Usually I was almost unaware of this being. I didn't know this God on any deep level. In my bones I didn't have much sense of God's greatness. Which left me fearing all sorts of things other than God. Which meant I couldn't rest well even when I took Sabbath.

A SENSE OF WONDER

Some years ago, Judy and I went to a free, outdoor concert. It wasn't just any old concert. Isaac Stern was playing a concerto with the Philadelphia Symphony Orchestra— Eugene Ormandy conducting.

Like I said, it wasn't any old concert. That kind of sound you get to hear live only a few times in a lifetime. Not often in the history of the world can more wonderful sound have been made.

In front of us sat half a dozen teenagers. Eating popcorn loudly. (When did you last hear popcorn eaten quietly?) They can't have heard much of the concert. At least, the rest of us couldn't.

That kind of sound has been made pretty often in the history of the world. But not often with Eugene Ormandy conducting. They might as well have been listening to a tin boombox. Or watching *Gidget Wears a Bikini*.

That event has become a metaphor for me. A metaphor of how we live in God's universe. With little wonder. Little respect. Most of us might as well live in a man-made garbage dump for all we appreciate the beauty and wonder God has surrounded us with.

Well, that's not quite right because we'd complain if we lived in a garbage dump. When things stink or are assertively ugly, we notice. And complain. We're gifted at complaining. But we miss the wonder. We seem scarcely able to distinguish between the Rockies and a plastic dresser.

Well, that's not quite right, either. Most of us have some appreciation of the Rockies. Like we have some appreciation of waterfalls. But we are not struck dumb by them. Which we could be. And if we are struck with wonder at the Rockies, we aren't struck by the everyday wonders that surround us—the sunsets, the full moons, the people, the little flowers.

No, we eat popcorn. Loudly. And turn up the boombox.

Fear

The Elizabethans had a different word than "wonder." They talked about "fear"—by which they meant a mixture of deep wonder and serious respect: "The fear of the Lord is the beginning of wisdom" (Prov 9:10). We've lost that meaning for "fear." What's worse, we've nearly lost the idea itself. We have deep respect for little or nothing. We eat popcorn while one greater than Eugene Ormandy conducts.

Sabbath is stopping eating popcorn and watching and listening.

Some years ago, our family rode mules down into the Grand Canyon. Given that a slip could have been a quarter of a mile straight down, that the mules were as uncooperative as mules are said to be, that it was early spring with ice still on the trail, that the Grand Canyon is wondrous . . . Well, given all that, let's just say we developed a serious respect for the Grand Canyon.

Our, uh, respect increased when Judy's mule began to munch on a bush three feet below the trail. The mule's back, with Judy on it, pointed at a forty-five degree angle straight to the bottom. By then, an element of fear was entrenched. It may have been mostly the modern sense of the word, but it was mixed with wonder, and I suspect it came close to what the Elizabethans meant.

The illustration is not perfect because much of our fear was caused by the mules' ungodly behavior and not by the godliness of the Grand Canyon. But I'm sure that riding those mules gave us a more accurate reading of what the Grand Canyon is like than if we had observed it mainly from our car at an overlook. It has a terrible majesty.

The Grand Canyon is not designed for ease of human use but as a display of the grandeur of God and God's creation. It's the kind of place that should strike us dumb and give us a sense of our smallness and creatureliness. The kind of place that can return us to reality after the shallow existence we accept as normal living—to the reality of Isaac Stern's violin after the noise of the boom box of daily life. The kind of place where you can easily experience joy and peace—and easily get killed.

As a friend said about Canada's Banff National Park, you shouldn't mess with whoever made that. And what would it be like to rest in his hands, to be saved by faith?

ON TAMING LIONS

But modern people are liable to think that that sounds too Old Testament. We are beyond fearing God because we have learned about grace and love. We moderns emphasize compassion and gentleness. Right?

Wrong. We emphasize eating popcorn. People who eat popcorn while God is conducting just don't have enough sense to be afraid. If we realized the depth of the Grand Canyon, we'd be afraid. The reason we're not afraid is the same reason we don't rest: we're insensitive to the terrible majesty and power of God and God's creation.

The terrible majesty of God is no less in the New Testament than in the Old. We just don't know the God of the New Testament. Remember Ananias and Sapphira? Or how about the way Jesus treated the Pharisees? Not exactly a modern Jesus, meek and mild. Nor was Paul especially kindly in his treatment of the Judaizers. And John has more blood shed in Revelation than Clint Eastwood sheds in *Magnum Force*. Those people sensed the majesty of God and the consequences for those who flout God. As C. S. Lewis put it of the Christ of Narnia, "Aslan is not a tame lion."

But we treat everything as tame. We throw beer cans into the Grand Canyon and discuss its prospects for commercial development. We suspect people of idolatry if they kneel before the cross as they leave a church building. We have nearly lost the ability to revere things, to sit in silent wonder, to have deep respect, to recognize majesty, to rest.

It's not entirely our fault. Our culture has taught us that little or nothing deserves respect. And in our culture, that's almost right.

Who are we supposed to respect? Who was the last president who deserved respect? Should we respect the royals? The latest crop of news anchors? Television evangelists? Whoever's on the front of *People* magazine?

In college many of us were taught to debunk most everything. The American Revolution was senseless bloodshed. The guy who wrote that all men are created equal kept slaves. In the name of fighting for liberty against communism, our country kept half the world enslaved for half a century. The rich get richer, and all our lofty ideals are really about sex. Don't waste time on the classics. Plato, Shakespeare, Beethoven—they're DWEMs. So we shouldn't admire any of them. We don't need to subject ourselves to their wisdom, to the wonder of the classics. Just listen to our hearts and express ourselves. You're as good as any of them. All we need is discussion groups, and even if the topic is Goethe, all we really discuss is ourselves.

That was the point of my professor who used to say, "This is a seminar on the thought of Luther, not on the thought of John Alexander. When your thinking is worth knowing, I'll schedule a seminar on you. Meanwhile figure out what Luther thought."

An eccentric man.

But I'll bet God also feels that way about his students sometimes. About me anyway. God's love isn't sentimental. And it's important to understand Luther deeply before I start correcting him.

Our democratic training increases the problem. When Americans decided we'd no longer bend the knee to King George or to the nobility, we were mostly right. But emphasizing equality can easily turn into: "No one and no thing is better than I am, and if it were, it wouldn't be fair." Then we refuse to see greatness when it appears. And what we suspect of being great, we tend to belittle till we have hacked it down to our size. It's exhausting.

And don't forget the way we rush around. Remember, you don't earn any money contemplating mountains. But people always in a hurry don't have time to see beauty, wonder, majesty. Which blinds us to anything great enough to trust. What are we to do? Keeping alive requires work, and we get caught up in that work and don't take time (Sabbath) to feel the things that make living worthwhile. And so the urgency of the daily grind pushes out the importance of Sabbath.

As a result, we revere nothing—not God, not sex, not personal relationships, not mountains. It's a terrible loss—eating popcorn while one greater than Eugene Ormandy conducts an eternal concerto of wonders.

MORE POPCORN

Without a sense of wonder you also have a diminished sense of horror. In a way the worst part of those teenagers eating popcorn at the Stern concert was that they probably didn't know they were doing something terrible. They may have realized they were breaking a rule (a rule like not making noise while the principal speaks in an assembly), but they probably didn't realize they were doing something almost sacrilegious. It's like peeing on a Rembrandt—without noticing.

Without a sense of the wonder before human beings, we will have little sense of the horror of war and racism. Or the horror of economic oppression and sexual abuse and environmental degradation and all the other evils we perpetrate. We will just think a rule is being broken—against making noise during an assembly. So when genocide begins, we will carry on with business as usual. No wonder means no horror means no response. While people are murdered wholesale, we'll chomp some more popcorn. No wonder, no horror, no response, no rest, more popcorn. It's like being dead and not noticing.

The fear of the Lord is the beginning of wisdom. I have spent much of my life denouncing oppression and injustice. And I don't regret that. But I would like to spend much of the rest of my life trying to increase people's sense of wonder and majesty, helping myself and others get the scales off our eyes. People with a sense of wonder, those who see the grandeur of the universe, those who feel the terrible majesty of God—such people will not participate in oppression. Having been struck dumb with wonder before creation, we will be ignited with horror before evil. And we will know that someone greater than ourselves is in charge, and we will also rest once in a while.

Seldom feeling wonder may be bad, but more to the point, it's sad. Those teenagers at the concert were blind to a whole section of reality. They were unable to hear the difference between Isaac Stern and a boombox. And that's sad. The inability to revere things cuts us off from so much depth and grandeur and majesty. We could be rich, but instead we choose poverty. Emotional, intellectual, aesthetic, moral, spiritual poverty. Why don't we open ourselves to the awesomeness of God's creation? To the wonder of trees, waterfalls, strawberries, forgiveness, Rembrandt paintings?

> "O LORD, our Sovereign, how majestic is your name in all the earth! You have set your glory above the heavens. . . . When I look at your heavens, the work of your fingers, the moon and the stars that you have established; what are human beings that you are mindful of them, mortals that you care for them? Yet you have made them a little lower than God, and crowned them with glory and honor." (Ps 8:1, 3–5)

REALITY THERAPY

Now, I don't mean we can lecture ourselves about our feelings and change them. As you've probably noticed in your own life, it does little good to work directly on feelings. What I'm suggesting is changing the subject, and within limits we can do that. We can change the subject from how I'm feeling to God. And then my feelings begin to change. I call this reality therapy—God's reality.

I start feeling worried about the future, and at 2:00 AM. I realize (perhaps correctly) that things could really go bad. Then if I start haranguing myself about relaxing, I just get worse and start feeling bad for not being at peace. So I change the subject. I start thinking about the greatness of God. I recite Psalm 46 to myself:

> God is our refuge and strength, a very present help in trouble. Therefore we will not fear, though the earth should change, though the mountains shake in the heart of the sea; though its waters roar and foam, though the mountains tremble with its tumult. Selah. There is a river whose streams make glad the city of God, the holy habitation of the Most High. God is in the midst of the city; it shall not be moved; God will help it when the morning dawns. The nations are in an uproar, the kingdoms totter; he utters his voice, the earth melts. The LORD of hosts is with us; the God of Jacob is our refuge. Selah. Come, behold the works of the LORD. . . . "Be still, and know that I am God! I am exalted among the na-

tions, I am exalted in the earth." The LORD of hosts is with us; the God of Jacob is our refuge. Selah. (Ps 46:1–8a, 10–11)

This may sound odd, but I trust God not because I feel trusting, but because God is great and he loves me. This often leads me to feel trusting, but it isn't my feelings I trust: it's God. It's like with fear of flying. If you're afraid of airplanes, what you need to do is trust your feelings less and airplanes more. However I may feel, I trust that God will make everything work out for good for those who love him (Rom 8:28). And in time, that helps how I feel. The knowledge of God's greatness moves me toward my center in God's peace.

This isn't an ethical point, and that's crucial to understand. It's a metaphysical point. A point about the nature of reality. God is great. If people don't experience much inner peace, we don't need to work on their feelings as much as we need to help them understand the nature of reality, the nature of our great and wonderful God.

This may not be quite the same thing, but I visualize what I've just said this way. I can't create inner or outer peace, but God has already created it. First at Eden, and then on the Cross. God's peace is here. I don't need to make it. What I need to do is open the door and step into the peace God has already created. And I visualize myself opening a door and stepping in to a room full of peace and rest. Full of shabbat shalom.

Activism, passivity, or . . .

The Bible is full of a certain sort of language foreign to Western ears.

> Wait for the LORD; be strong, and let your heart take courage; wait for the LORD! (Ps 27:14)

> Be still, and know that I am God! (Ps 46:10)

> . . . Return to your God, hold fast to love and justice, and wait continually for your God. (Hos 12:6)

> Abide in me as I abide in you. Just as the branch cannot bear fruit by itself unless it abides in the vine, neither can you unless you abide in me. I am the vine, you are the branches. Those who abide in me and I in them bear much fruit, because apart from me you can do nothing. (John 15:4–5)

We tend to be able to understand these verses only as some sort of passivity, and so we ask: When do we wait, and when do we act? These verses (and there are dozens besides the ones I quoted) are calling us to open that door and enter the room filled with God's peace. They're calling us to learn what we can do and what we can't. We can do the jobs that God has given us, do them to the best of our ability, and leave the outcome to God. That will usually involve being active, but we do that from within the room of God's peace. And then the time comes to stop altogether and listen for God. Rest in his arms. We can only do the little things. God will be the one who saves us. Our task is to wait eagerly for him to do that.

That is waiting for God. That is abiding in the vine.

The fruits of the Spirit embody the same idea. The *fruits* of the Spirit are contrasted with the *works* of the flesh. The language mildly implies that we can choose to produce the works of the flesh, but the fruits of the Spirit are something that grow rather mysteriously—perhaps as we put ourselves in a place where the gardener can water and fertilize us and cultivate the land around us. It wouldn't help much for the tree to start a to-do list: grow an apple today, tomorrow a pear. Mostly trees and vines just have to wait, peacefully absorbing the nutrients and water that the gardener makes sure are present. Then the fruit grows naturally.

That's part of the point of Jesus' parable: "The kingdom of God is as if someone would scatter seed on the ground, and would sleep and rise night and day, and the seed would sprout and grow, he does not know how. The earth produces of itself, first the stalk, then the head, then the full grain in the head" (Mark 4:26–28). We aren't responsible for the growing. We do our part and leave everything else to God. Then we begin to experience the something more, the normal Christian life.

WALKING BY THE SPIRIT

In several places Paul says that our part is to set our minds on the things of the Spirit, not on the things of the flesh. (This is explicitly stated in Rom 8:4–9, but it's also in Col 3:1–3 and to lesser extent in Gal 5:13–25.) Flesh and spirit, things above and things on earth, are sharply contrasted throughout Paul, and we are responsible to choose between them. Paul says we choose substantially by turning our minds to the one or the other. It's an active choice of what we spend our time thinking about, dreaming about, planning for.

Now the meaning of setting our mind on the flesh is obvious. If we spend our time daydreaming about getting rich or getting laid or getting even (the big three?), that's who we become. That's the fruit we bear. (You may have other preferences: getting comfortable, having the perfect family, becoming famous, whatever.) We know these well. However, when I ask people what Paul means by setting our minds on the things of the Spirit, they get a little tongue-tied. They tend to say something like "church" or "heaven" or "Bible verses" while looking a little lost. Now those aren't bad answers, but they aren't what Paul goes on to talk about in Romans 8.

What Paul goes on to talk about is the love of God, how God is our daddy, the presence of the Holy Spirit, how if God gave his son, he'll also give us every other good thing. Now that's what this book has been about. Our part is to turn our minds to the love of God and to keep doing so. That's the nutrient that makes the fruit of the Spirit grow.

We can't make fruit grow, but like the farmer who cares for his orchard, we can care for our minds. We can establish habits of meditating on the love and trustworthiness of God. Then when we get worried or self-protective, our habit of turning our mind to the father will enable the fruit of the Spirit to grow in us, and we will move toward God's shabbat shalom. Otherwise, "the cares of the world, and the lure of wealth, and the desire for other things come in and choke the word, and it yields nothing" (Mark 4:19).

Now, I know people who think I'm still underemphasizing the Holy Spirit, that I'm overemphasizing habits.[2] They believe that the fruit of the Spirit is more mysterious than I'm saying: "The wind blows where it chooses, and you hear the sound of it, but you do not know where it comes from or where it goes" (John 3:8a).

But Paul seems to me to talk about habits. He tells us to set our minds on the Spirit. And that sounds like establishing a habit to me. And in Romans 5 Paul combines habits and the Holy Spirit: ". . . suffering produces endurance, and endurance produces character, and character produces hope, and hope does not disappoint us, because God's love has been poured into our hearts through the Holy Spirit that has been given to us" (Rom 5:3–5; see also Jas 1:2–4, 19–21). We need to establish habits that lead to growth. But that doesn't mean that the Holy Spirit isn't involved. In the end it's the Holy Spirit who is pouring love into our hearts. However, we need to participate. We need to turn our minds to the wonderful care that God is giving us. And not out of duty, but because we love our father.

That is, we need to work as hard as we can to rest in God's grace and goodness. I love it. It's an essentially different take on life from efficiency or from self-absorbed hedonism. It's shabbat shalom.

LIVE-IN CHURCHES AND REST

When I was first involved in community, I had an extended conversation with some folks from the Bruderhof. I asked a thousand questions. They made a conscientious effort to answer me, but they didn't seem too interested. They punctuated the conversation with remarks to the effect that they didn't know how to do community. Community was a gift of God. Some things needed to be done and others avoided, but still sometimes community happened and sometimes it didn't. They didn't know why. Or rather they did: it was the Holy Spirit. Over whom we have no control. The Bruderhof might end tomorrow, and that would be fine.

I was frustrated and suspected them of mindless pietism. But twenty years later I began to understand, a little. I can't make live-in church happen. I know almost nothing about it that matters.

A pastor was recently telling me of the agony of a man who had confessed to severe sexual addiction. He said that he wasn't too worried about the man because he seemed to have come to the end of himself and was finally experiencing the greatness of God. The pastor said he was more concerned about an elder in his church who

2. They feel I'm being influenced by Aristotle more than by Paul. And it is true that I'm profoundly influenced by the work of Stanley Hauerwas and Alasdair MacIntyre, who are profoundly influenced by Aristotle.

wanted nothing to do with the addict; he'd messed up too badly. And the pastor wondered whether his elder had come to the end of himself enough to realize who God is.

As we realize that, we can rest. As a church realizes that, they can rest. As we figure
out that we can't figure things out and so decide to trust the sovereign God, then God
can make church happen. If he chooses. It is then the victory of God, not a function of
our getting it right.

Salvation is by faith. In almighty God. Body life will thrive as we rest in almighty
God. All will be well and all will be well and all manner of things will be well because
God loves us and is in charge of the universe.

God has done all that matters; we can relax.

BIBLIOGRAPHY

Alexander, John F. *The Secular Squeeze: Reclaiming Christian Depth in a Shallow World*. Downers Grove, IL: InterVarsity, 1993.

———. *Your Money or Your Life*. New York: Harper and Row, 1986.

Arnold, Eberhard. *God's Revolution: Justice, Community, and the Coming Kingdom*. Farmington, PA: Plough Publishing House, 1997.

Banks, Robert J. *Paul's Idea of Community*. Peabody, MA: Hendrickson, 1994.

Barth, Karl. *The German Church Conflict*. Translated by P.T.A. Parker. Richmond, VA: John Knox, 1965.

Bennett, William J. *The Moral Compass: Stories for a Life's Journey*. New York: Simon and Schuster, 1995.

Birkey, Del. *The House Church: A Model for Renewing the Church*. Scottdale, PA: Herald, 1988.

Bruce, F. F. *The Spreading Flame: The Rise and Progress of Christianity*. Grand Rapids: Eerdmans, 1954.

Clapp, Rodney. *Families at the Crossroads: Beyond Traditional and Modern Options*. Downers Grove, IL: InterVarsity, 1993.

Dickinson, Emily. *The Complete Poems of Emily Dickinson*. Edited by Thomas H. Johnson. Boston: Little, Brown, 1960.

Edwards, Tilden H. *Spiritual Friend: Reclaiming the Gift of Spiritual Direction*. New York: Paulist, 1980.

Elliott, John Hall. *A Home for the Homeless: A Social-Scientific Criticism of 1 Peter, Its Situation and Strategy*. Minneapolis: Fortress, 1981.

Etzioni, Amitai. *The Spirit of Community: The Reinvention of American Society*. New York: Simon and Schuster, 1994.

Gilkey, Langdon. *Shantung Compound: The Story of Men and Women Under Pressure*. New York: Harper & Row, 1966.

Gottman, John Mordechai, with Nan Silver. *Why Marriages Succeed or Fail: What You Can Learn from the Breakthrough Research to Make Your Marriage Last*. New York: Simon and Schuster, 1994.

Hays, Richard. *The Moral Vision of the New Testament: Community, Cross, New Creation*. San Francisco: HarperSanFrancisco, 1996.

Hodge, Charles. *Systematic Theology*. Cambridge: Clarke, 1960.

Kaylor, R. David. *Paul's Covenant Community: Jew and Gentile in Romans*. Atlanta, GA: John Knox, 1989.

L'Engle, Madeleine. *A Ring of Endless Light*. New York: Farrar, Straus, and Giroux, 1980.

Lewis, C. S. *Mere Christianity*. San Francisco: HarperSanFrancisco, 2001.

Lohfink, Gerhard. *Jesus and Community: The Social Dimension of Christian Faith*. Philadelphia: Fortress, 1984.

Luther, Martin. *Martin Luther's Basic Theological Writings*. Edited by Timothy F. Lull. Minneapolis: Fortress, 1989.

Micks, Marianne H. *The Future Present: The Phenomenon of Christian Worship*. New York: Seabury, 1970.

Niebuhr, H. Richard. *Christ and Culture*. New York: Harper and Row, 1951.

———. *The Social Sources of Denominationalism*. New York: Holt, 1929.

O'Conner, Elizabeth. *Call to Commitment*. New York: Harper & Row, 1963.

Piper, John. *Desiring God: Meditations of a Christian Hedonist*. Portland, OR: Multnomah, 1986.

Bibliography

Putnam, Robert. *Bowling Alone: The Collapse and Revival of American Community*. New York: Simon and Schuster, 2000.

Ratzinger, Joseph Cardinal. *Introduction to Christianity*. San Francisco: Ignatius, 2004.

Reston, James Jr. *The Last Apocalypse: Europe at the Year 1000 A.D.* New York: Doubleday, 1998.

Rice, Chris. *Grace Matters: A True Story of Race, Friendship, and Faith in the Heart of the South*. San Francisco: Jossey-Bass, 2002.

Rice, Tim. "Simon Zealotes Poor Jerusalem." Music Andrew Lloyd Webber. *Jesus Christ Superstar*. Decca US, 1998. CD.

Richardson, Alan. *A Biblical Doctrine of Work*. London: SCM, 1952.

Ryken, Leland. *The Liberated Imagination: Thinking Christianly About the Arts*. Wheaton, IL: Shaw, 1989.

Ryle, Gilbert. *The Concept of Mind*. New York: Barnes and Noble, 1949.

Stahl, John, director. *The Keys of the Kingdom*. 20th Century Fox, 1944.

Stedman, Ray. *Body Life*. Online at www.pbc.org/ray/library/series/10274

Thiselton, Anthony C. *The Two Horizons*. Exeter: Paternoster, 1980.

Thoreau, Henry David. *The Portable Thoreau*. Edited by Carl Bode. New York: Viking, 1976.

Troeltsch, Ernst. *The Social Teachings of the Christian Church*. Translated by Olive Wyon. New York: MacMillan, 1931.

Vonnegut, Kurt. *Timequake*. New York: Putnam, 1997.

Vonnegut, Kurt. *Wampeters: Foma and Granfalloons*. London: Cape, 1975.

Westley, Dick. *Redemptive Intimacy: A New Perspective for the Journey to Adult Faith*. Mystic, CT: Twenty-third Publications, 1981.

Wright, N. T. *The New Testament and the People of God*. Minneapolis: Fortress, 1996.

Yoder, John Howard. *The Politics of Jesus*. Grand Rapids: Eerdmans, 1972.